Praise for Andray Abrahamian's

Being in North Korea

"By far the most informative book I've read on life in North Korea. Andray Abrahamian writes very entertainingly and knows what he's talking about. This is a rich and surprisingly revealing portrait of a super-secretive society."
— **Michael Palin**

"Quite simply, a must-read for anybody going to North Korea. For everybody else, it is a literary excursion of the best kind — humane, funny in ways you will never expect, grim when it should be, and rich beyond belief with hard-won expertise." — **Evan Osnos**, Staff Writer, *The New Yorker*

"Each page of *Being in North Korea* is a fresh revelation. Andray Abrahamian has spent more time in North Korea than anybody I know and he's such a knowledgeable and amusing guide that you'll feel like you've had the privilege of an exclusive tour by the time you finish reading his book."
— **Barbara Demick**, *Los Angeles Times*

"Few North Korea watchers have the breadth and depth of experiences like Andray Abrahamian. Ranging from running a nonprofit training North Koreans on entrepreneurship to undertaking academic studies as a PhD-trained scholar, the author's work highlights his valuable perceptions about North Korea's society and markets. *Being in North Korea* captures Abrahamian's experiences in a way that informs and entertains." — **John S. Park**, Harvard University

"What is it like over there? This simple but at the same time immensely difficult question is what Abrahamian seeks to answer. Having worked in North Korea and speaking the language, he is the right person for such an endeavor. He identifies himself as an "engager," but he is far from being apologetic. Based on years of hands-on experience working with an NGO that offers capacity building to North Koreans, he paints a remarkably colorful, detailed, and multifaceted image of what Westerners, in his words, often experience as a 'no' society."
— **Rüdiger Frank**, Professor, University of Vienna

Being in North Korea

Being in
North Korea

Andray Abrahamian

Stanford | Walter H. Shorenstein
Asia-Pacific Research Center
Freeman Spogli Institute

THE WALTER H. SHORENSTEIN ASIA-PACIFIC RESEARCH CENTER (Shorenstein APARC) addresses critical issues affecting the countries of Asia, their regional and global affairs, and US-Asia relations. As Stanford University's hub for the interdisciplinary study of contemporary Asia, we produce policy-relevant research, provide education and training to students, scholars, and practitioners, and strengthen dialogue and cooperation between counterparts in the Asia-Pacific and the United States.

The Walter H. Shorenstein Asia-Pacific Research Center
Freeman Spogli Institute for International Studies
Stanford University
Encina Hall
Stanford, CA 94305-6055
http://aparc.fsi.stanford.edu

Being in North Korea
may be ordered from:
Brookings Institution Press
https://www.brookings.edu/bipress/
books@brookings.edu

Library of Congress Control Number: 2020941299

First printing, 2020
ISBN 978-1-931368-56-8

For Uli

In 2016, I helped you start a tuberculosis project in North Korea. You'd been traveling the world, showing how the traditional Asian medical technique of moxibustion can boost the immune systems of patients with tuberculosis. It was one of the passions of your final years, helping forgotten people with this forgotten disease.

Your gentle, smiling face, smothered in a beard and crowning six-feet-five-inches worth of limbs, was enough to put the North Koreans at ease right away. You immediately started evangelizing about your treatment method, winning hearts and minds. I'd suggested I'd play the bad cop that trip, you the good cop. But you weren't playing, you were just nice.

When we were visiting a TB facility and were told we couldn't visit the people in the ward up the hill because they were taking naps — even though we could clearly see them standing outside their rooms — your charm and composure helped. You replied, "Oh no, it's fine, I can see them!" and just start walking up. We laughed as a staff member *ran* past us to shoo them into their rooms, to "nap." It was too late, of course, the patients refused to go in. They'd seen you, too, and wanted to talk to this lanky Englishman who seemed to be there to help.

You'll be missed. Every time I throw a frisbee, every time I tut at the inferiority of simplified *hanzi*, every time I see how much Nana has grown. But you'll also be missed by the North Koreans you helped, and missed when the country decides it's ready for more cooperation, more openness, more joy, but you won't be there.

Songdo, South Korea
July 2020

Contents

Acknowledgments

I have too many people to thank. Victoria, who supports everything I do. My parents, who said I could do anything, and may have been wrong, but who gave me plenty of opportunities to try. My sister, who always has my back. My mother-in-law, who picks me up from the Palm Springs airport.

Gi-Wook Shin and the amazing Korea-focused folks at the Shorenstein Asia-Pacific Research Center, which supported me with a Koret Fellowship that gave me the time to write this. Noa Ronkin and George Krompacky, who stewarded this manuscript to completion. I learned much from Joyce Lee, Dafna Zur, Yong Suk Lee, Bob Carlin, Sig Hecker, and Allison Puccioni, among others. Laura Bicker was also hugely helpful to me during this period. Jacob Roy critiqued early versions of many chapters and Barbara Demick had a crucial semantic intervention.

Geoffrey See, Simon Cockerell, Nick Bonner, James Banfill, and Jean Lee have been absolutely crucial to shaping my experiences in North Korea. Jenny Town, Ambassador Kathleen Stephens, Keith Luse, and Jisoo Kim have helped me understand Korea's place in the DC universe.

James Pearson, Sokeel Park, Jacco Zwetsloot, Chad O'Carroll, and Christopher Green have made particularly crucial and frequent contributions to my understanding of North Korea. Many others have supported me or provided "on-the-spot guidance"* to my work in recent years, including Soyoung Kwon, Hyonsuk Kim, Ian Bennett, Steven Denney, Peter Ward, Andrei Lankov, and the NKNews team, Curtis Melvin, Bernhard Seliger, Jan Janowski, and Dean Ouellette. Ryu Jong-sun stewarded me as I became professionally interested in Korea.

There are of course, others. In particular, many North Koreans who explained much to me and who are resilient and good and will hopefully get the chance to make their country a better place someday. I hope one day to be able to thank them by name.

I accept no responsibility for any errors in this book and instead blame all these people.†

Andray Abrahamian
Seoul, South Korea
June 2020

---

* Sorry for this crap joke.
† And this one.

Being in North Korea

A Note about Accuracy

Nearly all names and other identifying descriptors of North Koreans have been changed. In some cases, the names of foreign interlocutors have, too. Locations, dates, and contexts for many conversations or interactions have been altered. However, despite being anonymized, all attributed statements and experiences are accurately described.

PREFACE

Pyongyang to Palm Springs

I step off the plane, grab my bags, and step out onto the curb, blinking in the bright. The desert heat is making the tarmac dance. Impractically large SUVs pull up, collect loved ones, and roar off. My family arrives, swoops me up, and bundles me into the car amidst hugs and questions and laughter. You must be tired, someone says.

I stare out the window. We zoom on wide boulevards past massive strip malls and obdurate golf courses, their deep greens defying the desert valley landscape. Among the Cadillacs, Mercedes, and SUVs zips the occasional golf cart, ferrying plump retirees to pharmacies, clubhouses, or restaurants where the menu invariably includes something called "surf and turf."

I am, of course. Tired. I've just flown straight from Pyongyang to Palm Springs, with layovers in Beijing and San Francisco, a twenty-hour trip. In my sister's neighborhood in San Francisco, there are plenty of eclectics — everyone is free to wear feathers, bow ties, beards, sequins, sparkles, leather, makeup, moustaches . . . whatever they like. Though most wear Old Navy, to be honest.

Yesterday I got out of bed in the Democratic People's Republic of Korea, more commonly called North Korea. As it is on every weekday in Pyongyang, a city-wide public address system spirited us awake at six o'clock in the morning, spectral, operatic music wafting as if carried by the dawn itself through the mist and coal dust. We got in a van with our minders, who were responsible for our behavior until the moment we passed immigration. We passed men wearing a mix of Mao suits and Western suits, their choices far more limited, their lives far more proscribed than they would be if they had been going to work in California. As they streamed out of subways and buses, heading to gray or pastel office buildings, we drove past monumental structures and shrines to ideologies and leaders, sparkling in the morning light.

But tonight, I'll sleep in California. And as America zooms past, I find myself shaking my head: how can these two places exist on the same planet? Sun-baked California, which spins dreams for so much of the world, and North Korea, which occupies the dark corners of our imagination? What do people in Palm Springs and Pyongyang know of each other?

"Wow, that Kim Jong Un is pretty crazy," someone will tell me later that week, knowingly, over a surf and turf sandwich. Also, "Do they want to attack us? Will they really nuke Los Angeles?" And of course: "Whoa. What's it like over there?"

That, of course, is the hardest question of all. What *is* it like? And who am *I* to try to tell you? What gives me the right?

Well, I helped set up and run an organization that trains North Koreans in economic policy and entrepreneurship. In North Korea I've run sports tournaments and assisted an NGO start-up focused on tuberculosis prevention. I speak Korean, sometimes with a Pyongyang accent. I have a piece of paper that says I have a PhD in international relations and I've read or written something about North Korea nearly every day for the past fifteen years. I've spoken with as wide a range of North Koreans as any Westerner I know.

With this book, I'll join a long and dubious heritage of Westerners who have traveled to the "hermit kingdom" and taken it upon themselves to interpret the place to a Western audience. It's a difficult challenge. I can't fully extirpate my "Westernness" or all the traditions of the United States, United Kingdom, and Armenia that have informed my worldview. I can't avoid the power that comes with describing a subject, regardless of what that subject wants. And I'll be trying to describe a place that is extremely difficult to access. It is, after all, the most closed, mysterious, confounding, blah blah blah . . . you've heard that all before. At the end of this book, let's check in with those other explainers of Korea and see how I fit into that heritage.

But first, come fly with me.

1

I'll Never Reach Gold Status

or, How I Learned to Stop Worrying and Fly Air Koryo

Getting to Pyongyang usually requires a flight on Air Koryo, named for the dynasty that ruled Korea from 918 to 1392. The tails of their Russian-manufactured Tupolev 204s carry a stylized image of a crane, a Korean symbol of longevity and, well, flight, one supposes.

Is a passenger's longevity risked by flying Air Koryo, which Skytrax long ranked as the worst airline in the world? I've not heard of any significant harm caused by the airline, though two friends of mine have had the pleasure of an emergency landing as the cabin filled with smoke.

I say "no harm" but that doesn't include the displeasure of being forced to listen to a concert or movie with the sound piped throughout the cabin. (They don't provide earphones.) It also doesn't include the mild unease one might feel after eating a surprisingly gray in-flight burger. It also doesn't include the mind-numbing wait to check in and collect bags because every North Korean returning home seems to be bringing a flat-screen TV or fridge with them.

Before 2012 you might have flown a 1960s-era Ilyushin or Tupolev, a delectable throwback experience. The seat headrest covers were like doilies, the kind your grandmother might have had on her sofa. There were cloth curtains over the windows. The luggage rack was open, like that on a bus or a train. The planes were rickety, however.

Once I saw the plastic frame from the central air vent peel off and hang down into the aisle. The flight attendant wasn't tall enough to fix it and it took a foreign passenger's efforts to wedge it back in place. The stewardess looked mortified. North Koreans often take great pains to make sure everything appears perfect in front of foreign guests. This was embarrassing.

They looked less embarrassed and more angry one time when I snapped pictures of the staff stacking luggage on seats in the rear of the plane. "This is fine," they told me. "This is allowed under international regulations," answering a question I hadn't asked. "Delete your photos." Flight attendants will also instruct you not to take their picture or any picture on the plane. This ends up being a discussion on every single flight.

It's a good introduction to the idea that North Korea is a "no" society. Unless something is explicitly permitted, its best to act as if it's forbidden, just to be on the safe side. Also, unlike many other places, when things are forbidden, you are not entitled to an explanation. That's just how it is.

I can speak Korean quite well, so I'd try to chat with the staff when not being reprimanded for taking pictures. One particular flight attendant, Ms. Nam, seemed particularly taken by me. Over the course of several flights, we'd have a chat if there weren't many passengers. She had a lovely smile, big bright eyes, and wore too much makeup, as all North Korean flight attendants seem to.

She had a younger brother who was studying tourism management at college. She wanted to get married in two years. Most conversations we had, no matter the topic, would result in her delivering an official explanation.

"That looks like a sports team back there," I noted once. "Do they play volleyball? Soccer?"

"Well, we get lots of sports teams going abroad for competitions because under the leadership of Kim Jong Un athletic fervor has reached new highs," she replied. "The party has instructed us to build a sporting powerhouse. The whole society is striving to achieve this goal."

Her slogan-driven explanations were tiring. We moved on to English language tips that would be helpful to her. Using "sir" and "madam" or "miss" is always nice, I taught her. Useful tools in her trade.

A less-outgoing flight attendant had somehow picked up a nice language quirk, which I left uncorrected: instead of asking "What do you need?" or "May I help you?" she'd march up to someone struggling with the overhead bin or blocking the galley and say, "What's your problem?" In her high-pitched Pyongyang accent, it sounded mocking and confrontational. "Me?" I nearly replied the first time I heard it, "what's *your* problem?"

I realized she didn't mean it to sound that way and from that moment always tried to listen out for it and chuckle. I saw her on flights for years after that, using that adorable, cruel phrase long after the more pleasant Ms. Nam had disappeared. I guess Ms. Nam got married. Or perhaps our schedules just stopped lining up.

When you fly across the Amrok River that separates Korea from China, you'll hear a voice announce that fact and that by making that crossing, "we are all reminded of the glorious exploits of Great Leader Kim Il Sung," who lived in exile for twenty years before returning to Korea in 1945. Another good aide-mémoire of where you're going. Then you cruise southward along the coastal plain of North Pyongan Province and touch down at Sunan International Airport.

The immigration forms for the Democratic People's Republic of Korea are unexceptional, except for one question asking for your race — they basically care if you're ethnically Korean or not — and another asking if you've brought "exciters" or any other drugs with you. Once you pass passport control, you grab your luggage and join a queue to get your bags x-rayed for contraband or sensitive equipment.

My colleagues and I once had a printer confiscated — or rather, kept at the airport until our flight out. A printer, after all, is a sensitive piece of equipment, able to reproduce and potentially disseminate all kinds of ideas. If you have a lot of camera equipment or other electronics you might have to explain why.

The authorities also log any printed material you are carrying and, if they aren't too busy, might flip through your devices. Over nine years I've messed up at this stage twice. The first time, I'd recently been to an exhibition in Seoul and taken a photo of the front page of a 1994 newspaper that read "Kim Il Sung Dead." As the border guard swiped onto that image, my stomach knotted. I immediately leaned in toward him and started apologizing in my heaviest Pyongyang accent. I recently visited the "village down there," I said, using a North Korean euphemism for South Korea. This was at a museum and I didn't mean to bring it and I know he must be so busy and I don't want to waste his precious time and I'm sorry, I'm sorry, I'm sorry.

"Just delete it," he said. Relief coursed through me like an exciter rushing through my veins.

The second time was shortly after I'd been to a conference on DPRK–Southeast Asia relations. I'd forgotten I had the conference summary still in my bag. The agent pulled it out and somehow, almost impossibly, randomly flipped to a page and pointed at a sentence that discussed how the Myanmar government had helped try to remove from the country's shops "DVDs of *The Interview*, an ostensible comedy film about the assassination of Kim Jong Un." Honestly, it was absurd, the chances of her landing on perhaps the most incendiary sentence in the whole booklet. Her fingers slowly traced the word as she mouthed the English: "ass-ass-in-ay-shun." My stomach knotted again. This time I played dumb. "I'm not entirely sure what's in there," I fibbed. (I'd in fact written that bit.) "I went to some presentations at a university and they were giving those out. You can throw it away, I don't care."

That seemed to work. They waved me on. But I was nervous for a few hours after that, wondering if my guide would get a call about it.

The most important thing they check is your phone. They take it from you and jot down the model and serial number alongside your name. This is so that if it turns up in the hands of someone who isn't supposed to have it, it can be linked to you, and in turn linked to your guides or partners. They could then face consequences, especially if the device has been used to try to contact the outside world, as difficult as that might be.

As a foreigner, every visit you make to the DPRK has to be at the invitation of some entity. And that entity and in particular the people assigned to look after you are responsible for your behavior. They will send two guides/partners/minders to meet you. The image of a "minder" might suggest someone relentlessly enforcing the rules and stopping you from doing as you like. In fact, the system means that when you visit, your behavior has consequences for your partners. I have been with someone who took pictures of a street that happened to include a couple of soldiers. This was reported and later in the evening the guides had to sit down with him and delete some photos.

They didn't *want* to do this, but it had been reported and they were instructed to take care of it. Indeed, much of the time, if you have a good relationship with your partners, you find yourselves working to find solutions to problems that the system throws at you. Fundamentally you're cooperating to accomplish tasks that aren't against rules, but constrained by them. Your minders, while part of the system of constraints, are also gently pushing against those constraints; they are often working with you to accomplish shared goals despite being in a system stacked with barriers to success.

And the system is sensitive about pictures, about how North Korea and its people are portrayed in general. Mostly, they ask you not to take pictures of anything connected to the military, any construction sites, or anything indicative of poverty. "Only beautiful, please," a guide might say.[1] Should you snap a picture of a highway military checkpoint, or even just have your camera out as you pass it, delays and arguments inevitably follow.

In February 2016, a tourist traveling with Young Pioneer Tours did a handstand for a picture in front of the Kumsusan Palace of the Sun. Kumsusan was once the offices of Kim Il Sung. It is now a vast mausoleum, where the preserved bodies of Kim Il Sung and Kim Jong Il lie in state. It is akin to a holy site, the very center of a mythology the binds the state together. It is the most solemn and immaculate place you can imagine. In fact, it almost certainly exceeds whatever you're imagining.

The tourist's handstand photo op was noticed and reported. Shortly thereafter his Korean guide was fired. She'd grievously lost control over her guests and was duly punished. Someone has to be responsible, after all. There have to be consequences. It may not be a case of being sent "straight to the gulag," but minor things can cause real disruption to people's lives.

Surprisingly, they aren't terribly strict about pictures in the airport, relative to other places. The airport itself was for several years a temporary structure, like an eighty-meter long hanger. It was freezing in the winter and too hot in the summer. And dark. A single light like a post-apocalypse harvest moon hung over the place, except of course for two lights illuminating the smiling portraits of Kim Jong Il and Kim Il Sung at the far end. It made for a poor welcome to the country for a first-time visitor.

The building of a new terminal began, haltingly, around 2012; it had the uneven lines and misshapen concrete that defines modern North Korean construction. In 2014 Kim Jong Un even scolded those overseeing the construction, saying that they had "failed to bear in mind the party's idea of architectural beauty that it is the life and soul and core in architecture to preserve the Juche character and national identity."[2]

Slightly ambiguous criticism, though he may have been right: After the cladding and interior were completed, it looked like a modern, if unremarkable, small airport terminal anywhere in the world. It is pleasant enough and Kim came around to it, it seems. He visited after it was completed in June 2015 and said it was "well-built as required by modern architectural beauty and national character." There is a picture of him in the boarding area, next to a chocolate fondue set.[3]

There is a darker side to the travails of the airport's construction. Part of it is the fact that Ma Won Chun, in charge of major construction projects as the head of the Designing Department of the National Defense Commission, disappeared from public view for nearly a year after Kim's criticism of the airport. People are punished there, and it can be capricious.

The other part is the glee with which some news agencies highlight stories of cruelty or weirdness in North Korea. The DPRK occupies a very real function for us as Western news consumers in the West: it can always be held up to remind us that we are "normal," while they are not. This leads to Western news companies trumpeting that "Kim Jong Un EXECUTES New Airport Architect — Because He Didn't Like the Design," or the slightly less breathy, "Kim Jong-un Shows Off Airport Designed by Architect He Likely Had Executed."[4]

Ma Won Chun showed up again in October of that year. He was almost certainly castigated for whatever was displeasing about the airport, as well as perhaps for other problems associated with its construction. The cycle of punishment, reform, and redemption through loyalty to the state is not an uncommon one in the DPRK.

And architecture and construction are a serious business in today's North Korea. Indeed, "Construction" is the name of a subway station and of a popular low-grade brand of cigarettes. As you drive into Pyongyang from the suburb of Sunan, you can't help but notice that a great deal of design and planning have gone into creating the city.

There are no checkpoints on the way into Pyongyang from Sunan Airport, as there are on many roads. Instead, you'll see tidy three- or four-story apartment buildings. They are concrete and tired, but not grim. They have often been cheered up with pastel paint jobs and plastic made-in-China flowers on their balconies. You may catch someone hand-sweeping the road if you arrive in the morning. Not the sidewalk — the road.

You'll pass paddy fields and train lines; this is the breadbasket of Korea after all, such as it is. North Korea is some 70 percent mountains — particularly unsuited to supporting a population of twenty-four million people. Then, as you approach Red Star Subway Station, the apartment buildings get taller.

Shortly thereafter epic, monumental Pyongyang emerges. First the April 25 Performance Hall on your right and the forty-meter-tall Immortality Tower boldly proclaiming that "Comrades Kim Il Sung and Kim Jong Il will live with us forever!" Behind this rises the gleaming towers of Ryomyong Street, with 70- and 82-story apartment buildings, bright green and intriguingly shaped, with distinctive bulges and flourishes. Then through the Arch of Triumph, bigger than the one in Paris (of course). On your right, the winged-horse Chollima monument. To the left some green space, Moranbong Park.

Ahead you glimpse the Taedong River, while the driver follows the law and slows down as he drives past gigantic twenty-meter-high bronze statues of the leaders at Mansudae. There they stand, forever surveying their domain, smiling benevolently. If you follow their sight line many kilometers across the river, you'll see three huge stone fists, gripping a hammer, sickle, and brush, celebrating the founding of the Korean Worker's Party. Just past the leaders is another new neighborhood of towers, blue this time, then after a couple minutes you see Kim Il Sung Square, a place you instantly recognize from countless news broadcasts of soldiers goose-stepping in a perfection of purpose.

The first time you drive through all this it is hard to believe you're there in this place that captures so much attention relative to its size. This abstraction, this weird cult, this nuclear state, this garrison society is real! There are actual people moving about, living their lives. People sometimes remark how humorless the Koreans on the street look, like "robots." I've noticed this impression tends to form when the weather is bad or when people see commuters. Turns out, like any large city, people on their way to work look cranky. And people in winter are cold.

I've seen people influenced the other way, also, if they arrive on a weekend, when people are relatively relaxed and enjoying leisure time, shopping, playing sports, enjoying the rivers. "They look so happy and content!" Turns out, like anywhere, people fishing and playing volleyball with their friends look pretty happy. And when it's sunny, people smile more. Visitors place undue analytical value on the little they get to see, forming broad conclusions on limited experience.

I find Pyongyang a beautiful city, however. It has been planned, of course, to be a showcase city. It was built from scratch after the Korean War. There is a lot of green space and the city is sliced open by two rivers. The Taedong is the bigger of the two, wide enough to have islands in it, on which there are stadia, funfairs, and a dolphinarium. (Of course there is a dolphinarium. Of course.) The riversides have a number of sports facilities. These have all been built under Kim Jong Un, reflecting his goal of creating the "sporting powerhouse" and the "civilized socialist country" about which Ms. Nam had soliloquized.

Pyongyang has Kim Il Sung Square, of course, which sits across the river from the striking granite Juche Tower. The top of the tower has a twenty-meter-high plastic torch, lit up at night and shining all the brighter for the lack of illumination around it. There are a number of less dramatic buildings that are pleasing to the eye. The apartments behind the Party Foundation Monument are designed to look like a red, fluttering flag, for example.

Then, of course, there is the Ryugyong Hotel. Construction began on this 105-story monster in the late 1980s. The collapse of the Communist Bloc and North Korea's subsequent economic crisis meant that it sat, frozen and gray like a gigantic troll, for two decades. Visible from everywhere, it was a humiliating symbol of the country's failures. In 2009, however, Orascom began finishing its exterior as part of their deal to create a mobile phone network. Still, it remained an embarrassment: in 2013 a British diplomat told me he once mentioned to a Korean colleague that over the weekend he had gone to a restaurant right next to the Ryugyong. The colleague feigned that he had never heard of the place. As of 2018, the hotel featured a huge LED lightshow on one side, and finally became prominent in domestic propaganda. The inside remains unfinished and probably always will be.

There are four churches. One of them, the Russian Orthodox Church set up in 2006, is used by Russian embassy staff and has a prominent gold onion dome. The other three appear to be mostly for show: some kind of congregation exists, but it isn't clear what services are like when foreign delegations are not around. This is a far cry from the early 1940s, at which time Northern Korea had about three thousand churches and three hundred thousand Christians,[5] and Pyongyang was called the Jerusalem of the East. Christianity was popular both before Japan took over the country in 1910 and after, as it offered gathering places away from the Japanese overlords.

When Japan was defeated in World War II, the Korean Peninsula was divided into Soviet and American zones of control. As leaders, the Americans installed Syngman Rhee, the Soviets, Kim Il Sung. Neither side was interested in cooperating with the other and war broke out in June 1950. This event claimed the lives of several million Koreans, or something like 10 percent of the population.[6] The war has framed the lives of North and South Koreans ever since.

And there is a reason, of course, why there are so few churches left and why the Koreans were able to build a city from scratch. The Americans bombed the country into oblivion between 1950 and 1953. The Koreans are fond of saying of Pyongyang that "only three buildings were left standing after the war." Whether or not that is exactly true, it is undeniable that "following China's entry into the war in November 1950, [US Air Force bombers] began to strike North Korean cities and villages even more harshly, designating them as *main targets* for destruction."[7]

Some 635,000 tons of bombs were dropped on Korea, more than on Japan in World War II.[8] Napalm was used, for the first time, in Korea — thirty-three thousand tons of it — burning and choking perhaps hundreds of thousands of people to death.[9] General MacArthur, hero of World War II and architect of the Incheon landings, also considered using nuclear weapons in the Korean theater.[10] Nothing remained, leading to the sometimes-used North Korean slogan, "We started with nothing."

This is true enough, and the state tirelessly keeps the memory of the atrocious bombing campaign alive. It is a central tenant of its self-image as a righteous country at war with vicious thugs; keeping the United States as an eternal enemy also helps explain away a variety of the country's shortcomings. Fundamentally, the society is organized around having the United States as an enemy. But if the claims about the cruelty of indiscriminate bombing in the Korean War are generally true, the other central claim beggars belief.

If you visit the spectacular Fatherland Liberation War Museum, updated in 2013, you will stop and look up at a ten-meter-high full-color statue of a young Kim Il Sung, looking *remarkably* like Kim Jong Un. You will then watch a video arguing one of the main pillars of the North Korean national story: that the Americans invaded the North on June 25, 1950. The North Korean worldview is one in which the Korean people are engaged in a righteous struggle, beset on all sides by an outside world that wishes to destroy them. To believe North Korean historiography, you have to concede that the most powerful military in the world spent months planning the surprise invasion of the North, launched its attack and then within hours was in full disarray, retreating in the face of Kim Il Sung's military genius.

In contrast, the rest of the world agrees that after lobbying Stalin and Mao for months, it was the Korean People's Army (KPA) that crossed southward that day. The South Korean army disintegrated like wet paper and the KPA roared down toward the very southern tip of the peninsula. The Americans intervened just in time to defend the port of Pusan, leading the United Nations forces that they had cobbled together.

A few months later, in September, the United States turned the tide by landing forces at Incheon, severing Northern supply lines and forcing a KPA retreat. The North Koreans took flight in disarray and UN forces pushed forward all the way to the border with China. This was a huge mistake, in retrospect, as the just-founded People's Republic of China sent soldiers pouring into Korea in response, pushing UN forces back to the thirty-eighth parallel. This, tragically, was basically where the war began. Even more tragically, for the next two and a half years, the two sides fought mostly over this line. A staggering three to four million civilians and well over a million combatants died between 1950 and 1953.[11] The war ended in an armistice, not a peace treaty.

The Northern part of the peninsula really had become a scorched wasteland and the North Koreans are rightfully proud of the pace with which they rebuilt their shattered infrastructure and industries. They hit their targets during a three-year plan to reconstruct, and then again in a five-year plan from 1957 to 1961. This was done partly through Soviet and Chinese aid — little mentioned in the North — but also because the populace responded exceptionally well to exhortation and encouragement, something mentioned *a lot* in the North.[12] There are limits to that model, you'd think. You can't exhort and coerce people into working hard forever, can you?

It isn't all exhortation — people largely work for wages these days, but North Korea still leans on its traditional method of mobilization from time to time, holding periodic "speed battles" in different sectors. In 2013, they had a "harvest battle," for example. Also, factories or other workplaces are often called "battle zones" or "battlefields." In 2016 on either side of the

Korea Worker's Party Congress they had a 70-day and 200-day nationwide "speed battle." Imagine, essentially, the whole country putting in overtime, either in their workplaces or outside, being mobilized for beautification or construction projects. These speed battles are exhausting to the citizens involved, which incidentally contributes to social control.

Those new neighborhoods you see on your way into town, Ryomyong and Changgon, were all built super-fast to meet political deadlines: the 100th and 105th anniversaries of Kim Il Sung's birth, in 2012 and 2017 respectively. (Or in the North Korean calendar, Juche 100 and 105. The calendar follows...you get it.) Mirae Scientists street, further along the river, saw over two dozen buildings constructed in under a year from 2014 to 2015, the tallest being fifty-three stories.[13] Indeed, the North Koreans have cycled through slogans, but two prominent ones have been "Pyongyang Speed" and "Chollima Speed," both callbacks to slogans from the era of reconstruction in the 1950s.

Unfortunately, buildings built during these sorts of campaigns look pretty shoddy within a year or two of completion. Tiles chip, lines are uneven, and stains appear. It turns out mobilizing office workers and using poorly trained soldier-builders does not produce the best results. The buildings are made with local, low-quality concrete and rebar, not steel, even those over 70 stories. ("No. No f — ing way," a Canadian architect I told once exclaimed as we drove past.) The electricity supply is unreliable, so people don't want to live too high up in them. Water supply can also be an issue.

They look impressive from a distance or when lit up at night, however. This creates an interesting split. If you're from Pyongyang, you know that they look pretty bad. If you're from elsewhere in the country and have only seen them in magazines and on TV, they must seem pretty amazing: monuments to the "golden era of construction ushered in by Kim Jong Un," as North Koreans describe the current period.

When leaving Pyongyang, the train is an option, for those with the time to saunter up the economic spine of Korea. Most visitors fly out. On Air Koryo, of course.

This is almost always fine. Almost. One time it wasn't fine was when my colleague, Geoffrey, and another friend who worked for an NGO were flying back to Beijing. Twenty or thirty minutes into the flight, while the attendants were preparing the selection of dodgy burgers, noses started twitching as passengers began to perceive an acrid smell. Then smoke began to fill the cabin and the plane started dropping.

As befits a low-information society, no announcements were made, other than by the flight attendants, who were by now rushing about, telling people to sit and declaring that there was "no problem." My friends had been in North Korea enough to know that there was. Oxygen masks dropped as the plane began to shake from the rapid descent, and the passengers' ears began to hurt and to pop.

Geoffrey sat there stewing; after all he'd sacrificed, setting up an NGO, leaving a lucrative consulting career, all the time and energy, North Korea was going to kill him. My other friend, trying to find zen and fight back her tears, chose to think about the last time she'd had sex: feeling positive and connected to someone, happy and relaxed. It was literally her last day in Pyongyang, having lived there four years. She couldn't believe it.

The plane limped its way down to Shenyang, where it made an emergency landing. Passengers were put in a holding room while Air Koryo staff went off to do things, without explanation. The airline obviously hadn't prepared for such an eventuality and it seems they couldn't get anyone with authority on the phone to tell them what to do with the customers. After a few hours, Geoffrey took the train to Beijing, wondering if someday they'd offer compensation, an apology, or even just an explanation.

He's still waiting.

Notes

1 John Everard, *Only Beautiful, Please* (Stanford, CA: Shorenstein Asia-Pacific Research Center, 2012).

2 Justin Rorlich, "Kim Jong Un Unhappy with Construction of New Airport Terminal," NK News, November 1, 2014, https://www.nknews.org/2014/11/kim-jong-un-unhappy-with-construction-of-new-airport-terminal.

3 Adam Taylor, "North Korea Unveils a Gleaming New Airport Terminal Featuring High-End Stores and Chocolate Fondue," *Washington Post*, June 25, 2015, https://www.washingtonpost.com/news/worldviews/wp/2015/06/25/north-korea-unveils-a-gleaming-new-airport-terminal-featuring-high-end-stores-and-chocolate-fondue.

4 Steve White, "Kim Jong Un Executes New Airport Architect — Because He Didn't Like the Design," *Mirror*, June 28, 2015; and Jessica Ware, "Kim Jong-un Shows Off Airport Designed by Architect He Likely Had Executed," *Independent*, June 30, 2015, https://www.independent.co.uk/news/world/asia/kim-jong-un-shows-off-airport-designed-by-architect-he-reportedly-had-executed-10354051.html.

5 김양선 [Kim Yangson], 한국기독교 해방 10년사 [A ten-year history of Korean Christianity liberation] (Seoul: Yaesu Gyojang Rohui, Jonggyo Gyoyukbu, 1956), 160.

6 Bruce Cumings, *The Korean War: A History* (New York: Random House, 2011), 35.

7 Taewoo Kim, "Limited War, Unlimited Targets," *Critical Asian Studies* 44, no. 3 (2012): 469. Emphasis in original.

8 Charles K. Armstrong, "The Destruction and Reconstruction of North Korea, 1950–1960 北朝鮮の破壊と再建1950–1960年," *Asia-Pacific Journal* 7, no. 0 (March 16, 2009): 1.

9 Hugh Deane, *The Korean War* (London: China Books, 1999), 149.

10 See Roger Dingman, "Atomic Diplomacy during the Korean War," *International Security* 3, no. 13 (Winter 1988–89): 50–91.

11 Wada Haruki, *The Korean War: An International History* (New York: Rowman & Littlefield, 2014), 287.

12 Joungwon Alexander Kim, "The 'Peak of Socialism' in North Korea: The Five and Seven Year Plans," *Asian Survey* 5, no. 5 (1965): 255–58.

13 J. H. Ahn, "'Pyongyang Speed' Touted as Finished Scientist Street Revealed," NK News, November 4, 2015, https://www.nknews.org/2015/11/pyongyang-speed-touted-as-finished-scientist-street-revealed.

2

Getting Involved

This goalkeeper is terrible," I thought after the second goal. "He moves funny, like a twelve-year-old, wearing a uniform two sizes too big." Shortly thereafter: "Okay, the third goal wasn't his fault, it was the back four. They're bad, too."

By the time Cristiano Ronaldo accidentally bobbled the ball on the back of his neck and head on the way to slotting home the sixth, it was clear it was the fault of every DPRK player and the coach as well. But as Portugal pounded North Korea in that 2010 World Cup match, an interesting thing happened. With each goal, the foreigners around me in the Seoul sports bar would gesticulate with glee: "Yeah! Suck it, commies!" They were genuinely elated that North Korea was being humiliated. The South Koreans were much more hesitant. Some shook their heads in disappointment that their compatriots were getting embarrassed on the world stage, even if they *were enemies*. The match ended 7–0.

You may have read that North Korean athletes who lose receive harsh punishments. Headlines like "North Korea's Key to Olympic Medals: Refrigerators for Winners, Labor Camp Threat for Losers," or "Freedom of Choice for North Koreans at London Olympics: Win and Get a Refrigerator, or Lose and Go to Work Camp" encourage that idea.[1] Actually, that kind of thing doesn't really happen, though it's pretty likely that players "who participated in the World Cup were subjected to a session of harsh ideological criticism" in front of four hundred participants and that the coaching staff lost their jobs.[2] This would, of course, happen in most countries. The firing, that is, not the ideological criticism session. Regular criticism sessions, in the twenty-first century, are a uniquely North Korean ritual.

The real tragedy from Pyongyang's perspective was that this game was the first they'd ever broadcast live: the authorities prefer a broadcast delay, to maximize control over images and narratives. But before the Portugal game they'd given Brazil a run for their money in their first group match, losing 2–1. This must have inspired the authorities to go live for the next match. They thought they had a chance. They were confident. They were wrong.

I'd been to North Korea just once at this point, earlier that year. My group didn't get to see a football match, but we did watch an entertaining ice-skating event. ("Was that a competition or a performance?" we asked a Ukrainian skater whom we ran into afterwards and who'd received a medal. "We're not sure!" she happily replied.)

I'd been studying the country for several years, however. I was living in South Korea and at the nadir of a PhD in international relations in 2009. My advisor, a sort of nicotine Buddha, was off on sabbatical and I found myself feeling isolated without his calm guidance, wondering why I was doing this work. Was it to sit behind a computer and bang out turgid analysis of a faraway place? To get a job in government and promote inadequate policies, or fail to get better ideas heard? What was I doing, I thought, studying this country that occupies such a weird place in the global imagination? I decided I should at least visit this country to which I was devoting so much thought. So a childhood friend and I booked a trip with Koryo Tours and off we went in February 2010.

And it was reinvigorating. There is no substitute for seeing a place. You see the New York skyline on TV, but it's not the same as standing among its towers. You can see pictures of a sunset over the Black Rock Desert, but it isn't the same as having it stretch 360 degrees around you. You can hear a song about heartbreak, but it doesn't make sense until after you've been dumped and left quivering in the fetal position on a mattress in an empty new apartment.

North Korea is an intense experience and describing it is a challenge. You can read about North Koreans' fear of speaking out, but it is more real to hear your guide falter and unable to answer when you ask, "Do you think that your country sends spies to South Korea?" You can read about a personality cult, but it's not the same as seeing it manifest in pictures, slogans, and other media from morning to night. For me, the most striking thing about that initial trip was seeing for the first time what it is to be poor and cold. That may seem a callow observation, but the only poor countries I'd visited up to then had been in warm climates. To see people suffering through the winter, unable to be productive, unable to relax, was upsetting. It is miserable.

Still, my guides and other Koreans I came across were charming, had their own individual opinions, and were immensely curious about the world. I came back from that trip thinking I wanted to be involved *with* North Koreans somehow, not just write *about* them. But as far as I could tell, other than tourism, the organizations interacting with North Koreans were related to the UN or national agencies that I probably wasn't qualified to work for, or religious groups that for other reasons I'd struggle to work for.

I needed advice, so over the following months I started reaching out and connecting to people in the Korea-watching community. One such person invited me for a beer at that same Seoul sports bar a few days after the Portuguese shellacking. He said, "Let me introduce you to a former student of mine who's interested in North Korea, too."

That former student was Geoffrey K. See, a Singaporean graduate student at Yale, who said, "I'm starting a project to teach North Koreans about business. We plan to take groups in to do workshops."

"Interesting," I wondered. "Why?"

Geoffrey was young. He finished university early to save money, then chose Yale over Harvard for graduate school. His dad was a hawker — a food-court vendor of drinks — and his mother was a nurse. He was the first in his family to go to university. He was interested in how organizations work and how to build successful, large-scale companies. He had an extremely keen mind, which compensated for a slightly youthful awkwardness and relatively modest family background. He was one of those lucky few who are able to leap social classes by force of intellect and hard work alone.

Three years before, in 2007, he'd visited North Korea while he was in business school. His guide happened to be a young woman who wanted to start her own company, "to show the men that a woman can do just as well in business." This struck a chord with him and he started thinking there was a whole class of people he'd never read about in the media whom he could potentially help. He started fishing around for a contact in North Korea who'd be interested in helping, finally finding someone in 2009 and organizing a workshop for fall of 2010.

I said, "I'd love to be involved." And that was that. We both noticed that as well as North Korea's well-studied bottom-up marketization, there was an increasing interest in marketization and management flowing from the top. We thought the military-first era — in which the economy was largely abandoned and the Korean People's Army was given primacy — would be coming to an end.[3] I started helping Geoffrey plan programs and build awareness amongst journalists, academics, and potential funders.

We ran a few in-country workshops on a volunteer basis using a very low-cost model and donating our own time. This was getting tougher for Geoffrey, who had joined a major consultancy in the United States, the kind of job where they work you to death and where if you're sleeping more than six hours a night, your male colleagues will ridicule you for being soft. The kind of job where they give awards to the associate who spent the most nights in hotels that year, and the number is always well over two hundred.

But after we'd won enough funding in 2012 for the both of us to come on full time, we had difficult decisions to make, more him than me. After all, I'd be stepping away from an academic path I was already ambivalent about. My wife was interested in living in China, too, so we were personally excited about the prospect of moving to Beijing. Geoffrey would have to step off a corporate fast-track, one that promised things like a *Friends*-sized apartment in Manhattan, restaurants that have gold leaf on the desserts, and suits made by impossibly posh London tailors. He chose a life less ordinary.

"Why are you here?" the short Korean with a kind face asked Geoffrey and me in the café in the Pyongyang Hotel. This was in early 2013.

"We're here to plan our year's programs with you and your colleagues."

"No," he replied, "I mean, what is *your purpose?*" He wasn't glaring, but his question carried a whiff of suspicion, a sentiment that the North Korean system encourages.

We were visiting Pyongyang for three days of planning meetings. And now we were wondering what this kindly, elderly man was doing. The meetings were with a Mr. Kim. We'd worked with him several times in the past, but now that we were planning on ramping up the frequency and size of our training, there was much to discuss. We'd already received positive responses to our proposals via email. But this other, older gentleman was joining our meetings, and we weren't sure why. He was connected to the committee we were working with and had spent some time in Europe. He was very genial and warm. He'd clasp your shoulder and inquire about your night's rest in the morning. But why was he there?

"We want to help teach Koreans so that they can run companies better and improve the economy," I answered him.

"That's it? *Why?*" It dawned on me that his whole purpose was to check on us before we mapped out a whole year of projects. We thought we'd already explained ourselves. For a second my heart jumped. Geoffrey and I had both just moved to Beijing specifically to run Choson Exchange! Were our partners now suddenly unsure? Did the State Security Department send this guy to vet us? Were the stakes at this meeting far higher than I'd anticipated?

"Yes, we think that peace, stability, unification . . . all these things are only possible after economic development." North Korea was becoming, in spite of its rhetorical commitments to mid-twentieth-century socialism, a market economy. People needed to know how to run companies better and the government needed to know how to make better rules for businesspeople to succeed.

It was a good answer. He nodded in agreement and we relaxed. We walked him through our plans for a few in-country workshops and one or two study trips to Singapore. He *was* there to try to assess if we were genuine; to see that we weren't spies or evangelicals. By the end of our meetings he was on board.

The next morning, Geoffrey and I went for a run. I was awake exceptionally early for some reason, before the light, before the ghostly city-wide alarm, an eerie theremin rendition of a revolutionary opera song, "O! General Where Are You." A light snow had fallen. It was a thick, dry snow, not slippery. It was an inch thick and my feet beat out a perfect rhythm — crunch crunch crunch — like brushes on a snare drum. Breath would billow out of me then I'd run through it, emerging through my self-generated cloud on the other side. There were no cars and almost no one on the street. I imagined other early risers peeking out from their windows at me, watching disbelieving at this big Armenian dude making his mark in the virgin snow.

With our first full-time year's plans laid out, we got to work. An early volunteer with us was an accomplished businessman based in Shanghai, but who had some excess office space in Beijing. He said we could use it and we moved in to a space on the eleventh floor of a nondescript tower in the Chaoyangmen neighborhood of Beijing. On the ground floor of the building was a karaoke place called Party World. There was a Starbucks, as there is everywhere in Beijing. There was a view of the Ministry of Foreign Affairs, an imposing curved monolith, and the Second Ring Road, which runs where beautiful ancient city walls once stood. Chairman Mao had them torn out in order to build a more modern, revolutionary capital. Most days a silvery haze would blanket the city, coal dust and car fumes creating a contemporary, malodorous backdrop. Mao would have liked it.

Geoffrey and I planned to work together out of this Beijing office, but within a few months we realized we needed a presence in Singapore. We planned to have at least five or six in-country workshops per year in Pyongyang, where we'd take volunteers to teach for two to four days and through which we could select North Koreans to take to Singapore for study trips abroad. The logistics of two-week trips to the city-state required someone on the ground. More importantly, we had donor and volunteer relationships to maintain in Singapore. We needed someone there, so Geoffrey moved back.

I moved to a different apartment, a bigger space with room for a home office and a spare room where Geoffrey or other volunteers could crash as they passed through Beijing on the way to Pyongyang. Once we had the whole in-country team of five people stay over, several on the floor in sleeping bags, before we got our visas at the DPRK embassy in Beijing and went to the airport. It was like a base camp before striking out to summit Everest. Cramped, but full of excitement at doing something new. Regardless, I was grateful for the move: our first apartment in Beijing was a 1950s era low-rise where the insulation was made of either paper or something more ephemeral, like revolutionary spirit. My wife and I froze that winter.

Geoffrey and I traveled a lot. When we weren't going to North Korea, we were crisscrossing the northern hemisphere, visiting South Korea, the United States, and Europe, looking for a united front, so to speak, but also looking to build credibility. We needed to make sure people around the world didn't think we were spies, fellow travelers, or smugglers.

Guess how many times people have joked that I'm a spy after I describe what I do. Go on, guess. Okay, I don't actually know the answer, but it is a lot. And always *hilarious*. It is a joke I put up with for the most part, pointing out I'm too much of a chump to be a spy. Once, however, an incautious workshop leader made a joke to that effect while we were in Pyongyang. I growled at him to shut up.

Hilarious jokes aside, a North Korea–related startup is bound to draw scrutiny. Geoffrey and I gave talks at trade associations, think tanks, and community groups. We ran a blog with pictures and talked to the press a lot, trying our best to reshape the discourse on North Korea. Fundamentally, we were saying that, yes, much remains the same in terms of human rights or political norms in North Korea, but the authorities have a new interest in the economy and in using markets. At the individual level, people were primarily concerned with making money, and finding careers that could deliver financial security. (We'll discuss the causes of this in the next chapter.)

We thought this new interest was profoundly important, but it was being overlooked. The North Korean regime strives to project an image of a unified state where one leader controls everything. Unfortunately, it often seems outside observers fall into the trap of viewing North Korea through that lens, rather than as a complex society of twenty-four million people struggling to survive or thrive within a very difficult system.

It also seemed as if many people were stuck viewing the DPRK through the lens of its famine years, which peaked in 1996 and 1997. The country was no paradise in 2013 and in myriad ways it still hasn't recovered from the economic collapse of the 1990s, but the grimness of that decade had abated by then. Indeed, in some ways the culture has relaxed from that dark, martial period. (In some ways it remains the same.)

Things had changed. By way of example, we'd been told by several NGO people who'd worked in the DPRK in the 1990s or early 2000s that once we brought people on study-abroad trips, they'd disappear back into the system and we'd not be able to contact them again; indeed, that trying to do so would be dangerous for them — they'd be seen as perhaps too devoted to ideologically impure foreigners. To our delight, following our very first study-abroad trip in 2011, we found this not to be the case.

Another example: at the end of 2011, Kim Jong Il died. We'd heard that for three months after the 1994 death of Kim Il Sung virtually no foreigners were allowed into the country, save for diplomats already stationed there. The Korean Central News Agency even put out a bulletin making clear that "no foreign delegations would be invited" to Kim Il Sung's funeral. The country shut down. In 2011, the leadership apparently realized that such a move would not be beneficial. We penned a very respectful letter to our partners acknowledging that they needed to mourn and we expected programs to be delayed. Just two days later — instantaneously in North Korean terms — we got a reply: "Of course we are sad, but we must also push on and keep working together."

Overall, fewer ideological statements were made to foreigners than in the past. Once, foreigners could expect that any meeting or discussion would be kicked off by lengthy speeches on the genius of the leaders or on party policy. By 2011 this seemed to have been reduced to a couple of perfunctory sentences. North Korean counterparts still had to give a quick shout-out to their system, but most seemed to want to speed through it and get down to business.

Still, these changes were not fundamental to the system; our media output was still regularly monitored, and this occasionally became a pain point. Security services would sometimes spot something I'd written or said that they didn't like, then bring it up with our partners, who would then have to talk with us about it.

"Did you put pictures of construction on your website?" I was asked once in a hushed tone by Mr. Kim.

"Yes," I said. "I wrote something wondering why the supposedly seven-star hotel being built next to the Koryo Hotel doesn't seem to be moving forward. I had a picture of the site."

"Construction is very sensitive in my country," he said. This is, as best I can figure, partly because they don't want people to know what projects are underway. The instinct to control information is high in North Korea, as we will later see. It is also partly out of a sense of pride: North Korean construction materials are shockingly bad and are as uneven as an open-mic night. Building sites look poor and haphazardly slapped together, and they don't want pictures of them.

More than security services, we came to realize, it was pro–North Korean foreigners who were monitoring our media output and then reporting it back to Pyongyang. (More on this strange cohort later.)

Early on, my choice of wording, in the media or on our blog, also became a problem.

"Did you say we are 'reforming?'" asked Mr. Kim.

"Yeah, your government is changing the rules for running companies. I wrote about it."

"Please don't use that word. Use other ways to explain our country."

Reform implies, after all, that something is broken and needs remaking.

"Can I say 'policy changes'"?

"Yes."

"Can I say 'policy experiments'"?

"Yes."

"Can I say 'new economic rules'"?

"Yes."

"Can I say 'adjustments to policy'"?

"Yes."

"Can I say 'economic restructuring'"?

"Yes."

"Can I say 'amendments to economic policy'"?

"Yes."

"Just not 'reform'?"

"Yes."

I became a master of saying "reform" without saying it. Look at any article I've written or contributed to and you'll find an orgy of euphemism. But that word illustrates the ambivalence about markets in Pyongyang. They really *had* embarked on a dramatic program of reform from 2012, but unlike the Chinese in the 1980s, whose "amendments to economic policy" were clearly labeled "reform and opening," the North Koreans were — and still are — reluctant to discuss what is going on. Some elements of the system are bothered that the state doesn't control nearly everything in the economy the way they once had.

Another pain point early on in our enterprise was money. Generally speaking, if North Koreans think you are a one-time visitor, they will try to extract as much money from you as possible. The thinking is, "Well, if we're not going to have a relationship, what does it matter if I squeeze these guys for a few extra bucks?"

With our limited funds, we had to be on guard for hotel prices that seemed higher than they should be, extra dishes on menus, spurious requests for printer ink cartridges, and that sort of thing. The first time I was there completely on my own, I couldn't tell which costs were real and which were being inflated. This was before foreign visitors could get mobile SIM cards, so contacting Geoffrey or anyone else was difficult. With a limited amount of cash, I was worried I would run out, given the unexpected costs that were popping up. It was incredibly stressful.

Even worse, I had files on my computer that could potentially aid in hacking Choson Exchange, reading our emails or digging into our finances: all things to be concerned about. I was green and stupid about data security. Could they get around my screenlock password? Could they install things on my computer? I didn't know, but it was starting to freak me out. What if they found correspondence with an institute they objected to, combined with the fact I had a US passport? What if they accused me of being a spy, and not as a joke? Was that likely? Was I being paranoid? I couldn't tell. And because this was 2012 and I couldn't get online, I had no one to talk to about it. A few days of thinking like this and I was starting to feel physically ill.

My wife, who happened to be leading a tour group into North Korea as kind of a part-time gig while she was studying Chinese in Beijing, arrived the night before I was due to leave Pyongyang. She was staying at the same hotel as I, which was fortunate; otherwise, meeting up would have been nearly impossible. Getting permission to move off-itinerary can be very difficult. For hours I'd been lingering around the marble lobby of the Yanggakdo Hotel, skulking around an aquarium that housed a depressed turtle. When her group finally arrived, I rushed into her arms, buried my face in her cheek, and whispered, "I'm so tense—I think they're ripping me off and stealing data off my computer."

I'd never been more relieved to see anyone in my life. She helped calm me down.

Shortly thereafter Geoffrey arrived in Pyongyang for a planning meeting and had a similarly stressful and isolated experience. We resolved that there should always be two Choson Exchange staff on any trip. At that point, that meant both of us.

Notes

1 Joohee Cho, "North Korea's Key to Olympic Medals: Refrigerators for Winners, Labor Camp Threat for Losers," ABC News, August 2, 2012, http://abcnews.go.com /International/north-koreas-key-olympic-medals-rewards-winners-punishment/story ?id=16907983#.UJoAQ-PZ8ii; and John Clarke, "Freedom of Choice for North Koreans at London Olympics: Win and Get a Refrigerator, or Lose and Go to Work Camp," *Forbes*, August 3, 2012, http://www.forbes.com/sites/johnclarke/2012/08/03 /freedom-of-choice-for-north-koreans-at-london-olympics-win-and-get-a-refrigerator -or-lose-and-go-to-work-camp.

2 "World Cup Team Shamed, Reprimanded," Radio Free Asia, July 28, 2010, http:// www.rfa.org/english/news/korea/worldcup-07282010173446.html.

3 Andray Abrahamian and Geoffrey K. See, "Economic Performance and Legitimacy in North Korea," *Harvard International Review*, August 2011.

3

Famine, Nukes, and Marketization

Mr. Bae Ho Nam was one of the kindest, most genuine men I'd ever met. He was a smart guy, a youngish official who spoke English and Chinese. He was slender and loved doing pull-ups and push-ups. He'd grown up in Haeju, several hours to the southwest of Pyongyang. His family was "nothing special," he once told me, but he'd been good at school, gotten into a local college and then moved on up to the Pyongyang University of Foreign Studies, the country's second most prestigious institution, after Kim Il Sung University. (PUFS graduates will contest this ranking.)

He was very hard working, too. He'd make sure he understood our workshop materials inside and out so he could better explain the content to participants. If you said, for example, you wanted to try to buy a particular book or poster, he'd go out of his way to help you. He was always smiling. He'd have made a wonderful bureaucrat in any system, wherever he was born.

Above all, he was fantastically earnest. Once as we drove past Tongil Market, a sprawling one-story covered market on the east side of the river, the size of several football fields, one of our group asked him. "Do you shop there?"

"No, he said, there is a closer market to us, we use that one."

"For most things?"

"Oh yes," he answered. "We are using markets as a solution on our way to a more socialist system." It wasn't clear if he meant what he said, which was the official and impossibly hopeful explanation of the marketization of North Korea. Now there are over five hundred official markets in the country, where individual vendors rent booths from the local authorities and sell everything from toothpaste to televisions.

The old state-controlled model collapsed in the 1990s and was gradually replaced by a market economy. Markets are here to stay in the DPRK. The state will never be able to supplant them again.

Kim Il Sung died in July 1994 and within a couple years the country was in economic free fall. He'd always dreamed of economic self-sufficiency, but in reality that was well out of reach. Like other socialist states, Kim had created a command economy that was very good at reconstruction after the Korean War — it leapt ahead of the shambolic South Korean economy in the 1950s — but eventually succumbed to massive inefficiencies. Although the Soviet Union had assessed by the early 1980s that the DPRK economy was stagnating, Moscow saw Pyongyang as a necessary bulwark against American power in Asia and so allowed a large trade imbalance to develop, subsidizing the economy.[1] When the Soviet Union disappeared, it took with it a range of support.

This precipitated what might be the "most arresting tale of economic failure from modern times," as one observer puts it.[2] North Korea's impulse to restrict information couldn't prevent news of catastrophic floods leaking out in 1995, by which time Pyongyang was desperate enough to request aid from the international community. The floods returned in 1996, damaging both industry and the country's tenuous food production system, which even during good years was not producing enough to feed everyone.[3] Some provinces had been enduring food shortages since the late 1980s. This time, a full-blown famine, referred to as the "Arduous March," began.

Estimates of the tragedy vary wildly, but sober and realistic assessments put the total number of deaths between six hundred thousand and a million people or from 3 to 5 percent of the population. That alone was an utter catastrophe, but bear in mind that that number only reflects the deaths due to starvation or associated diseases. It doesn't capture the increase in malnourishment, physical underdevelopment, psychological issues, crime, displacement, or other problems that arose as a result of the famine.[4] The whole structure of society was profoundly upended, beginning with bodily health, but extending to social and economic life, also. We need to spend a minute looking at the famine and its aftermath because the character of the North Korean system and of North Koreans today has been so deeply shaped by this trauma.

Kim Jong Il is sometimes referred to as the "Great Defender of Socialism." As the official narrative goes, in the 1990s the "unnatural" collapse of the socialist bloc took place. (Unnatural because Marxist teleologies claim that history is moving inevitably in one direction: toward communism.) Only Kim Jong Il was visionary enough, the story goes, to do whatever it took to protect Korean socialism. The people suffered in this defense, of course, but they were all in it together against an outside world that was expecting and encouraging their system to collapse.

There are plenty of hero-myths from this period, too, harkening back to the struggle of Kim Il Sung and his guerrillas. The one most commonly referenced in propaganda is *Hamnamui Bulgil* or the "Burning Road of Hamnam." The slogan references an industrial region in the country's northeast where factory workers and their families supposedly banded together, sold their personal possessions, and donated metal and fuel from their homes — even though they were suffering — in order to keep struggling factories operating for the good of the people. It's unclear if any of this is grounded in the lived experience of Hamnam citizens.

At least one North Korean American does not recall this as a time of solidarity,. He writes that "to build their statues, the government would ask starving families to donate copper or iron or cement. You had to sacrifice your pots and pans for the glory of Kim Jong Il, and if you didn't have any, you had to spend precious time searching for scrap metal when you could be hunting frogs.[5]" Frogs, rats, insects — almost anything was food in these dark years.

One late-1990s study of North Korean migrants who'd fled the country found that "60% migrate for food, and that 40% of households relied primarily on foraging" for food.[6] The authors couldn't generalize from that survey, but it hinted at how people were surviving, or failing to. It was in this period that thousands of North Koreans annually fled the country across the border. Before the famine, numbers were low.

Birth rates dropped in the mid-90s also, as some women avoided getting pregnant or married, and sometimes sought abortions.[7] Under conditions of such hardship a pregnancy could easily threaten the life of the mother, and adequately providing nutrition for a newborn was nearly impossible. Malnutrition also impacted fertility.

The social classes of the North Koreans I mostly interacted with — middle and upper-middle — did not starve, but they suffered also and their relatives who lived outside of the capital even more so. The few times I've discussed the famine with them, the conversations are generally curt. Older people recall losing weight, being cold, and worrying about their children. "It was so hard," a middle-aged man once told me, shaking his head. "We were always hungry." This was over a bountiful spread in Singapore. I offered a toast: "Well, I'm glad we can be here together and eat so well." Middle-aged North Koreans that I've taken abroad still take the opportunity to eat as much meat and dairy as they can. The memory of privation is strong.

Yet Pyongyangers who are now in their late twenties or younger barely remember the Arduous March. They recall their parents worrying a lot and eating the same simple foods over and over again, not seeing meat for months at a time. One young lady told me that she recalled her family managed because of their "good family background," but the neighboring family didn't have enough food. Her family shared what they could.

Solidarity was not always to be found, however, especially lower down the social ladder where the stresses were greater and stakes higher. Children begging for food, few at first, eventually became so common that there were just too many to help, especially when one's own family was struggling to survive. "Charity begins with a full stomach," some would say.[8] Before thinking about helping desperate strangers, they'd sometimes already be choosing who in their own family would eat or go hungry, or even who would live or die.

Corruption also blossomed during this period. Various government agencies and other authorities stopped working together. Central government officials started being dispatched to the provinces to crack down on bribery, but eventually mostly ended up getting sucked into the system of rent-seeking as well.[9] ("Rent-seeking" is an economics term that describes extracting wealth without actually producing anything.) The DPRK went from being probably the least corrupt country in Asia, where money practically got you nowhere, to a market economy without proper rules but with a huge state sector whose employees needed to find money somehow. It was the perfect recipe for corruption.

Personally, I've never really seen much corruption in North Korea, although I was given the impression that if we were to buy cigarettes from duty-free shops as gifts for our partners, those could be regifted at dinners where our partners were seeking permission for programs.

The only blatant attempt at extortion I've been confronted with was at immigration. I'd led a marathon-running group to help out my friends at Koryo Tours during a busy period. A sullen (or at least tired/hungover) Australian in his early twenties was put on my bus to head to the airport, for some reason leaving Pyongyang earlier than the rest of his tour group. After my group had been checked in and had gone through immigration, he and an immigration officer, wearing the trademark oversize hat and green uniform, came up to me. Tourist visas are issued on a piece of paper, not attached to passports, and the officer told me the Australian had lost his, and furthermore, he said, "the fine for that is $400."

"Do you have that much money?" I asked the sullen kid. He shook his head and appeared somehow even more sullen as we discussed where his visa might have gotten lost.

"Then you or someone has to pay," another immigration officer said. Something about this brazen and seemingly made-up fine annoyed me.

"Well, I don't have that much money," I lied. "So . . . I guess he lives here now? Please give me some contact information I can pass on to his family and to his government."

This was not the response they were expecting; they asked again for the money, but I insisted we didn't have it. As the two immigration officers conferred, to everyone's great relief someone came running in from outside the building, waving the visa. It had been dropped in the parking lot.

Another time, some small error was made on my and another visitor's visa, as we were entering the country. We were both pulled aside and had to stand around waiting for a while. This mistake — a misplaced number or two — was neither of our faults, but after around twenty minutes the immigration officer returned and claimed it was a $40 fine. When our North Korean partner explained that I was a frequent visitor, the immigration guy waved me away and said "Fine, just go." The other guy had to pay.

As well as the vagaries of rent-seeking, the country's unwillingness to dramatically reform its economy and system created a massive social and public health crisis. But the domestic crisis was also linked to the high-profile strategic and geopolitical crisis of the mid-1990s. In a very real way, North Korea's darkest hour negatively affected the first-ever attempt by the United States and the DPRK to cooperate.

This was because North Korea's descent into disaster coincided with the first nuclear crisis, which erupted in 1993. It was at this time that American intelligence, cooperating with the International Atomic Energy Association, discovered that the North Koreans had produced more fissile material than they had acknowledged when they reported on their activities to the international community.[10]

The backstory to the two-decade-long nuclear crisis started much earlier. The Koreans saw what the bomb had done to Japan, even if in their version of history, the Japanese were mostly defeated by Kim Il Sung. They also experienced devastating bombing by the US Air Force during the Korean War from 1950 to 1953. At the time, they worried that nuclear weapons would be used on them. To some extent, they still worry.

Pyongyang began lobbying Moscow for help in nuclear research and the Soviets reluctantly agreed to help establish a nuclear research center in Yongbyon in 1959.[11] The North Koreans wanted to expand beyond the small, experimental reactor at the research center, but no one would assist them.[12] Eventually, in order to get more help, North Korea agreed to join the Treaty on the Non-Proliferation of Nuclear Weapons (NPT), signing on in 1985; in return, Moscow pledged to help build four additional reactors from which weapons-grade material would be hard to extract.[13] The essence of the NPT is that states without nuclear weapons permanently swear off developing them. In return, states that possess nuclear weapons pledge not to use them against non-nuclear states, and to share the benefits of peaceful nuclear technology. Oh, and also to disarm, a promise that has proven difficult to keep.

The nuclear crisis with North Korea was averted in 1993 through negotiations, but mutual mistrust and acrimony caused it to resurface the next year, when in May 1994 North Korean scientists removed the fuel rods from their 5-megawatt nuclear research reactor, without international observers present. This not only gave them fuel that could be used for weapons but also destroyed the historical record of their activities.[14] For Washington, this was a red line. Suddenly President Clinton found himself considering two courses of action. The first was sanctions, which the North Koreans had labeled an "act of war"; the second was airstrikes, which probably would have actually started a war.

With no one backing down and a military conflict seeming more and more likely, an unlikely hero (or anti-hero, for the American and South Korean right) swept in: former US president Jimmy Carter. He flew to Pyongyang, met with Kim Il Sung, and single-handedly brokered a deal, going beyond the remit that the Clinton administration had given him.[15]

A plan called the "Agreed Framework" came out of this breakthrough. The United States formed a consortium with several allies and agreed to supply North Korea with two light-water reactors, which are difficult to extract weapons-grade fuel from. The United States also agreed to annually supply five hundred thousand tons of heavy fuel oil until the reactors were completed. Full inspections would resume, North Korea would remain a part of the NPT, and the United States would have greater access and input into the storage and reprocessing of fuel.[16] The United States, North Korea, South Korea, Japan, and others formed the Korean Peninsula Energy Development Organization (KEDO) to oversee the program.

During this period, normalization of relations between the DPRK and the United States was actively discussed, but some bad luck would interfere.[17] Kim Il Sung died in July 1994, so the founder of the DPRK wasn't around to influence the process. Even though Kim Jong Il was essentially in control by the time of his father's death, losing the elder Kim was a profound shock and made bold policy choices more difficult.

Then, the Democrats lost control of both the House of Representatives and the Senate just two weeks after the Agreed Framework was signed. Republicans in Congress were highly critical of the Clinton deal, and Congress made it difficult for the administration to secure funding for the heavy-fuel shipments. Moreover, the quality of the fuel sent to the Koreans was especially low. It had a high sulfur content, making it corrosive and damaging some of the North's power station equipment. The Americans tried to explain that it was a bureaucratic error; the North Koreans believed it was intentional.[18]

Clinton created his own distractions. His rampant libido cost him a great amount of political capital.[19] What he had left he was choosing to spend on the Middle East and Irish peace processes that he was trying to broker. The Korean issue simply occupied third place in his hierarchy of international peace-building efforts.

The general feeling in Washington (and elsewhere) was, however, that North Korea was on its last legs. Its founder was dead, its economy had collapsed — how long could it be before the whole system went? Months? A year? Many thought that it didn't make sense to waste time and resources on something that wasn't going to matter in the near future.

Pyongyang began sending signals that it felt the United States was not living up to its end of the bargain.[20] Then the North Koreans started clandestinely buying up components for uranium in around 1997, kicking off a second-track nuclear weapons program. (Their first pathway to the bomb was plutonium.) Both sides gradually gave up on the deal, in essence.

The famine in a very real way contributed to the failure of the deal, on both sides. The Americans felt that North Korea would have to capitulate sooner rather than later. The North Koreans felt more isolated and vulnerable than at any time since late 1950 and became even more determined to boost their deterrence capability with nuclear weapons.

These were issues for practitioners of high politics, however. The famine's greater impact was on ordinary people, who had to turn to market activities to survive. People were making, trading, buying, selling, and hustling on a scale that was new. Previously, farmer's markets existed where surplus crops could be sold, but they were limited in scope. These markets would sometimes expand to meet people's food needs during periods when the public distribution system failed to operate well, most notably in rural areas. Black-market activities would pop up, too. This happened in the mid to late 1980s, along with more goods being illegally imported from China.[21] A fortunate few were thus being trained to survive in a monetized society before catastrophe hit. Those who weren't and expected the state to continue to provide for them were set up for tremendous suffering.

When the North Korean command economy was working properly, money was not really necessary for most people. The system, from a citizen's point of view, was simple. You worked hard for and were loyal to the state and the ruling Kim family. In return, the state took care of everything for you. The state had a public distribution system for food and provided you with food coupons to use through your workplace. It provided your work clothing as well as suits or other nicer items for formal or special occasions. It adjudicated whether you went to university or not and what your choices were for subjects. It provided your housing and chose where you lived. It provided healthcare to you. It gifted you luxury items if you or your work team did well: radios, refrigerators, and televisions for the fortunate few.

In North Korea, you can go far on talent. If you have aptitude for science and do well in school, you can get into a good university, join a prestigious organization, and be allocated better housing and better rations. If you are athletic, you might be picked out to train for a certain sport and, again, better-quality provisions would be made available to you.

There is a darker side to the state deciding your social prospects: the *songbun* system. This is, essentially, a loyalty metric that the state applies to you, based in no small part on your family history. The three main classes to the system are Core, Wavering, and Hostile, but a report found that as part one of several North Korean "projects" for investigating and classifying the population, North Koreans were further divided into fifty-one subcategories during 1967–70.[22] Some now suggest there are five main categories: Special, Core, Basic, Complex, and Hostile.[23]

There is some mobility, but the social class to which you belong depends in large part on the actions of your parents and grandparents. Were your forebears guerrilla fighters with Kim Il Sung? Then you start life with incredible advantages. Were they landlords who resisted the communist takeover or fled south during the war? Then educational opportunities and good bureaucratic jobs are probably out of your reach.

The idea of the state deciding whether or not you are worthy of a good life is discomfiting to a Western observer. We prefer to let market forces handle the distribution of inequality. After all, if your grandparents were millionaires you are unlikely to end up working class. And if your grandparents were working class, the odds are against you moving into the upper-middle class. This has been a robust system for organizing society and it does seem less unfair than having a bureaucrat look at a file and decide your whole life's prospects. The social contract was simply dictated to you by the state.

In many ways it still is, but when the famine came much of the social contract was shredded. The state just couldn't provide what it once had, so people had to fend for themselves. People scrapped and hustled to survive:

> They were desperate to find food and needed money. So they went to the river or sea to hunt fish and sell in the market. Some people even bred domestic animals and butchered them secretly.
>
> People running restaurants or hotels were often involved in prostitution and brewing illegal alcohol to make money. Some of them even tried to dismantle infrastructure, machinery and ammunition and sell it to the Chinese. Almost every market in North Korea became overflown [sic] with Chinese goods.... [24]

Obviously, the collapse of the public distribution system for food was most catastrophic. It was the people who couldn't find creative ways to make up for the shortfall who died. For those who survived, a new worldliness emerged. The state's control over information had been punctured. As more people crossed illegally into China to work and trade, they came back with new perspectives and ideas. Smuggling media on DVDs and then USBs became common. People who were running private businesses to survive also spread news and market information from town to town and county to county. Penalties for distributing media illegally can be severe, but the authorities have been unable to stamp it out.

As the years went on and the state couldn't resurrect the old system, a new reality emerged and gradually set in. Mr. Yang, a low-ranking official with whom I spent a few days in Wonsan in 2015, told me, "These days the government provides my family with coupons for rice and cooking oil. Everything else we have to buy ourselves." He raised his eyebrows, wrinkling his weather-beaten face, and gave a that's-how-it-is shrug.

Mr. Yang had two huge gold fillings, which he said were provided by a government dentist, but not 100 percent covered. Gold fillings are common in North Korea as they are more durable and simpler than the fancy white resin used in developed countries. He went on to say his wife had some stomach problems, but the government either couldn't or wouldn't provide the right medicine, so he was having to save for it. He said this matter-of-factly; he wasn't begging or asking for sympathy. I found his stoicism so impressive I slipped him fifty dollars and told him not to tell his more senior colleague, a man whom I didn't trust and who I thought would try to take part or all of it.

Where loyalty was once the currency of social life, now money is paramount. I should have given more. Would I have felt a pinch if I had given an additional fifty dollars? He was a good man and could have used that money well. As with the majority of the North Koreans I've met, I have no realistic way to get in touch with Mr. Yang. I remember him from time to time and hope he is well and that his wife recovered.

One person I met back in Pyongyang, and of a significantly higher social class than Mr. Yang, also complained about the difficulty of obtaining good medical treatment; the country's medical system, like its distribution system, never fully recovered after the famine. He said he was thinking of getting his ailing mother some "ice."

"What's that?" I asked.

"It's a drug that gives you energy." Then, in a whisper: "It's illegal, but everybody can get it and it's cheap."

"What! You mean *crystal meth*?" I said through clenched teeth. It was a question, but I knew the answer. I'd heard that it was widely used in the country.

"Maybe," he said. He'd not heard that name.

"Listen," I argued, "don't do it. It's really, really bad for you. It may make her feel better for a bit, but it will make her condition worse overall." Even I, the kind of doctor who can write a social science essay — pretty useless — knew that "ice" wasn't a good prescription.

"We have a huge problem with this drug in my country," I said. "It really messes people up."

"Really?" He was surprised by this claim. "We think it is pretty good." Indeed, laborers across Asia are getting hooked on this cheap drug that helps them stay alert and provides energy as they engage in exhausting, menial work.[25]

I'm not sure what he ended up doing. Nor do I begrudge people taking an ultimately harmful drug to help them through their incredibly difficult lives. The rise of meth use coincided with the famine, not only because rule of law broke down but because of the nature of the drug: it gives you an energy boost while suppressing appetite, perfect for the malnourished, in a very short-term sense.

At least one far healthier trend came out of this period: *injogogibap*. *Injogogibap* means "fake meat and rice." The fibrous dregs that come when you press soybeans to get oil get turned into a paste, then dried in strips. They are rehydrated, stuffed with rice, and slathered with a spicy sauce. During the famine this was survival protein. Now, it has become a part of the cuisine.

It reminds me of a dish in South Korea called *budaejigae*. This means "base stew" and features processed meats like spam, sausages, and other odds and ends like baked beans and sometimes cheese. It was based on food scrounged or bought from the US military during and after the Korean War. A dish that once represented extreme poverty, it is now part of the national cuisine. The dish can be enjoyed today without shame, from a position of wealth.

Injogogibab is similarly enjoyed more by choice now in North Korea. As Cho Ui-sung, a North Korean now living in the South, puts it: "Back in the day, people had *injogogi* to fill themselves up as a substitute for meat . . . now people eat it for its taste."[26] This may not be from a position of "wealth" as such, for privation and hardship are still widespread. But it has entered the national cuisine in a positive way. Ironically, a friend in the tourism business tells me they don't promote it to tourists because of the association with the famine, a connection the vast majority of tourists would have no idea about.

I'm a vegetarian and this dish was once being discussed by our group of volunteers in our van as we cruised around Pyongyang. One of our North Korean partners, a spritely young woman, turned around from the front and said, "Actually, being vegetarian is quite popular in our country these days."

"Sure," said Henry, one of our workshop leaders, "but not by choi — ." He caught himself about to say something impolitic and cut himself off.

"Aha! I heard that," I said, laughing.

A few hours later, Henry was delivering a presentation in front of forty-five North Korean officials and academics. One of his slides used the Big Mac Index to explain purchasing power parity around the world. (The Big Mac index was invented by *The Economist* in 1986 as a rough way to judge prices between countries and whether currencies are being valued properly.) In the late 1990s, this might have seemed a cruel way to illustrate an economic issue that needed discussing. By 2013, it was fine.

"We have this kind of thing here now," said one participant, referring to a hamburger restaurant in Pyongyang set up by a Singaporean investor. Someday, perhaps, there will be an actual McDonald's in Pyongyang. Though when that day comes I sincerely hope that people will not eat there, will continue to support local businesses and choose to eat *injogogibap*. Most sellers of that tasty fake meat are sole proprietors or small family businesses; they make the food in their homes and sell it at market stalls or to bigger shops.

Notes

1 Nick Eberstadt, *The End of North Korea* (Washington, DC: AEI Press, 1999), 35.

2 Nick Eberstadt, *North Korea's 'Epic Economic Fail' in International Perspective*, (Seoul, Korea: The Asan Institute for Policy Studies, November 2015), 8.

3 Marcus Noland, Sherman Robinson, and Tao Wang, "Famine in North Korea: Causes and Cures," *Economic Development and Cultural Change* 49, no. 4 (July 2001): 746.

4 Stephen Haggard and Marcus Noland, *Famine in North Korea: Markets, Aid, and Reform* (New York: Columbia University Press, 2009), 76.

5 Joseph Kim, *Under the Same Sky: From Starvation in North Korea to Salvation in America* (New York: Houghton Mifflin Harcourt, 2015), 68.

6 W. Courtland Robinson, Myung Ken Lee, Kenneth Hill, and Gilbert M Burnham, "Mortality in North Korean Migrant Households: A Retrospective Study," *Lancet* 354, no. 9175 (July 1999): 294.

7 Andrew S. Nastios, *The Great North Korean Famine* (Washington, DC: USIP Press, 2001), 64.

8 Barbara Demick, *Nothing to Envy: Ordinary Lives in North Korea* (New York: Random House, 2007), 167–68.

9 Ishimaru Jiro, *Rimjingang* (Osaka: Asiapress International, 2010), 32.

10 Victor Gilinsky, *Nuclear Blackmail: The 1994 U.S.-Democratic People's Republic of Korea Agreed Framework on North Korea's Nuclear Program* (Palo Alto: Hoover Institution, 1997), 6.

11 Walter C. Clemens, "North Korea's Quest for Nuclear Weapons: New Historical Evidence," *Journal of East Asian Studies* 10, no. 1 (2010): 129.

12 Clemens, "North Korea's Quest," 131–33, 144–45.

13 Vladimir Orlov, "Russia's Nonproliferation Policy and the Situation in East Asia," The Nautilus Institute, March 05, 2001, http://nautilus.org/nuke-policy/russias-non proliferation-policy-and-the-situation-in-east-asia-2.

14 Joel S. Wit, Daniel B. Poneman, and Robert L. Gallucci, *Going Critical: The First North Korean Nuclear Crisis* (Washington, DC: Brookings Institution Press, 2004), 92.

15 Michael J. Mazarr, *North Korea and the Bomb* (New York: St. Martin's Griffin, 1997), 163.

16 Gilinsky, *Nuclear Blackmail*, 10–11.

17 Wit, Poneman, and Gallucci, *Going Critical,* 252–53.

18 Various conversations between author and US officials, 2010.

19 Mike Chinoy, *Meltdown* (New York: St. Martin's Griffin Press, 2008), 8.

20 Leon Sigal, "North Korea Is No Iraq: Pyongyang's Negotiating Strategy," *Arms Control Today* 32, no. 10 (December 2002): 11.

21 Choi Bong-dae and Gu Gap-woo, "북한 도시 '농민시장' 형성 과정의 이행론적 함의 - 1950~1980년대 신의주, 청진, 혜산의 사례를 중심으로 현대북한연구" [Implications for the process of forming the "farmers' market" in North Korea—a study on modern North Korea focusing on the cases of Sinuiju, Chongjin, and Hyesan in the 1950s and 1980s], 현대북한연구 [Contemporary North Korean studies] 6, no. 2 (December 2012): 180–81.

22 Robert Collins, *Marked for Life: Songbun North Korea's Social Classification System* (Washington, DC: The Committee for Human Rights in North Korea, 2012).

23 Fyodor Tertitskiy, "Songbun and the Five Castes of North Korea," NK News, February 26, 2015, https://www.nknews.org/2015/02/songbun-and-the-five-castes-of-north-korea.

24 Daniel Tudor, *Ask A North Korean* (North Clarendon: Tuttle, 2017), 94.

25 "Methamphetamines from Myanmar Are Causing Problems across Asia," *The Economist*, December 15, 2018, https://www.economist.com/asia/2018/12/15/methamphetamines-from-myanmar-are-causing-problems-across-asia.

26 James Pearson and Seung-Woo Yeom, "Fake Meat and Free Markets Ease North Koreans' Hunger," Reuters, November 3, 2017, https://www.reuters.com/investigates/special-report/northkorea-food.

4

A Walled Society

I have to go to the phone company to reactivate my SIM card," I said to Mr. Jang. "Is it OK if I walk the four hundred meters to the office and come back?" If you're a foreigner with an internet-enabled SIM, the phone company disables the card the day you leave the country. When you come back you have to set it up again. This is so that if you leave the card in the country, no local person can use it.

"Let me find someone to help; it will be more convenient if I find someone to go with you," replied our smiling prevaricator. We'd occasionally worked with Mr. Jang to organize workshops and he could be very friendly, but only up to a point. He was of the old school. He defended his country and his system with every ounce of his being and in eloquent staccato English. He propped himself up on platformed shoes to compensate for his diminutive height, much the same as Kim Jong Il used to do.

"Oh, that won't be more convenient." Obviously. "Everybody is busy running the workshop, but I have some downtime. I'll just go and come back."

"No, no, what if you have some miscommunication on the way?" he asked, attempting to sound helpful while being the opposite.

"Well, you know I speak Korean, so I'm sure that won't be a problem. Plus, I know where the building is and I won't talk to anyone. I promise."

"Perhaps people here aren't used to seeing foreigners, they might misunderstand something."

"Do you not trust me not to speak to anyone?"

"Oh no! It isn't that at all. It would just be much easier if someone accompanied you."

I knew at this point the inevitable outcome of this discussion but was annoyed with him and didn't want to let it go. In fact, I was the tolerant one when it came to Mr. Jang. Geoffrey would occasionally raise his voice when dealing with him and I'd have to smooth things over. Classic good cop/bad cop, except no one was really acting.

"Mr. Jang," I pushed, "Am I not *allowed* to go by myself?"

"No, no, it isn't that, but we have a very *organized* society, with certain expectations." His euphemism for controlled/repressed/forbidding was always "organized."

What was he worried about? When visiting on a non-tourist visa, as we were, sometimes we'd be allowed to do such errands unaccompanied or go off on our own to meet foreign residents. Had he been told this time to keep us on a short leash? Was his performance being watched? Was he genuinely worried I'd try something problematic, like talk to a passerby or go into a shop I wasn't allowed to?

"Listen," I tried, "if I'm not allowed to go by myself, I understand, but please . . . just tell me. Of course, I don't want to cause any trouble for you." I genuinely didn't.

I was trying to give him the chance to admit that we were working together in solidarity amidst difficult rules. I failed.

"Oh no!" he pantomimed, "There wouldn't be any trouble! I'm only thinking of the convenience of everyone involved."

Younger people aren't like this so much. Much more often they will simply admit that something isn't possible because of "the rules," even if they have been instructed not to fully explain what those rules are to you, the visiting foreigner. They might even give you a shrug or an eyebrow raise. The longer you work with someone of this younger generation, the more of that sort of cynical attitude might peek out.

Once a colleague of mine was returning with a group from Wonsan. She was having a slow, lazily paced road-trip conversation with her Korean counterpart. They knew each other well, having worked together several times. As the sun was setting over the bumpy highway, the Korean asked her, "Why do you keep coming back?" She responded diplomatically with something about having a love for Korea. A few minutes later they rumbled past yet another dark village. One house had a dim exposed bulb visible, its pale light struggling through the window. People lived by that bulb. Someone was reading or cooking or studying for a test. They'd likely lived their entire lives there, never having known twenty-four-hour electricity, or spoken to a foreigner, or perhaps even been to the nearest city. They both looked over at the forlorn, spectral scene.

"Doesn't this place make you feel depressed?" the minder asked. My colleague didn't bother with an answer this time.

If you're just visiting once, you are unlikely to get much beyond the official party line from any North Korean you encounter. I recall one meeting in Beijing with a lady who worked in renewable energy. She was originally from East Germany and was on her way into Pyongyang for a tour. We were meeting because she said she was interested in returning to North Korea to run a workshop with Choson Exchange.

She came back from her tour, five days later, in a sort of rage because her guides had never strayed from the official explanation for anything. "I used to host foreign groups when I was a university student in the German Democratic Republic," she told me. "We'd always communicated our dissatisfaction somehow, perhaps with the sarcastic tone of our voice or a roll of the eyes as we gave the party line. My guides didn't do that once. I couldn't get them to admit anything about their situation."

She was profoundly disappointed in this, having tried to map her German experience of living under a controlled form of socialism onto the Korean one. The fact is there aren't good equivalents elsewhere. In the European communist experience, Romania or Albania were the tightest-wound societies, but not as disciplined as in Korea. Peak Stalinism in the Soviet Union may have been similar, in terms of control and caprice, but again, it was hard to maintain that sort of discipline in a country that spans eleven time zones. North Korea is small, contained and "organized," to borrow Mr. Jang's term.

The German lady didn't return. She'd have *hated* Mr. Jang. He was steeped in a way of dealing with foreigners in which hiding as much information as possible—*even the fact that you are hiding information*—is the modus operandi.

"Externally, we must not reveal ourselves to the outside," Kim Jong Il is reported to have said, "but conceal ourselves as if Joson is inside [a] fog. We are to hide the politics of Kim Jong-il inside the fog."[1] "Joson" (also transliterated as Chosun, Joseon, or Choson) is the DPRK word for Korea. Kim is supposed to have said this to a group of officials in the mid-1990s, as they were working on a deal with the United States regarding the DPRK's nascent nuclear program. The country was also descending into famine, a vulnerability they wished they could hide from the outside world. The idea of keeping Korea inside a fog is at the heart of North Korea's worldview, and has been perhaps since its inception. In this view, the DPRK is a small country beset by hostile forces that want to see its destruction. By controlling information, the country creates an asymmetry: it can find out more about its enemies' societies, economics, and politics than they can find out about its own. This is, therefore, a key pillar of the DPRK's resistance to influence by the outside world.

Frankly, it makes sense, in terms of state survival. The United States, Japan, and South Korea would probably wish North Korea out of existence if they could. Relations with China are frequently tense. North Korea's most important ally, the Soviet Union, literally stopped existing. And the secrecy does give North Korea an asymmetrical advantage against its enemies. The "fog" means that human intelligence is extremely hard to come by. By contrast, United States, Japan, and South Korea are all relatively open societies, easier both to infiltrate by operatives and to understand through conventional research.

The "wrapped in fog" mentality means leadership changes at the very top are made without explanation; they are merely presented to the public. Many longtime Korea watchers are sure that while some information can be gleaned by paying attention to who is in power and who is out, there are real elite decision-makers and institutions that we never even hear about. Details of the leadership's actual lives are kept secret from the people. North Koreans don't even know where Kim Jong Un resides. They know who his wife is but knew nothing of the women in the lives of Kim Jong Il or Kim Il Sung, nor anything about their family trees.

"Kim Jong Un has an older brother?" a gentle workshop participant asked me in 2015.

"Yes," I said. "He lives in Macau."

"Is he smart?" was her first question, probing as to whether he had the genius ascribed to his father and grandfather. "Why is he in Macau?" was her second, asked with a furrowed brow.

I thought about how to answer. "Everyone seems to agree that it's better if he lives abroad for a while," I said, vaguely.

She nodded in understanding. Kim Jong Un's half-brother Kim Jong Nam was not smart enough to outwit the assassins that killed him in Malaysia in 2017.

The state hides information from both foreigners and citizens alike. The political instructions handed down to the masses are kept secret from outsiders. Every week all adults have to attend study sessions, wherein political ideas and objectives are promulgated. Foreigners rarely hear much about what is conveyed in such meetings. We see the *Rodong Sinmun* newspaper, but there are also hard-wire broadcasts—something akin to cable radio—piped into homes. These broadcasts cannot be intercepted from outside and we rarely know what messages are transmitted.

"The fog" also means that no meaningful economic data has been published since the mid-1960s, around the time when rival South Korea started to ramp up its economic development. As a North Korean told me once, "our enemies could use this information against us." The practice persists even to this day, despite North Korea acknowledging that attracting foreign direct investment is a goal.

It means that the whole country sometimes shuts down at the slightest pretext, such as during the Ebola outbreak (which never reached Asia) in 2014–15, or the SARS epidemic (which was right on their doorstep) in 2003. There are also periodic crackdowns on activities that lead to outside information coming in, as in 2014 when trade and trafficking along the border with China—whether in goods, people, or information—became much harder.[2]

Maintaining the fog requires keeping foreigners inside the country as isolated from the public as possible. Foreigners are sort of treated like a bacterial vaccine: a bit of bacteria is necessary for all sorts of bodily functions and can make the body stronger, but too much can risk disease. The "disease" in this metaphor is any idea or group of ideas that challenge the monolithic control of the North Korean state.

After all, every single visitor to North Korea is required to have a guide or a minder and a set itinerary that is cleared by a protocol officer at whichever organization authorized your visit and sponsored your visa. (There is some flexibility: you can drop in at a number of sites or restaurants without pre-approval; but any "serious location" requires clearance first, as does any meeting with a North Korean. It is not possible to just meet someone from a prior visit without some official pretext, real or concocted.) This has been the case since the early 1990s, when Pyongyang began inviting Westerners to visit as tourists, rather than as more formal delegates with some official purpose. For three decades they've maintained this model.

By contrast, China used essentially the same modus operandi from the mid to late 1970s, an extremely short period. China was completely closed during the Cultural Revolution in the late 1960s, but as that tumultuous period waned, the country began inviting people to come visit in groups, to enjoy "revolutionary tourism." This meant seeing revolutionary sites and interacting with "ordinary Chinese," but under very limited and controlled circumstances, very similar to how the North Koreans run tourism and other visits today.

In China the practice was abandoned by the mid-1980s, however, when foreigners were allowed the freedom to enter and conduct business, research, or just travel on their own.[3] Their system of minders for foreigners lasted barely half a decade because Beijing quickly decided that letting go of some control was worth it for the sake of economic development. Vietnam similarly required special permission and sometimes minders for foreigners leaving Hanoi or Ho Chi Minh City for other locations until the early

1990s. They kept that system up for perhaps five or six years from their *Doi Moi*—opening—in 1986, again, choosing economic development. Pyongyang, by contrast, has always leaned toward more control.

In the 1990s, as Vietnam was opening up and connecting to the world, some of us in the West were growing excited at the prospects of positive change brought by the internet. New technologies would drive democracy and be great levelers that would give everyone a voice as well as all the access to information and relationships that they would need. Or so we thought. Disappointingly, things have turned out differently. Mobile and internet technologies have become instead incredible tools for control.

In China the most intense example of this is being birthed in the form of a social credit system. Networked cameras with facial recognition technology, home computers, and of course mobile phones are being stitched together to build an unsurpassed surveillance system. Your social credit score will go up if you go to the gym, obey traffic laws, pay taxes on time, or join in volunteer work. Your score will go down if you have relationships with political activists, perhaps some foreigners or journalists. It could go down if you get in a fight, or consistently litter in your neighborhood, or buy alcohol too often. China is becoming the ultimate wired surveillance state. Xinjiang is becoming the testbed for this.

Meanwhile, North Korea is perhaps the ultimate unconnected surveillance state. It has a network of semi-professional informants acting as eyes and ears: "the bird listens during the day and the mouse does at night," goes a Northern proverb that exhorts caution in sharing opinions.[4] You always have to assume someone is watching or listening to what you do.

Historian Andrei Lankov believes that perhaps some 250,000 to 300,000 North Korean citizens are at any given time paid informers.[5] The country is thought to have a "one in five household" surveillance system.[6] This means the state regularly calls on 20 percent of people or households to inform on neighbors or co-workers to state security personnel. These people may not be paid but are regularly cooperative. If an offense is dug up, the target may be able to bribe their way out of trouble if the crime is not too serious. This is in stark contrast to pre-famine DPRK, in which this sort of corruption was nearly unheard of. Still, today, when a crackdown is happening, bribery may not work.[7] It is a capricious system.

Under such conditions, criticism and frank speech are things that are at best confined to one's immediate family or closest friends. Trust is extremely difficult to build in North Korea: people are constantly having to regulate what they say, careful not to contravene boundaries or standards that are often unwritten. So if you have doubts about something sensitive, say, perhaps if there is a TV news segment touting an amazingly successful infrastructure campaign in your hometown that you know has in fact been poorly constructed, you usually keep quiet on the matter.

The news you see as a North Korean is of course extremely limited. We'll return to that later. Suffice for the moment to say that there is nothing outside of official channels.

The most important tool for maintaining society-wide discipline is "organizational life." All communist regimes have or had some mechanism for transmitting ideology downwards, but in North Korea there emerged "a number of unique features not to be found in other communist countries."[8] Every single North Korean adult belongs to one of the following organizations: the Korean Workers' Party (KWP), the Youth League, the Trade Union, the Farmers' Union, or the Women's Union.

The Worker's Party is the master organization. Getting accepted as a party member is a big deal. It means you suffer greater scrutiny but it also improves your social and career prospects significantly.[9] An applicant has to have two party members sponsor them, then their case is discussed at a local party cell, then finally by a higher, more obscure committee. Once, a North Korean colleague of ours seemed a little bit more agitated than usual. One of his co-workers confided to us that he was in the process of applying for party membership but didn't think it was going well. It was stressing him out.

There are probably around 3.4 million party members.[10] If you aren't a KWP party member, you have no choice but to be a member of one of the other organizations. Every Saturday you will have a political study session with other members, where you'll also engage in self-criticism and mutual-criticism sessions.

During the study sessions there are lectures on politics, economics, and culture. People are expected to learn long passages by heart. Often you can see people in parks or at night sometimes hanging around under streetlights, memorizing these texts. There can be tests on recent party teachings. In no small part because of this system, North Koreans have amazing memories. It really is noticeable when you visit how little we remember compared to the Koreans. We're now so dependent on our mobile devices and the internet. I don't commit my calendar to memory because I can just call it up at any time. The Koreans can remember all sorts of details.

The power of recall is highly prized and people who can easily memorize and recite things genuinely have a leg up in life. Indeed, "every member of an organization is required to occasionally produce properly worded utterances on political subjects," meaning that organizational life turns participants into reproducers of propaganda.[11] This also means you end up hearing *remarkably* similar answers to questions you might ask North Koreans about their system. I've heard several visitors ask something like "are there Christians in the DPRK?" The answer is always something along the lines of, "Freedom of religion is guaranteed by our constitution, but we Koreans don't feel the need for Christianity." They *always* mention the constitution.

The criticism sessions, which we'll return to, are called *saenghwal chong-hwa* ("life harmony") sessions. These can be more or less frequent, depending on your position and organization. They can be intense, serious events, in which people attack each other and attempt to gain or use leverage. They can be, but this is generally not how they go. More often, they seem to be very perfunctory, ritualized affairs, in which people note things they could have done better and promise to try harder. Colleagues with good working relationships will criticize each other, but not so harshly as to damage relationships.

Still, North Koreans are constantly thinking about these sessions. Sometimes issues from months ago can resurface and cause problems for individuals. In most of our work lives in the West, usually if a mistake or incident arises, it is dealt with right away. If you are North Korean, however, an incident you'd been involved in—say a foreigner you were minding wandered off and tried to buy things from a street vendor—might be sat on by a rival for months. They could then bring it up at some point when they want to harm you or want to, say, distract from their own shortcomings.

It's not always so odious though. Indeed, one North Korean couple I know have their "marriage origin story" rooted in a mutual-criticism session. She was very competent at her job and felt that he was holding back her team: she called him out for being late too frequently and for being lazy. In that moment he felt some nerves—she was senior to him at their company—but he also became enamored with her badassery. This was the sort of tough woman that maybe he needed to whip him into shape, he thought. He convinced her of that idea, eventually. They've been married several years now and recently had a child.

That may be a happy ending of sorts but take a second to imagine what it must be like to participate in this ritual. Whether in normal times or times of high tension, every single week you'd have to consider your work in relation to goals set by the ruling party. You'd also have to consider your criticisms of others with regard to both their political and social positions and yours. Every group setting thus becomes political. The KWP mediates your personal relationships.

On top of being forced to engage in organized life, the state's interference and presence in your daily life is compounded by the fact that North

Koreans have no right to organize anything on their own, outside of state control. Markets, semi-private enterprises, and gray-area private owner-ship of assets have grown and even been encouraged under Kim Jong Un, yet there remains essentially no such thing as civil society in North Korea. People can meet friends to play volleyball in a park, for example, but they cannot organize a league.

I once asked a particularly musical North Korean, Mr. Shim, about what he could do as a musician; he was good enough to crush a karaoke session, but perhaps not elite enough to get into a music program somewhere.

"Could you make a band with friends?" I asked.

"Of course."

"Could you record yourselves around a laptop?"

"Sure."

"Could you make a CD of the recording and sell it or give it away?"

"Hrm." He paused. "I've never heard of such a thing. Maybe not?"

In all likelihood, there would be trouble if he tried. He'd have some explaining to do in his next "life harmony" session. Any sort of regularized group activity has to have permission, to be within the bounds of state activity. Cultural production all the more so.

A major report on North Korean human rights published in 2014, the UN Commission of Inquiry (COI) Report, puts it starkly: there "is almost complete denial of the right to freedom of thought, conscience, and religion as well as of the rights to freedom of opinion, expression, information, and association."[12] This unprecedented report was an attempt to put human rights in North Korea higher on the global agenda.

It worked, though North Koreans tend to react badly to having been singled out by a special UN report. "Why is this targeting just us?" one Korean complained to me at an international conference in 2018. "Every country has human rights problems! We know we do too, but so do China, the United States...every country!"

Regardless, the report found that suppression of freedom of religion was uniquely important to the state, concluding that since it was an overt ideological challenge, Christianity is prohibited and punishments for prac-ticing it are severe.[13]

Three show churches exist in Pyongyang— the protestant *Chilgol* and *Bongsu*, and a Catholic church—with some sort of local membership, though they appear mostly as an exercise in foreign-facing propaganda. When ques-tioned on theology by visitors with a genuine interest, the Korean Church staff invariably reply with a mishmash of Juche and Kim Il Sung–focused answers. A representative of the Bongsu Protestant Church in Pyongyang once told a US news crew that, somewhat amusingly, "in the era of science, we don't believe" in the virgin birth of Jesus Christ. She went on to bluntly say, "We think Kim Il Sung is God . . . he's a person who is like God."[14] This was in 1995—North Koreans are a little subtler now in many ways. I've never heard a Korean say the Kims are anything more than men. Great men, but men all the same.

The UN report also found some evidence of small-scale protests taking place around the country, but noted that rather than being political at heart, "these random protests are mostly about economic conditions rather than direct criticisms against the state."[15] A public display of disaffection with the state, the party, or the leadership remains nearly unthinkable in the DPRK on an individual level. Some of these small protests in response to relatively minor grievances against minor officials may flirt with criticisms of broader policies, but there isn't really evidence to suggest that develops into broad and explicit criticism.

Ensuring that no one can found an organization outside state control means that there are no institutions to act as a platform or channel to oppose the government in any real way. The limits on freedom of association and on communications technologies also limit the potential for mobilizing significant numbers of citizens or cooperating closely with people outside the country.

The limits on technology are manifold. And while the information cordon has been breached, as we saw in the previous chapter, the authorities still have tremendous power to shape opinions through their monopoly over permitted media.

With radio, for example, they keep it simple: there is a single radio station (for the most part). More extraordinary than that, all radios sold legally are physically fixed so that they can only receive the state channel. Tampering with the radio to make it capable of receiving other stations is a punishable offense. So is listening to foreign radio broadcasts on a smuggled radio. No other country has tried such a restrictive policy on radios.

That doesn't mean that listening to radios illegally doesn't happen. A 2004 survey of defectors found that 19 percent had used foreign broadcasts as their main source of news, while 21 percent claimed to know someone who had tampered with their fixed radios to listen to other broadcasts.[16] Other surveys around that time found over 50 percent of defectors had listened to foreign radio broadcasts.[17] Some activists suggest that 30–40 percent of people are listening to unrestricted radios.[18] A more recent study suggested "most respondents who listen to the radio at all listen to foreign broadcasts."[19]

These sources are self-selecting, but it is fair to assume that a significant minority of North Koreans now listens to foreign—primarily South

Korean—radio broadcasts. Certainly, while in Pyongyang, this was a sensitive enough subject that I never brought it up, nor has any information ever been volunteered to me on the issue. This is in contrast to foreign movies or TV shows, which were quite frequently discussed, even though the contents were often forbidden. I was privy to the sensitivity about radios on one occasion, however.

In 2011 I organized an ultimate frisbee tournament in Pyongyang, hoping to introduce the sport I loved to the country I studied. One of the players in our group, from Michigan, was studying Korean down south. She was engaged all week with her guide, using an electronic English-Korean dictionary to look up South Korean slang and idioms. She and the guide would laugh and compare terms between north and south. They both had bubbly, outgoing personalities and by the end of the week it seemed like they'd known each other for years.

The day before we were to leave, the guide had worked up the courage to ask if she could buy the dictionary.

The tourist, aware of the guide's relatively meager salary, came to me and asked, "Do you think it's okay if I just offer to give it to her?" I had a glance at it.

"That would be a lovely gift," I said, "but it has a radio function. So maybe just point that out to her when you offer it."

Back on the bus, the ultimate frisbee player scooted up next to the guide's seat and offered to give the dictionary to her, eliciting a huge grin. Then she explained about the radio function. The guide's smile evaporated into a composed neutral expression. "Actually, it's okay," she managed. "I'm not really studying much these days, but you are. You should keep it."

Of course, control extends to media beyond radio. The DPRK has comprehensive control over newspapers, which is made easy by how few there are: a handful in Pyongyang and one paper per provincial capital. There is no evidence of private newspapers, 'zines, or other variation of *samizdat*—underground publications—as there were in the Soviet Union or other socialist states during the Cold War.

Indeed, for one workshop, we wanted to run an exercise where participants would type up their conclusions, then we'd print them out and pass them out to other groups to debate, compare, and contrast opinions. We brought a printer for this purpose. It was seized at customs. We were allowed to have it back when we left a week later, but the worry was clearly that we were bringing a piece of technology that could be used to create and disseminate unapproved content.

Censorship over content that does get printed and distributed in the media is extremely tight—all publications and broadcasters are state-owned. In effect, the party's Propaganda and Agitation Department (PAD) first filters out personnel who might not be ideologically acceptable: all of the workforce are heavily vetted, so if you've been hired, you're already considered reliable. Staff focused on censorship at publications will approve content first, then send the material upwards to the PAD's sub-agencies (different for broadcast and print, for example) for further inspection. It is then sent back to the publication for a final check before being released.[20] This constant feedback and coordination mechanism ensures that nothing unwanted can sneak into print or over the airwaves.

Television in the DPRK is, as you might by now suspect, also state-owned. The main channel, Korean Central Television, broadcasts usually from three or four o'clock in the afternoon until sign-off at eleven o'clock. There are often three other channels available on the weekends, offering more global content and sports. Foreign content is heavily vetted, though they have showed *Bend it Like Beckham*, Bollywood movies, and Disney cartoons.

The level of control over traditional media is easy to perceive, but how far do digital technologies disrupt the state's control over information? We've seen that the pre-digital information cordon has been breached by marketization and cheap technology, but computers and phones still offer powerful tools for monitoring and control.

For computers, North Korea has developed its own operating system based on Linux, called Red Star OS. It is installed on computers sold in the country and sometimes installed on computers that Koreans bring in from abroad. It can scan for files or content deemed undesirable by keyword and perhaps other indicators and delete that content without the user's consent. It automatically watermarks files such as word processing documents, videos, and audio.[21]

The watermarking means that if you copy, say, a South Korean pop song from a USB stick onto your hard drive, it embeds code into that file. If that file is later copied to another USB and another computer, it repeats the process. In that way the authorities can track where a file has come from and what machines it has seen along its sharing journey. This allows authorities to investigate file sharers more easily. If files were being shared on the North Korean intranet, they could even map file sharing remotely, probably linking IP addresses to specific machines and users. Interestingly, the term *angae*, meaning "fog," is widely used in parts of custom code used by the Red Star OS.[22]

Of course, it is mobile phones that stitch people and markets together in the developing world in the twenty-first century, and North Korea is no different, even if it got a late start. North Korea has seen modest but significant mobile subscriber growth since 2008. That was when Pyongyang offered Orascom, an Egyptian company, the chance to set up and run a mobile network in the DPRK by forming a joint venture, Koryolink. Previously, Loxley Pacific, a Thai company, had done the same, but that network was largely shut down in 2006. Orascom has run into problems remitting its profits, though by 2015 subscribers had topped three million people.[23] Some estimates suggest that this had grown to over five million subscribers in 2018.[24]

North Korea monitors the communications of individuals of whom it is suspicious, even if it cannot monitor everyone. But the authorities can also rely on some restrictions that are unique. For example, each SIM is registered to a single phone. If it is inserted into another phone, however briefly, it is flagged to authorities, who can either immediately call to demand an explanation or who can quietly put the person on a list to monitor them more closely.

In 2014 a Choson Exchange volunteer I was traveling with in North Korea had a flip-phone with him, using it as an old-model burner phone. Our youthful, inquisitive, and ruddy-cheeked guide, Mr. Lim, noticed it as we were driving in the city one day.

"Oh cool, Samsung!" he said. "I've heard these are good phones. May I see?"

The volunteer passed it over and Mr. Lim poked around with it a bit, then out of curiosity decided to pop his SIM card in. It didn't work.

"It doesn't work," he said in confirmation. He swapped the cards back. Two minutes later his phone rang. He made a puzzled face at a number he didn't recognize.

"Hello? My name's Lim Yong Min," he said in Korean. There was a pause while a tinny little voice barked questions through his ear. "With a foreign delegation," he said. Another pause. "One of their phones . . . just to see." More tiny voice barking. "Tomorrow? Yes. Understood."

The next morning, he had to leave us briefly to go have a conversation with security services. He returned saying, "No problem, it's fine," but his face said he knew this was going to be logged as a black mark against him. He hadn't known how the government could monitor his SIM card.

It's not clear exactly what personnel or technical measures the authorities use to monitor people on the mobile network, though most devices won't allow non-government-approved files to be uploaded. Some devices also take random screenshots of the phone and store them to allow authorities to check browsing history.[25] (Through the domestic intranet, users can access newspapers or other information services.) Indeed, the fear of what's possible might be as powerful as the actual surveillance capabilities they might have. Defectors interviewed for one study agreed "that users would never say anything politically inappropriate or sensitive via cell phone, believing every single call is under surveillance."[26]

There are several Korean phone brands that are portrayed as being made in the DPRK, but in actuality appear to be made in China for the North Korean market.[27] They run Android and a range of domestically made apps are available from your local app store. And I do mean "local." App stores are actual shops, with walls. You go in and browse apps that are presented in a laminated booklet. Some, perhaps because the company paid a small fee, are displayed on the wall. You choose which one you want—whether a local version of Angry Birds, or an English-Korean dictionary, or an encyclopedia—plug your phone into a computer and have the app installed.

Foreigners have been able to purchase SIM cards easily since 2013 and have mostly unfettered internet access via the 3G network, though recently they've had to use a VPN to access services that are blocked in China, such as Twitter, Facebook, and Google. More importantly, they can only call other foreigners in-country or abroad. It is impossible to call a Korean mobile phone or landline. Just pause on that for a second: no other country on earth has tried such a restrictive system. You can buy a local SIM card, but you cannot call anyone in the country where you've just bought the SIM.

One time I had to contact Mr. Kim, who'd left us in the hotel while he went to run an errand. Our schedule had to change and I needed to communicate that to him. So I asked our other minder, Bae Ho Nam, to call Mr. Kim, since I was not allowed to. I proceeded to yell at Mr. Bae as he held the phone up:

"Mr. Bae!" I bellowed. "Please tell Mr. Kim we need to be back at the classroom by 1:30, not 2 p.m. One of the workshop leaders needs to set something up!"

Mr. Bae was smiling as he quickly confirmed that Mr. Kim had understood. "What a great solution!" he exclaimed.

"What a ridiculous situation. We shouldn't need a solution at all," I countered. But his grin was not to be deterred. He was just too relentlessly positive.

Another time, Mr. Kim had to attend to something, so he left the Choson Exchange group in a restaurant to dine alone. The appointed time to reunite came and went. The group waited and waited some more. After some more time passed, Geoffrey asked the restaurant to call Kim's mobile phone, which they did. Then, no doubt because the restaurant staff didn't know the rules, they passed the handset unbidden to Geoffrey, who was standing by for news. The two men exchanged just a couple sentences on when and where to meet up; Kim's discomfort at being in conversation over the phone with Geoffrey was clear.

Sure enough, Kim had to go into security the next day to explain himself. Like Mr. Lim, he said it was fine, but the way he shook his head indicated frustration. It was unclear with what or who exactly. Again, he couldn't or wouldn't explain further what it might actually mean for him. Those procedures must be kept in the fog, after all. I think he carried a grudge against that restaurant after that.

Sometimes this North Korean instinct to hide information extends far beyond what makes sense, from my perspective, anyway. For example, market activity, now pervasive in the DPRK, is still considered sensitive. There are now over five hundred official markets in the country. Foreigners are only allowed to visit two of them. From about 2014, however, most visitors were forbidden from going to the one in Pyongyang, though resident foreigners are still allowed. Visitors can still visit the market in Rason, though even there, no photos are allowed. One's partners still get nervous about foreigners wandering too far from the group as we move through the raucous and often humid building, which stretches out like a giant playground of commerce.

Why? What could we see or do? The answer requires a bit of speculation, but it is likely two-fold. First, markets are, as anywhere, fairly boisterous, freewheeling places. People bend rules to make money, and the government knows this. They may fear trade in sensitive materials or some other breach of the rules in front of foreigners. The most I've seen is a drinks vendor say "Hey, I have booze here if you want," nodding to a covered cabinet—market vendors aren't supposed to sell alcohol. I've also seen a persuasive chap talk a vendor into selling a *seanghwal chonghwa* —"life harmonizing"—journal to a foreigner, something they weren't supposed to do. The visitor made her an offer she couldn't refuse, something like ten times the normal price. On other occasions I've also tried to buy them and been refused even when offering much, much more money. That this pillar of their propaganda system is sold in markets and not distributed is perhaps in and of itself embarrassing.

Indeed, I suspect the other reason they don't want us to see markets is almost certainly a misplaced sense of pride. When they started to approve the construction of marketplaces in the early 2000s, the outside world became excited that this spelled a shift toward more capitalism. The North Koreans balked at this idea. But since then *they* know that *we* know markets have become pervasive and represent, essentially, the failure of their orthodoxy. Their system was once non-monetized: you worked for the state and the state provided you with everything. That was how it was *supposed* to be.

The state can't do that anymore, though conservative North Koreans wish it could, taking comfort in the old model. The system can't ever really go back, though the idea Mr. Bae once mentioned, that "markets are a solution until we can move to full socialism again," bounces around the system. The concept is that life dictated by markets is a failure, even if that sort of rhetoric is now massively distant from lived experience.

Once, our group was heading to Wonsan, on the east coast. At one point in the mountains the easterly road leads out of a tunnel right near a rest-stop pavilion atop a steep hill. Travelers often hop out there to stretch legs and backs that have been abused by the bumpy roads and take pictures. On this occasion, there were a handful of young women skulking shyly about by the pavilion, spectacular layered mountain views behind them. They didn't sport the fine garb of Pyongyang folk, but still wore makeup and warm blue or green coats. They also wore long trousers, something women in Pyongyang are discouraged from doing. Displayed in little cloth bundles, they clearly had fresh fruit, dried snacks, and other small items for sale to travelers. This was obvious. It could not have been more obvious.

Knowing that, I turned to Mr. Jang and playfully (okay, perhaps a bit cruelly) asked what they were doing up here.

"Uhhh. Perhaps they came here to rest," he offered.

"They walked their bikes several hundred meters up this incredibly steep hill to take a rest?" I asked, raising an eyebrow and probably wearing an expression mixing smugness and righteousness.

"I'm..." he couldn't find anything. "I'm not sure," he said with an awkward chuckle.

We bought some fruit from one of them, some sort of delicious Korean berries that seemed to be a cross between grapes and gooseberries. We left them to their rest atop the hill and went on about our lives. Like so many North Koreans I shall never meet again, I wonder how often they go up there, perhaps if they're up there today, as you read this. I didn't ask them too many questions, as that would have made them uncomfortable and Mr. Jang nervous.

Some days later I was on a fairly empty flight heading back to Beijing. My occasional conversational partner, the flight attendant Ms. Nam, was working that flight and in a chatty mood. "What's your favorite thing about my country?" she asked. I gave a perfunctory answer about the kimchi being the best in the world and about Pyongyang being a very beautiful city.

"And the people?" she prompted, with a smile.

"Well," I said, deciding to gently complain. "I can't really meet that many Koreans. There are a lot of rules that keep me from making Korean friends, so I don't really know."

She launched into an explanation of why the rules are necessary; without them Korea's enemies would infiltrate and cause the country to collapse. I stopped paying attention and zoned out. I was tired and had heard this spiel plenty of times before.

"Yes, yes, I get it," I thought. "You built these walls to keep us out so your republic could survive."

We overflew the border with China and the announcement came over the PA system saying that crossing it reminded them of the exploits of Great Leader Kim Il Sung in building their country.

"Well done. It's working."

Notes

1 John H. Cha and K.J. Sohn, *Exit Emperor Kim Jong-Il: Notes from His Former Mentor* (Bloomington, IN: Abbott Press, 2012), 74.

2 Christopher Green, "Wrapped in a Fog," in *Change and Continuity in North Korean Politics*, eds. Adam Cathcart, Robert Winstanley-Chesters, and Christopher K. Green (London: Routledge, 2017), 25.

3 Harry Harding, "From China, with Disdain: New Trends in the Study of China," *Asian Survey* 22, no. 10 (1982): 948.

4 Jae Young Kim, "Why Did We Never Complain? We Didn't Even Know How To," NK News, November 5, 2012, https://www.nknews.org/2012/11/why-did-we-never -complain-some-of-us-didnt-even-know-how-to.

5 Andrei Lankov, *The Real North Korea: Life and Politics in the Failed Stalinist Utopia* (Oxford: Oxford University Press, 2013), 50.

6 Ji-Min Kang, "Neighborhood Watch: Inside North Korea's Secret Police System," NK News, February 26, 2014, https://www.nknews.org/2014/02/neighborhood-watch -inside-north-koreas-secret-service-system.

7 Lee Seok Young, "Pyongyang Seeing Tighter Inspections," *Daily NK*, August 24, 2011, http://www.dailynk.com/english/read.php?cataId=nk01500&num=8094.

8 Andrei Lankov, In-ok Kwak, and Choong-Bin Cho, "The Organizational Life: Daily Surveillance and Daily Resistance in North Korea," *Journal of East Asian Studies* 12, no. 2 (2012): 194.

9 Lankov, Kwak, and Cho, "The Organizational Life," 197.

10 "'당 대표자 3467명 참석'… 노동당원 數 340만명 달할 듯 출처" ["3467 party representatives attend".... Labor party size likely to reach 3.4 million], Chosun.com, May 7, 2016, http://news.chosun.com/site/data/html_dir/2016/05/07/2016050700236 .html.

11 Lankov, Kwak, and Cho, "The Organizational Life," 203–04.

12 UN Human Rights Council, *Report of the Detailed Findings of the Commission of Inquiry on Human Rights in the Democratic People's Republic of Korea*, A/ HRC/25/CRP.1, Human Rights Council, Twenty-fifth Session, February 7, 2014, section 4, clause 259, 7.

13 UN Human Rights Council, *Report of the Commission of Inquiry on Human Rights in the Democratic People's Republic of Korea*, A/HRC/25/63, Human Rights Council, Twenty-fifth Session, February 7, 2014, 7–8.

14 "North Korea's Fake Church," Youtube, https://www.youtube.com/watch?v =O5GdYvpmJVo.

15 UN Human Rights Council, *Report of the Detailed Findings*, section 4, clause 239.

16 Stephan Haggard and Marcus Noland, *Famine in North Korea: Markets, Aid, and Reform* (New York: Columbia University Press, 2007), 280.

17 Koh Jung-Sik, *Is North Korea Really Changing?* (Seoul: Institute for Unification Education, 2014), 43.

18 Kim Seong Hwan, "30-40% of NK Thought to Be Tuning into Pirate Radio: How Do We Reach More?" *Daily NK*, September 14, 2015, http://www.dailynk.com/english /read.php?cataId=nk00100&num=13460.

19 Nat Kretchen, Catherine Lee, and Seamus Tuohy, *Compromising Connectivity: Information Dynamics between the State and Society in a Digitizing North Korea* (Washington, DC: Intermedia, 2017).

20 Yonhap News Agency, *North Korea Handbook* (London: M.E. Sharpe, 2003), 410.

21 Florian Grunow and Niklaus Schiess, "Lifting the Fog on Red Star OS," presentation at 32nd Chaos Communications Congress, Hamburg, Germany, December 27–30, 2015. https://www.youtube.com/watch?v=8LGDM9exlZw.

22 Grunow and Schiess, "Lifting the Fog."

23 James Pearson, "North Korea's Black Market Becoming the New Normal," Reuters, October 29, 2015, http://www.reuters.com/article/us-northkorea-change-insight -idUSKCN0SN00320151029.

24 Koo Bonn-kwon, "North Korea's IT Proficiency Attracts Attention Worldwide," *Hankyoreh*, July 30, 2018, http://english.hani.co.kr/arti/english_edition/e_north korea/855454.html.

25 Warangkana Chomchuen, "How North Korea Is Using Smartphones as Weapons of Mass Surveillance," *Wall Street Journal*, December 9, 2017, https://www.wsj.com /articles/how-north-korea-is-using-smartphones-as-weapons-of-mass-surveillance -1512719928.

26 Yonho Kim, *Cell Phones in North Korea: Has North Korea Entered the Telecommunications Revolution?* (Washington, DC: U.S.-Korea Institute at SAIS, 2014), 31.

27 Martyn Williams, "North Korea's Newest Smartphone Might Be Made in China," North Korea Tech, June 10, 2018, http://www.northkoreatech.org/2018/06/10/north -koreas-newest-smartphone-might-be-made-in-china.

5

Oh, the (Foreign) People You'll Meet

This state that has somehow persisted past the end of the Cold War and through a third-generation leadership transition inspires strong reactions in people. Most of the world thinks of North Korea as essentially the bad guy. Relatively few people outside the DPRK are pro–North Korea, though if you travel there enough, you'll end up meeting some of these foreigners. For many, their relationship with the country is extremely simple. Too simple. For others, it's extremely complicated.

The Moranbong Theater is a lovely concert hall nestled within a patch of cherry trees on Moran Hill. It is where a North-South joint convention was held in 1948 and where the Supreme People's Assembly first met, before it got its own grand building next to the Mansudae statues. The theater was rebuilt in 1957 and refurbished in 2006.[1] On my first trip to the DPRK, we went to see an orchestra perform such classics as "Our General is the Best!" and "Cantata to Comrade Kim Jong Il." It was Kim's birthday. He'd only be alive for one more.

Honestly, I don't remember much from the show, except for the gigantic clown-smile the tenor affixed to his face following his final bellow of "Our general is the best!" What I do remember is first walking up from the parking lot to the venue. As we did, we approached a group of about thirty female university students, dressed in the customary DPRK university uniform, which is a traditional *jogori* dress made up of a short white top with long sleeves and an elegant bow over a long blue skirt.

They were in a line, as you'd expect: Koreans do a lot of respectful queueing. But as we got closer, I couldn't help but notice that there was something different about them, compared to the other North Korean students I'd seen. They were openly looking at us, making eye contact—other groups of students had mostly pretended not to notice us. They were also chatting and laughing. Their body language was so breezy and open. At that moment I realized how restrained North Koreans are in the way they carry themselves physically. These girls were . . . relaxed.

When we got closer, I could hear why. Their Korean popped and lilted with Japanese accents. They were from Korea University, the pro–North Korean University in Tokyo.

Korea University is run by *Chongryon*, the General Association of Korean Residents in Japan, or *Chosen Soren*, in Japanese. During the Japanese colonial rule of Korea, from 1910 to 1945, hundreds of thousands of Koreans migrated to Japan. This was also when Kim Il Sung cut his teeth as an anti-Japanese guerrilla leader, an experience that informed the rest of his life and the shape of the state that he created.[2]

After the collapse of the Japanese Empire, a couple of organizations emerged to help Koreans who found themselves in the Japanese homeland: *Mindan* was pro–Republic of Korea and *Chongryon* was pro-North. Mindan got relatively little support from Seoul, but Kim Il Sung saw the potential value of Chongryon and helped it set up a school network and other social services.

In the 1950s Koreans in Japan suffered massive discrimination and desperately needed the help. In 1952 their Japanese citizenship was revoked and they just "disappeared—from the national census, from public service jobs, from national pension benefits," as well as from the list of wounded veterans and atomic bomb victims.[3] They were effectively blocked from most educational and career pathways.

A friend of mine whose family was heavily into Chongryon—her mother once met Kim Il Sung and cried her eyes out—recalls landlords would not rent a space to her parents, who were trying to start a bookstore, simply because they were Korean. She also recalls frequently getting into racially charged yelling matches with Japanese children. She remembers being really scared when public opinion turned on Koreans in 1987 after the North Korean agents who blew up a Korean Air flight were found to be carrying fake Japanese passports, pretending to be Japanese. "We were told not to wear our school uniforms for a while," she remembers, and "to be careful."

The agent who was caught, Kim Hyon Hui, confessed and said she'd been trained for years to act Japanese by a person called Yaeko Taguchi, who it seemed had been kidnapped and taken to North Korea for that very purpose. This led to years of right-wing Japanese accusations that various unexplained disappearances were kidnappings by North Koreans. Chongryon strenuously denied this was the case and the accusation remained a fairly fringe belief.

Still, North Korea–Japan relations were bad as the twentieth century closed. There'd been no reparations nor an apology for colonialism, something South Korea had received in 1965 and 1995, respectively.[4]

Japanese prime minister Junichiro Koizumi and Kim Jong Il used back channels to create a plan to overcome the decades of mutual suspicion and create a shift in the politics of the region. Koizumi would visit Pyongyang and apologize for the suffering caused by the colonial period; Kim would seek economic cooperation, rather than the politically more difficult compensation. Crucially, he would also admit that North Korea had indeed kidnapped some Japanese citizens. The two leaders put this plan into action, with Koizumi visiting in September 2002. At the summit Kim confessed to thirteen kidnappings by "some elements of a special agency of state" who were "carried away by fanaticism and desire for glory."[5]

Not only did this revelation shock the world, but it proved to be a tremendous political blunder by two seasoned leaders. Japanese public opinion *exploded* in fury:

> In the following days reports began to emerge of Korean female students having their school uniforms slashed on crowded public transportation, being verbally abused, or even being spat at. Many Korean schools hastily organized security measures, while parents feared for their children's safety. For months and years to come, Koreans in Japan, especially those who were affiliated with Chongryun, would be vexed with worry and fear about their present and future in Japan.[6]

Chongryon membership withered as Koreans were humiliated by the kidnappings, especially as it seemed probable that members of their community were involved. At the same time, many were losing belief in the ideologies of the DPRK. Chongryon once boasted over half a million members, but in 2016, the Japanese government estimated only 70,000 remained and more than half of those had taken South Korean or Japanese citizenship.[7] Chongryon also ran over 160 schools at its peak;[8] that number was down to about sixty by 2017.[9] The kidnappings have remained a hot issue in Japan ever since and a key stumbling block to relations between the two countries, adding a complication to the broader geopolitical strains caused by North Korea's nuclear and missile programs.

Regardless, when in Pyongyang, we at Choson Exchange tried to stay at the Chongryon-owned Pyongyang Hotel, whenever possible. The location was great and the staff were friendlier than at other international hotels, even if the furnishings were a bit worn and hot water unreliable. The hotel is a five-story building in the shape of a large, rectangular *U*. On the sides were guestrooms, on the corners restaurants and bars, and at the bottom of the *U* is the entrance and then some offices and shops on the upper floors. The hotel has the best coffee shop in Pyongyang. The coffee is truly excellent.

Chongryon Japanese Koreans almost always stay in the Pyongyang Hotel, including students from Korea University. The university students were always very sweet. Many of them didn't speak Korean very well or spoke it with a heavy Japanese accent. They'd be brought over for six to eight weeks, take classes in a lecture room in the hotel, learn patriotic songs, and go see historical sites. It was sort of like summer camp. "What is the worst thing about being here?" I asked a group of them once as we had snacks in the lobby bar. "No internet," was the easy answer.

"What is the best thing about being here?"

"Feeling all together, learning Korean history, being welcomed warmly everywhere."

A former student told me they called it "Pyongyang magic." They really would feel the glow and solidarity of being in their forebears' homeland. But it was temporary. They'd go back to Japan and before even touching down, they'd shed their DPRK uniforms like an old skin, and emerge, texting and laughing, plugging back into Japanese life.

Once there were a group of twenty and thirty-something business people who were a part of some kind of Chongryon youth business federation. I started chatting to one of them in Korean as he ordered at the bar. I explained our NGO and he seemed quite impressed and certainly intrigued by the fact we were conversing in Korean. So he invited me from the bar area to go sit at a table with his friends. One of his friends was on the larger side for a Korean. He looked like a wrestler, with maximum shoulder width and no neck.

He was significantly less impressed by my Korean. In fact, as soon as we started chatting he said "this isn't fun"—referring directly to me—and proceeded to actively ignore me. I talked to the other guy. At some point I bought a round of drinks, however, and the wrestler seemed to suddenly warm up to me.

Koreans have a phrase to describe themselves—*naembi gunsong*—or "boiling-pot disposition." It means that their feelings can heat up or cool down very fast. It's used to explain how public opinion polls can rocket up and down so fast in South Korea or how a celebrity scandal can be all-consuming and then be quickly forgiven. Was this the reason for the wrestler's change of heart? Or was it just that the path to a man's heart is his stomach? (And this man's stomach craved booze.) Regardless, after some friendly banter he asked if I would do an interview on-camera to show to his federation when they had their quarterly meeting back in Tokyo. I checked with Geoffrey to see if he thought it was a good idea and then agreed.

Stupidly, the next day, an hour before our appointment I thought I would try to squeeze in a bit of a workout. By this time I'd developed a personal rule for Pyongyang: exercise every day. Without it, the stress of constant group activity and surveillance could pile up. Many visitors, residents, and indeed North Koreans offset these pressures by drinking, but that creates a downward spiral of productivity and well-being. The other rule I developed was that each trip I'd take one evening off from the group to watch a movie on my laptop and have some alone time.

This time, however, the exercise was a mistake. I didn't leave myself enough time to cool down, so when I showed up to the interview, I was sweating like a drug addict at rehab. I looked, I'm sure, like a panicky wreck. The first few questions were friendly and innocuous; but then the wrestler started dropping inquisitorial bombs.

"What do you think of our socialist system?" His annoyed face was back. He was trying to catch me out, to get me in trouble.

"Listen," I said, "I think there are a lot of ideas that are very positive but there are also some limitations and many things that are inefficient. So, I'd like to help improve those things so the country can develop."

He then asked, "Which do you like better, North or South Korea?" My god. Going for the jugular. Maybe it was better I was sweating already, otherwise I might have started at this point.

"I'm lucky to have been to both," I replied quickly, "and for me it isn't about which one is better or worse. I like them both in different ways. I want to think of ways that the international community can help the two countries work more closely together and find more in common."

He nodded his approval as I wiped my brow, again. That was a good answer, his facial expression said. I added the sweeter, crunchier kimchi in the north is better, but noodles are better in the south. This is why they need to work together! We laughed and good-naturedly argued about whether that was the case. I stand by that controversial claim, despite a popular song called "Pyongyang Cold Noodles are the Best" and the existence of a "Cold Noodle Research Center" in the city, implying Northerners are not resting on their laurels. There's a lot of propaganda about northern cold noodles. (Don't fall for it.)

Pro-North Japanese Koreans, like the wrestler, can be in an extremely difficult position emotionally. This is because they do have some affection and patriotism for their country, the DPRK. But they've also seen the world. They know that much is not well with "our country," as they call it, but they feel compelled to defend it. They own the problems of North Korea in a way that other outsiders do not. I remember once when I was a teenager overhearing a friend of mine criticizing my mother. I burned with rage and yelled at him. What he was saying was true, but it didn't matter. *I* could say those things because I was on the inside. She's *my* mother. Outsiders don't get to talk about it in the same way as family. North Koreans will often describe their country to foreigners as a family, with their leader as the father figure, and everyone else with a role to play. Chongryon members are to some extent part of the DPRK family.

But Japanese Koreans are not *fully* part of the family because they didn't grow up in North Korea. They have been partially, but not fully, inculcated. When they visit, they *are* treated much more warmly and with greater affection than other foreigners. But they're still not free to visit their actual families as they please, nor are they able to travel freely. They still have very prescribed itineraries and are under a lot of limitations. They're like semi-foreigners. Or as my friend who grew up in a Chongryon family puts it:

"You feel insecure. You are taught that you're Korean but when you go there you realize you're not and you don't know shit." She hated being Korean in Japan, with the disadvantages that conferred, but also knew she wasn't Japanese. And her community in Japan still suffers from problems like alcoholism and depression. "Colonialism does generations of damage; dysfunction and trauma and identity crisis...."

You'll meet more clearly marked and identifiable foreigners visiting the country too, most commonly as tourists. Tourists range widely from extremely gullible to extremely cynical. The idea that the people on the subway are actors, for example, persists. They aren't. Or that the people in the bowling alley are actors. They aren't. Or that the people using computers in the library are actors. They aren't—but *are* probably put in place to do research for our viewing pleasure.

Indeed, once with Choson Exchange, we were taken to a research center on a Sunday, which was staffed with folks at their computers working on some scanning technology. Sunday is a day off, so I started asking people, "Are you just here for us?"

"Oh no," the first few said, implausibly, "We're very busy, so we have a lot to do. No days off for us!"

Finally, I reached someone who cheerfully replied, "Yup! We wanted to demo our projects to you." Put like that, of course, it seemed perfectly normal. But Pyongyang's instinct to stage things can create suspicions in visitors, suspicions that could be avoided if the North Koreans were a bit more honest about when they are trying to show off their best.

Of course, there is a group of people who are uniquely receptive to such staging or really anything that they're told by North Koreans: members of DPRK friendship groups, Juche study groups, solidarity committees, and other such entities. You can spot them because they'll often proudly be wearing the Kim badges on their chests, the ultimate shibboleth. These people are usually fantastically credulous.

The most vocal of these people is a corpulent fellow named Alejandro Cao de Benos. He appears to genuinely believe in Kimilsungism, but also makes a tidy package charging high rates to media or other organizations for access to the country, having claimed to have a DPRK passport, an apartment in Pyongyang, and various other things that strain the imagination. He sometimes wears a DPRK military uniform that appears to have been self-made. He literally plays dress-up as a North Korean.

He, and members of other DPRK friendship groups, seemed to hate Choson Exchange because we were possibly not sufficiently pro–North Korean. We definitely encroached on his claim to be an explainer of and access point to the country.

There was one occasion when I found myself deeply embedded among several hundred of these friendship group types: the sixtieth anniversary of the Day of Victory in the Glorious Fatherland Liberation War in July 2013. Actually, the normally boisterous Alejandro was relatively muted during this celebration because there were plenty of other foreigners around with even greater pro-DPRK credentials. They'd walk around with their orders of friendship and other medals draped around their necks. They'd be bussed around in official vehicles to various sites and events and for a week feel important, when back home they were almost certainly not.

I dropped into this milieu not really knowing what to expect and when our partners showed us the itinerary, I was pretty shocked. "Indignation Meeting," "Anti-imperialism Rally," and "Solidarity and Peace March" were all on the program. This made me feel extremely uncomfortable. And in true DPRK fashion, our partners never thought to communicate any of this to us beforehand.

"Look," I told them, "I can't be seen as a representative of Choson Exchange at an anti-American event. Nor do I personally want to express myself this way." Serious faces all around.

I continued: "You understand, right?"

They said they did, but also made it clear that it would reflect extremely badly on them if I didn't take part. After all, they were responsible for my behavior in-country. They would have some explaining to do if I didn't go. This is part of the pressure the system puts on you and your partners: if you care about them, you are compelled to try to keep them out of trouble.

I left the issue of my participation hanging, but when I saw television cameras at the "Solidarity and Peace March" my nerves tingled and I got a lump in my throat. "Peace" at such events just means anti-Americanism. I said again, "Guys, I really don't want to be on TV at this thing."

My minder pondered this for a minute, then said, "Okay, you have that big iPad, right?"

"Yeah."

"When you see a camera nearby, just hold it up in front of your face." He raised his eyebrows in a "whaddayathink?" expression. I sighed and rubbed my temples.

So, if you come across footage of an iPad walking along in a march in Pyongyang in 2013, that's me. I'm in the foreigner section because, of course, Koreans and foreigners were kept in separate groups at this "solidarity march" lest, perhaps, we find too much in common and discover some actual, personal solidarity.

Meanwhile, the foreigners seemed to be getting weirder. I overheard a mustachioed head of the Pakistani Juche Study Group tell a local dignitary, "I've raised my daughters to refer to Kim Il Sung as their grandfather." He had Kim's picture on his living room wall, he said. At dinner a tiny Philippine lady stood up and in practically one breath made and approved a formal motion to toast to the health of the Marshal. "I think we should all unanimously support this idea. Does everyone agree? Yes? Good." Clink! She didn't wait for a response. Democracy!

I'm not sure if she knew Marshal Kim Jong Un's name, which is, well, Kim Jong Un. Others certainly struggled with Korean names. One Aussie kept referring to the military-first idea, *songun*, as "*shogun*."

"Ah," he nodded at one exhibition," "*Shogun* was the idea of Kim Il Jong," also conflating the names of the country's two icons.

"Kim Il Sung," his guide politely replied.

"Kim Il Jung?"

"No, Kim Il Sung."

Not everyone was sufficiently inculcated enough for these people. One of the Australian delegates on our bus told his friend with some disgust that he "overheard someone from the Slovakian group saying 'Oh, it's just like a religious cult'."

"Well, they should keep their bloody traps shut," said his bogan seatmate in the heavy enunciation of rural Australia. "Some of us are trying to enjoy this!" he grumbled.

The common thread for nearly all the people in these friendship groups was anti-Americanism and a real cynicism about US power in the world. And one can understand that sentiment—there are many reasons to be suspicious of US hegemony and the way America has exercised its power during the Cold War and beyond. But then these folks arrive in North Korea and seem to say, "Well, this is the answer!" Whatever cynicism they had about the United States is not applied in the DPRK. It just evaporates. They uncritically accept everything they are told. It is an exercise in extreme credulity.

We spent a lot of time on buses, me and the non-cynics, repeatedly going to events with Marshal Kim Jong Un in attendance. This meant taking nothing but our room key onto the bus, waiting for perhaps an hour, driving to a second location to go through a security screening, and then moving to the event: a concert, the unveiling of the new war cemetery, the opening of the new, larger war museum. Often, the venue and event were kept secret from us until the last minute.

It was at the last location I ran into Kim Jong Un himself, almost literally. Usually at these events, he would inspect something, then he'd leave in his Mercedes, and then we'd be allowed to look around. This time as we waited behind a cordon in front of the building, the monitoring of the several hundred foreigners just kind of . . . broke down. Several of us noticed some other people walking toward the museum further along the cordon, so we just decided to go.

A vexed look crossed the face of one of our other local partners, a petite young lady called So Mi. "Wait, wait," she implored. "They haven't told us we can go in yet!" It was too late. We were gone.

We entered the lavish museum, taking in the top-notch construction materials, dioramas, and displays. I've heard several people call it unforgettable, the best war museum they've ever seen. I won't forget it, because on that day suddenly there was cheering and commotion and then, there I was, right next to Supreme Leader Kim Jong Un, in a throng of people. He looked at me as we moved past and I gave him a kind of "what's up?" nod. Actually, my first instinct was to reach out and touch his arm or something, I was so surprised. I'm glad I didn't. That would have been weird.

His powerful uncle, Jang Song Thaek, also brushed past me. He was a man who'd married Kim Il Sung's daughter. The couple had a rocky relationship.[10] Still, Jang held a number of powerful positions and was assumed to be something of a prince regent, overseeing his young nephew's development.

He would be dead five months later. He was executed for being a "traitor to the nation" and engaging in "anti-party, counter-revolutionary" acts. Some people thought he tried to initiate a coup. He certainly built up a powerful business empire and plenty of strong ties to China. We'll probably never know exactly why Kim had him killed. Regardless, the execution illustrated the Machiavellian court politics in the DPRK system. It also shocked Korea watchers. Jang was married to Kim Jong Il's sister; people expected he might be pushed aside someday, but not so soon and so brutally.

And no, he was not executed by a pack of wild dogs.[11] Though if you've read that, it would perfectly illustrate some of the problems with media coverage of the DPRK. There is a huge demand for news about North Korea that is salacious or weird. Moreover, there's no cost for getting it wrong. The execution-by-dogs story originated in a joke social media post in Hong Kong and ended up being copied by news organizations around the world.

The most famous and persistent of such stories is that North Koreans think Kim Jong Il was the world's best golfer. This may have first shown up in a 1994 *New York Times* article, in which a single North Korean guide seems to have discussed Kim Jong Il's incredible score of 34 over eighteen holes.[12] A *Telegraph* journalist who played a round of golf in Pyongyang in 2006 after posing as a businessman to get a visa wrote about the "amazing 11 hole-in-ones . . . given jubilant publicity by the country's propaganda machine, and [which] has gone down in the annals of abridged socialist history as another example of Kim Jong-il's prowess at all pursuits."[13] This fantastic feat persisted after Kim's death in 2011, with the *Christian Science Monitor*'s pseudo-obituary headlined, "Kim Jong-il: Legendary Golfer and Mythical Powers Even in Death."[14]

Thus, a single minder's idle boast became fact in the West. My first trip to Pyongyang I asked my guide if she knew Kim Jong Il was so good at golf. "What?" I've never heard of that."

I explained that most foreigners think that they think he got eleven holes-in-one.

"What? That's . . . crazy," she ventured.

I've asked a couple other North Koreans about it, too. In each case I was the first person to have informed them of the fact that they thought Kim Jong Il was the world's greatest golfer.

The new Victorious Fatherland Liberation War Museum has a huge statue in its expansive courtyard. It is a Korean People's Army soldier, mid-yell, rifle on his back, holding a flag and exhorting his comrades forward with an outstretched arm. It is an image of glory. By contrast, in Seoul, the central statue at the war museum is called "Statue of Brothers." It depicts a northern and southern solider in an embrace, crying. It was only recently pointed out to me, however, that the ROK solder stands erect, while the smaller North Korean figure grasps upward for comfort and help. This was a disappointing discovery.

Outside Pyongyang's museum, generally Westerners are shown some US planes that were shot down, then the USS *Pueblo*, a spy ship captured in 1968 off the east coast of Korea. Then they are taken into the museum itself, where cameras are not allowed. There is a towering full-color wax statue of the young Kim Il Sung, who looks so much like Kim Jong Un (circa 2012) that one guest I was with pointed at it and asked why there was a statue of Kim Jong Un.

Then they are shown a video that makes the case that, after plotting for months, it was the Americans who started the Korean War in June 1950. This is at the heart of North Korea's self-image as a righteous country struggling against an imperialist power. Everywhere else in the world, the question of who started the war was settled once the Soviet archives were opened in the 1990s.

Those archives show that Kim Il Sung lobbied Stalin in March 1949 for a war of unification, but Stalin, wary of the continuing American presence, refused. In the summer of 1949, the Soviet leader became concerned about the possibility of an attack from the south and Kim again agitated for a limited campaign. Stalin decided against it.

When the two leaders met again in the spring of 1950, however, Stalin had decided that "the international environment now made it possible to undertake the invasion," though he warned the North Koreans "that they must win the war quickly, before the United States would have time to enter."[15] The archives show "in excruciating detail the oversight Moscow exercised over North Korea" and "that it would have been utterly impossible for the DPRK to mount an attack" without Moscow's approval.[16]

The North Korean people genuinely believe it was a defensive war; even for many defectors, most of whom are somewhat cynical about the DPRK, the fact that it wasn't is the hardest thing for them to accept. One such person writes that, "Even if you try to tell the truth about the war to North Korean people, no one would be likely to believe it. It was unbelievable even for someone like me, who voluntarily left North Korea."[17] Another called the revelation "the most surprising thing she learned after moving to the South."[18]

History in Northeast Asia is alive and where you're from hugely impacts what you are taught.[19] It is contestable, especially around the events that created the contemporary order. That order is in no small part defined by the Korean War, the Chinese Civil War, and the abrupt conclusion to World

War II, before that. Imagine: on August 5, 1945, Japan's position in Korea seemed secure. The empire was being pushed back in several theaters, but it looked as if the war would drag on for months, perhaps years, even. The fate of Korea was not a hot topic. Ten days and two atomic bombs later, Japan surrendered unconditionally.

In one of many twists of fate that would define Korea's future, the USSR declared war on Japan on August 8, two days after the first atomic bomb was dropped on Hiroshima and just hours before the second bomb obliterated Nagasaki. The Japanese surrendered on August 15 and the Soviets came down the peninsula, bringing along a young guerrilla fighter called Kim Il Sung. They thought Kim would be a pliable leader. They were wrong.

Surprisingly, given that the Americans were considerably further away, in Okinawa, Stalin accepted a proposal to divide control of the former colony. The Americans put forward the thirty-eighth parallel as a dividing line, with the main priority of keeping the capital, Seoul, in the American zone.[20] They installed Syngman Rhee in the South while the Soviets ensconced Kim Il Sung in the North: both men sought to unify the country on their terms. At a political impasse, South Korea held its own, separate elections in 1948. North Korea followed suit in 1949. This solidified political differences.

Kim Il Sung was convinced that a quick invasion would spark an uprising in the South, allowing him to take over the country. Stalin, as mentioned, was wary of this plan, but by 1950 the Chinese Communists had won their revolution and the Soviet nuclear bomb test had been completed the previous year. Stalin was ready to give Kim the green light.

When Korean People's Army troops poured over the temporary border on June 25, 1950, the South Korean army fell apart like leaves off a dead tree. The Northerners rapidly pushed all the way to just outside Busan before Washington rallied the United Nations to provide a legal fig leaf for an American intervention. In September, the enigmatic corncob-pipe–toting General MacArthur caught the North Koreans off guard by landing at Incheon, behind enemy lines. This crippled the North Korean operations. They retreated in disarray and President Truman had by the end of September resolved to counterattack into North Korea.[21] The US-led UN forces chased the Korean People's Army all the way to the border with China, when the year-old People's Republic of China decided this was too close for comfort. They sent tens of thousands of ill-equipped soldiers streaming across the Yalu River border with Korea, battering UN forces back to the thirty-eighth parallel—basically where the war began. (Actually, UN forces lost Seoul again and then re-took it.)

For two-and-a-half more years the war ground on with little territorial advantage to show for it. US forces had air superiority and they flattened the North. Pyongyang's propagandists claim only one building was left standing in Pyongyang, a slight, but not massive exaggeration. If their claims about who started the war are basically false, their collective memory about the American bombing campaign is basically true.

Two months into the war, a US general said that "practically all of the major military industrial targets strategically important to the enemy forces and to their war potential have been neutralized."[22] As the months dragged on, the US Air Force switched to bombing just about anything that had economic value.

The aerial campaign was widespread, cruel, and devastating. General MacArthur, a World War II hero and the man who'd both turned the tide against the North Koreans, but whose aggressive pursuit had dragged the Chinese into the war, even considered using nuclear weapons.[23] Thankfully, this didn't happen. Still, in the end some three to four million civilians and well over a million combatants died between 1950 and 1953.[24]

Pyongyang's war museum is huge, and even though I've visited it several times, there are massive expanses of it I've not seen. There are whole separate sections focused on the Chinese and Russian experiences that are shown when groups visit from those countries. Those are the two countries that have had the deepest ties to North Korea. These relationships are rooted in that experience of war, but also what took place after the armistice—not a full peace treaty—was signed in July 1953.

The Chinese and Soviets became the DPRK's main patrons, pouring aid and assistance into the devastated socialist state that had suffered so much in providing these two massive countries with a strategic buffer against the Americans. This allowed Kim Il Sung the political space to play the two great powers against each other during the Cold War, but also meant deep ties were formed between the North Korea and the Soviet Union.

The collapse of the USSR was a huge shock to the Koreans, who still maintain this to be an historical aberration and only a temporary setback for socialism. The Russian state still maintains its large embassy and geopolitical interests in North Korea, but economic ties between the countries are now meager. As sanctions have isolated Pyongyang from most normal trade and investment opportunities, the Chinese have emerged as the dominant economic power in North Korea. The country does export weapons, statues, and coal around the world, but by 2016, over 90 percent of North Korea's trade was with China.

As such, Chinese people are the most easily spotted foreigners in North Korea. There's a business community that centers around the semi-dilapidated and semi-refurbished Changgwansan and Haebangsan hotels. Businesspeople from China generally are in the DPRK running companies that have textile operations, food processing facilities, or other light manufactures.

There are also *hwagyo* Chinese, who have longstanding residential rights. Some tens of thousands of ethnic Chinese were living in northern Korea at the end of World War II and they were given permanent residency that has been passed down to their children and grandchildren.[25] There are now perhaps fewer than five thousand remaining in this community, because as Chinese citizens they had the right to move back to China. As Chinese wealth and opportunity has increased in recent decades, this became an increasingly attractive option, though during the 1960s and 1970s the DPRK was a haven of prosperity and stability compared to the People's Republic of China.

Those who have remained in Korea have seen their fortunes ebb and flow, but in general they have been given many of the same rights as North Korean citizens, with far fewer of the downsides. They can, for example, freely leave and return. As the economy marketized in the 1990s and 2000s, trade relations crept beyond state control and these ethnic Chinese living in Korea were perfectly positioned to take advantage of this. They became "one of the most prosperous social strata in North Korea," enjoying greater wealth and fewer political pressures.[26]

Hwagyo tend to speak perfect Korean and can only really be picked out because they don't wear a loyalty badge on their clothing; those clothes can also sometimes be too casual for the average North Korean. North Koreans dress very formally when out in public: jeans and sweatpants are not to be found.

Finally, there are also Chinese tourists. Most are coming on what are essentially nostalgia tours, as in "Ah yes, we remember the simple times when our country was like this." They can sometimes be very condescending toward the North Koreans. "Don't you want to give this up and get rich like us?" many ask. Chinese tourists are not allowed in the mausoleum where Kim Il Sung and Kim Jong Il's embalmed bodies lie in state. Chinese tour groups in North Korea, as everywhere, are rowdy. Too rowdy for such hallowed ground. (That said, the tourist I mentioned earlier who performed a handstand at the mausoleum was a Westerner; his Korean guide was subsequently fired.)

Russian visitors are far fewer. A few times I spotted Russians or some other Slavic-looking and speaking gentlemen in suits in the more distinguished and iconic twin-towered Koryo Hotel. They were clearly not tourists. Once I asked why they were visiting Pyongyang.

"Meetings."

End of conversation. In general, non-Chinese businesspeople visiting Pyongyang are not eager to share their itineraries. So much of North Korea's trade with the wider world is on the margins of legality or acceptability, all the more so as sanctions grew tight from 2015 to 2017. Before that period, even when their activities were benign, most Westerners doing business in North Korea just didn't want publicity. The image of the DPRK is such that it can only be negative.

Moreover, Russians resident in Pyongyang mostly operate in their own world. I must confess, I only ran into Russian diplomats twice. Once one was picking up kegs of beer from a hotel for a party. The other time, a more social young chap was at The Friendship bar, having drinks with other expats.

Foreigners resident in Pyongyang make up a peculiar milieu. If you live there, running a business, an NGO, or an embassy, you are unable to make friends with North Koreans in a normal way. You cannot visit their homes or go out for dinner with them. You can't help their kids study English or set up play dates with your kids.

Thus, your friends are the other foreigners who live in Pyongyang. They tend to be quite quirky. And very few in number: there might be at any time a couple hundred Westerners, about the same number of Russians, and perhaps a couple thousand Chinese people living in Pyongyang. There isn't much overlap between these communities.

There are currently only twenty-five embassies in Pyongyang. In place of having an embassy, most countries choose instead to have an ambassador in Seoul or Beijing who is accredited to Pyongyang. There are also six UN agencies and a handful of NGOs with full-time offices and employees.

A real treat for those of us who flit in and out of Pyongyang is hanging out with friends in this community. This is not only because they are often pickled eccentrics, but because we are allowed to hang out with them without our Korean minders around. Tourist visa holders don't have this privilege, but when on a service visa we'd be given the luxury of getting picked up by a resident, telling our partners where we were going and what time we expected to be back, and off we'd go. This feels remarkably free.

Our partners didn't love us doing this: it meant extra reporting for them and a bit of vulnerability while they couldn't contact us. At the end of the day, they were responsible for us; the wider range of people we met with, the more explaining they'd have to do. And of course, if we were out of their sight, there was always the chance that we'd say or do something that would draw the ire of an onlooker, who'd report us. When such things happen when a minder is present, they can sometimes diffuse the situation on the spot. When they are not around, they don't get that chance.

If we were in the Munsu Diplomatic Compound, the Koreans were not even allowed to be with us at all. It was unclear if they were allowed to join us for dinner at a restaurant with a locally resident foreigner: at any rate, they always refused such an offer.

The Munsu Diplomatic Compound is a gridded neighborhood in East Pyongyang, where almost all the foreign embassies exist. (The massive Chinese and Russian embassies are elsewhere and there is another small compound on the east side of the river.) It is a compound designed in a communist fashion, enclosed and full of mid-twentieth-century Stalinist architecture. The Polish embassy is a fortress, with windowless walls and outdoor features designed to be defended during a second Korean War. It once had forty or fifty diplomats. Now it houses four or five. The erstwhile East German embassy now houses not only German diplomats, but also the British and the Swedes.

The compound also has a small primary school, flats, and a medical clinic. Perhaps most importantly, there is an entertainment and shopping complex. I say "complex"; I mean a supermarket the size of a Pizza Hut and a building that houses a barber and restaurant on the top floor and a bar, recreation room, and pool table on the second floor. Some rooms were separated by bead curtains that gave the impression of a college sophomore decorating his first apartment or of a kitschy BBC show from the 1970s set in a Turkish brothel. This is The Friendship.

Once at the upstairs restaurant I leaned on the dinner table, which turned out to be only resting on the table legs, not joined together. My weight caused my end of the table to drop; the other end rocketed upward, flinging food and tableware into the sky like a dinnerware fireworks display.

Friday nights the bar would open. Sometimes one would only find a lone, desperate NGO worker quietly drinking their sorrows away at the bar. Other times, often birthdays or some other pretext, would inspire a whole motley crew of NGO workers, diplomats, and businesspeople who called Pyongyang home to come out. These parties could get rowdier than a Chinese tour group.

The young ladies who staffed The Friendship spoke great English and were extremely flirtatious. Other North Korean girls can be flirty, but in a Christian summer camp kind of way. These girls could be outrageously so: touching arms, sharing drinks, giving nicknames, and laughing riotously. It was widely held that they were there to collect information on the foreigners.

Indeed, embassies had all their local staff supplied by a branch of the foreign ministry called the General Services Bureau. Those staff may have helped with various non-sensitive tasks at the embassies, but we also assumed they were reporting everything the foreigners did. This presumably included cleaners, who helped tidy up apartments but also gleaned as much personal information as possible. The Koreans could never come over for a meal, nor could the foreign staff visit their Korean colleagues' homes. As one diplomat who lived in Pyongyang for three years put it: "I couldn't say I had any North Korean friends. The ones that got closest to us . . . they were trained and had a job to do."

Still, "the more difficult the place, the more the support" among the tiny foreign community. There were frequent barbeques or events such as pool parties at the gigantic concrete Polish embassy compound.

Residents had some freedom to roam: they could venture as far as the cities of Wonsan or Nampo, but this could take weeks of planning to get permissions. Amongst the people I met, younger couples without kids seemed the best positioned to enjoy themselves. School-aged children created complications. On the compound there is only a small primary school, so some diplomats sent their children to international boarding schools in China. Parents would worry about the state of healthcare, also. There is a small clinic for foreigners, but it is limited.

Being single and looking for love could also be a challenge. The dating pool was tiny and obviously dating a Korean was out of the question. Once at the Pyongyang Hotel's fifth-floor bar I came across two hefty Germans drinking alone. Their forearms were too muscular and their bellies too pronounced to be NGO or diplomatic staff. Indeed, they were not. What they were was extremely excited to see a Westerner.

"Mein Gott," one of them said, after handshakes. (Okay, fine, he probably said "My God" in English, but I *feel* like it was "Mein Gott.") "Ze Ko-reans have us trapped in here!" he exclaimed, spitting the first syllable of "Korea," as is the German fashion. "All we see is our workplace and this hotel. They say we can't leave and they don't take us anywhere!"

"How long have you been here? What are you here for?" I asked.

"Three weeks," and "to install printing presses at the main newspaper."

"The *Rodong Sinmun?*" I asked.

"I guess so," one responded. "Is that the main one?"

Then, as if to emphasize how unprepared these two were for life in Pyongyang, one asked: "Where do you go to meet girls here?"

"Um. Beijing?" I suggested.

"Mein gott!" (I think he actually said it this time.) "Zis is terrible!"

"How long are you staying here?" I asked.

"Five months," one responded glumly as he shook head in disbelief.

I pitied them and thought it terribly unfair that their Korean partners expected them to just work and stay bottled up in the hotel for five months, so I started to make a list of restaurants and recreational facilities that foreigners were allowed to visit. I told them of the bowling alley, a great place to be around young North Koreans relaxing and having fun. I told them about Cafe Pyolmuri, where one can get good goat's cheese pizza or fondue. I also told them about The Friendship and how on Friday nights the local expats gather for drinks.

This may have been a mistake. They latched onto the idea in a way that seemed unhealthy.

"It sounds amazing," one said. I assured them it wasn't.

Every time we saw them as the week went on it was the same: "We can't wait to go to The Friendship . . . we can't wait." It had become a place of myth, where all their Pyongyang problems—the loneliness, the claustrophobia, the alienation—would be washed away.

I didn't see them after that Friday, so I don't know if they found their redemption there. I suspect they would have felt nearly as misplaced as anywhere else in Pyongyang. Though perhaps they ran into the Nigerians, who also didn't fit in easily with the NGO/diplomatic set. The one Nigerian diplomat I met a couple times at The Friendship had a scar and a hat that combined to give the impression of old-timey gangster activity. I initially silently scolded myself for such a prejudiced thought until he quickly started berating a couple young ladies for not wanting to talk to him. He spoke to them like an enforcer for a minor underworld boss.

The Nigerians would have probably been there to facilitate oil sales to North Korea, possibly in exchange for weapons, though this is just a guess based on circumstance: there isn't evidence of either. At one point in the early 2000s, Nigeria was "losing" five hundred thousand barrels of oil a day: they were either stolen outright or somehow disappeared from accounting systems.[27] One might assume at least a few of these made it to North Korea. The DPRK and Nigeria signed an information technology cooperation agreement in 2014, though it isn't clear if that has led anywhere.[28] The two countries have been friendly since the 1960s, as they both sought to navigate the Cold War.

Indeed, North Korea has had good relations with a number of African countries. Tanzania, Angola, the Democratic Republic of Congo, Eritrea, Mozambique and Namibia, Benin, Botswana, Mali, and Zimbabwe have all had longstanding arrangements to purchase North Korean weapons and training. Those countries all came under scrutiny in 2017, given that as of March 2016, UN sanctions forbade arms sales or the hosting of DPRK military trainers.[29]

Another export from North Korea to Africa and other places was also banned in 2016 by the UN: art. North Korea's top art studio, Mansudae, has an overseas projects arm that has created technically impressive large-scale projects around the world, perhaps most notably the Angkor National Museum in Cambodia and the African Renaissance Monument in Senegal. The latter is a titanic statue of an African man clutching a baby (that is pointing toward the sky) and leading his wife (presumably) toward the future. At least fourteen other African countries have had statues or monuments built by North Koreans.[30]

The Iranians have a presence in Pyongyang, also. In fact, on their embassy compound sits the only mosque in the DPRK. Again, that country's relationship with North Korea is based on oil going one way, weapons the other, framed by the warm glow of anti-Americanism. Specifically, North Koreans helped Iran with their missile program to a "significant and meaningful" extent, though "there is no evidence that Iran and North Korea have engaged in nuclear-related trade or cooperation with each other."[31]

I'd occasionally meet one of the handful of the Iranians living in North Korea on planes or in hotels. I'd sometimes say hello to them, introducing myself by sharing that my dad was born in Isfahan.

"Do you speak Farsi?" would come the obvious question.

"No, he's Armenian. We spoke Armenian at home."

"Oh, too bad."

That may have been a letdown for the Iranians, but it was usually how I'd frame my identity when talking to North Koreans after they'd ask, "Where are you from?"

I'd say, "Well, my dad is Armenian..."

"Ooooo, great! Armenia, part of the Soviet Union," often accompanied by a thumbs-up.

"...but he and his family are from Iran," I'd say.

"Iran! We love Iran!" Of course you do.

"But I'm British."

"..."

A neutral response, though on occasion there might be a mention of the greatness of Shakespeare. After 2016, you were more likely to hear pity expressed over Brexit-related political turmoil in the United Kingdom.

"I was born in the United States, so I'm American," I'd continue very rarely; only if I thought the person in question really needed to know.

The response to this final revelation was always disappointment, my conversation partner usually sighing or shrugging with regret. It wasn't anger or rage. Disappointment. The equivalent for me would be if I'd found out someone I like turned out to be an Amway salesman. But not like finding out someone is a Nazi.

North Koreans authorized to interact with foreigners have a well-rehearsed line: "Of course we respect and like the people of America, it's just their government that has unacceptable policies. Though of course governments can influence their people."

Choson Exchange had never been able to take US passport holders to North Korea. There is a separate bureaucratic channel for dealing with Americans and our partners simply did not have the organizational right to invite and mind US citizens. This was a shame because we always had a great deal of interest from the United States, in particular from Silicon Valley.

North Korea occupies a fraught space in the imaginations of most of us: its opacity, its prison camps, its collective life. For techies the added idea of a country without the internet adds to that imaginary space. Here is a country that is fundamentally resistant to the defining technology of our age.

"Has anything changed regarding US citizens?" we'd always ask our North Korean partners. The answer was always no.

Until the one time it wasn't. "We've gotten permission to try," they said.

And it was here that we made one of our worst mistakes. We got too excited. Over the years, we had had dozens and dozens of Americans ask us if they could come. "Let's get as many Americans as we can," Geoffrey and I agreed. We should have started with just one or two.

Instead, I flew to Silicon Valley, had several meetings, and gave a couple of talks. Geoffrey reached out to the numerous expats in Asia he knew. We assembled a team of over twenty people. It was going to be amazing. Two simultaneous workshops, like a real conference, with participants choosing which one to join.

We sent the visa application materials to Pyongyang and then settled in to wait. After ten days or so our partners who'd submitted the materials had heard nothing. It had been sent to the DPRK mission to the United Nations in New York, they said.

The mission to the UN is often called the "New York channel" in the North Korea–watching world. Americans and North Koreans tend not to sit down with each other too often to discuss policy. When it happens, it is often in "Track 2" discussions or "Track 1.5" discussions. "Track 2" generally means discussions between academics or other non-government people who have connections to actual government officials or institutions; "Track 1.5" means a mix of government representatives and non-government researchers.

The New York–based mission is responsible not only for UN activities, but also any dealings with Americans, including these sorts of talks and NGO activities. Neither country has official diplomatic relations with the other, but they've usually had this method of communication since 1991, when both Koreas joined the United Nations. I say "usually" because sometimes communications break down. When tensions were running high in 2016, for example, the North Koreans shut the New York channel down. This effectively meant not answering emails or phone calls from US officials. In 2017, as the White House's aggressive rhetoric ramped up, the channel was used frequently for working-level diplomats to explore ways out of the tensions.[32]

We called New York. They didn't know about it. We called Pyongyang. Our partners went to work, navigating the Kafkaesque bureaucracy. (Note: I have now fulfilled the obligatory reference to Kafka.) We called again and they said it had been sent to New York. We called New York. They said they'd processed it and sent it back to Pyongyang. Indeed, the second secretary at the UN mission seemed very positive on the idea. Then nothing. We called back. No news from Pyongyang. We missed a deadline with the workshop leaders who'd signed up. I wrote them and asked them to please hold on. More days went by. Still nothing.

Then the second secretary went on some kind of business trip. No one else knew what was going on. There were no replies to emails, or calls. With just three weeks to go before the workshop, I had a friend in New York prepared to go in person to the North Korean mission to try to find something out, when I finally heard back from the traveling diplomat: nothing. No news.

We'd entered a bureaucratic black hole. The visas weren't rejected. Nor were they approved. We decided to write the volunteer workshop leaders and say, "Hey, with deepest apologies, this trip cannot go ahead. But I will organize a tour with Koryo Tours that will at least get you into the country, will look at economic sites, and will still be a good learning experience." Sixteen or so people agreed to go on those terms.

Our partners kind of stuck their necks out to try to invite Americans. It was a bit of a risk and we'd failed them by trying to bring too many people. For their risks, there were some benefits: the chance to bring influential Americans to their country, make connections with them, and push the boundaries of what is allowed in the DPRK. But for whatever unnamed bureaucrat in the Ministry of State Security or the North American department of the Ministry of Foreign Affairs, there must have been only risk, with no upside.

Taking a large group of (mostly) Americans has its quirks. Americans are able to visit as tourists easily, except when banned by the US State Department. The DPRK's UN mission almost always approves the travel permit, though

US travelers are (arbitrarily?) not allowed to do certain things other tourists can: homestays or train travel, for example. Visitors from the United States tend to be on the more suspicious side, convinced that everything is set up for the benefit of tourists and are, for example, the most likely to think that the people riding the subway are actors.

When riding the subway to see two of the rather spectacular Moscow-style stations, a common tourist activity, I'll sometimes say to my travel partners, "Move over to make room for these actors getting on." This usually draws a laugh. Once it drew a rebuke: "I think you're wrong, these people aren't actors. You shouldn't call them that." I explained it was a joke, and thus accidentally humiliated the objecting visitor who didn't get it.

This group did visit Moranbong Park, which was packed with families relaxing and drinking, as is common when it is a day off and the weather is nice. Several drunk people waved us over, offering beer or burning clear soju to these foreign guests. A soccer-obsessed member of our group started kicking a ball around with some kids. After several days of being shooed away from talking to people or being ignored by Koreans on the street, some of the group put their suspicion antennas up.

"Are they here for us?" one asked. "Is this real?"

Several years later I met one member of this group who looked back on this experience as perhaps the most valuable. He recalled thinking it was a setup, but upon realizing that it wasn't, was struck by the genuine human warmth and hospitality that was being displayed. "People are people everywhere," he told me, "and of course you know that already, but to see these people who just happened to be born in a very different society from ours . . . that had an impact on me."

The cultural and ideological divide is vast. These little human interactions have to go up against a lifetime of indoctrination and propaganda. And that's true for the North Koreans, too.

To combat that, whenever a positive interaction would take place, I'd always emphasize to the Koreans that the foreigners were Americans. (I have intentionally said that once or twice even if they weren't.) A lifetime of propaganda is hard to counteract, but when the only direct interaction a North Korean has with an American is a positive one, that must leave some kind of impression. A Korean guide once told a friend of mine that "Americans are the best *and* the worst visitors." They're more likely to be combative or try bending the rules, but they're also more likely to go out of their way to be kind and understanding, knowing they are a sort of citizen-diplomat.

On this trip, I suggested to the soccer nut that he should give his ball to the kids, that they'd remember him forever for such a gesture. He did so and we walked away up the hill waving and feeling good about ourselves. A minute later another guy from our group came up behind us holding the ball. "Hey," he said, "I saw those kids had your ball so I grabbed it from them."

"Nooooo!" the soccer guy and I lamented in unison: our efforts at citizen diplomacy were coming unraveled. We rushed down the hill and explained that the other guy was just confused and not some cruel, heartless Yankee bent on ruining their fun. The other guy was of Chinese ethnicity, so the Koreans probably just thought of him as Chinese anyway. Theirs is a highly racialized worldview, after all.

I got a chance to bridge the cultural gap once more on this trip. A few days later we were in Pyongsong, the city that borders Pyongyang. It is an important place, home to many factories and the State Academy of Sciences. It also has the DPRK's biggest market and biggest bus depot. Most North Koreans don't have the right to enter Pyongyang—it requires special permission—so this neighboring town has become the logistics hub of North Korea. Regardless, all these places are closed to tourists. Instead, tourists are allowed to visit a middle school that grooms ping-pong prodigies, a high school for smart kids, statues of the leaders, and the Jangsusan Hotel.

It was at this aging hotel that a hose behind the toilet in one of the rooms came free and began spraying water everywhere. The soccer guy and his roommate were both in there getting absolutely soaked through as they attempted to wrangle this vomiting metal serpent under control and back into place. A couple other people and I were drawn by their yells and whoops.

This was 2015, so of course smartphones came out and recorded the affair as we all laughed at the hilarity of our friends getting dowsed. Some staff quickly arrived and got it under control and then left. Shortly thereafter our guide, Ms. Ha, was summoned to the lobby, however. The staff and the manager of the hotel were deeply humiliated: not only was it embarrassing that their facilities were substandard, but they thought the Americans were laughing *at* them. They were demanding that the tourists delete the videos and even pay for breaking the hose.

Face saving is an important concept in Korean culture and East Asia generally, though it is often overused to explain Korea. It is essentially the value of avoiding humiliation and preserving dignity, even when it is difficult to do so. In Korean it is called *chaemyon*, the characters meaning body *and* face: the concept is of the same value as literally one's whole physical being.

The North Korean media frequently rails against insults to its dignity in statements such as: "Infringing our sovereign rights and dignity is an act of insult and crime that can never be tolerated."[33] It is a sociological concept we have in Western societies, too, of course, and it is very much a part of the tortured relationship between the United States and the DPRK. When a relationship between two states is so negative, there is a strong imperative not to be humiliated by the opponent. Moreover, because there is no trust, almost any action is interpreted as an attempt to not only "win" an interaction, but to dominate or embarrass.

Most importantly, this negative dynamic and lack of understanding has shaped the nuclear crisis between the United States and North Korea. In 2002 the Americans had gained evidence of Pyongyang's uranium program, which was in violation of the 1994 Agreed Framework that the two countries had signed to mitigate the first nuclear crisis. President George W. Bush dispatched a team to Pyongyang to confront the Koreans. To the American delegation's surprise, the Koreans sort of acknowledged a uranium program, saying something along the lines of "it's our right" and that "they regarded the Agreed Framework as 'nullified'."[34]

A gentler approach that didn't directly accuse the North Koreans of cheating might have opened the space to negotiate on the matter; however, the Bush administration was eager to pull the plug on the Clinton-era deal with North Korea.[35] They didn't care or understand that confronting and embarrassing the Koreans was going to limit options for negotiations.

For their part, the North Koreans sometimes rub American noses in it as well, testing an intercontinental ballistic missile on July 4, 2017, for example, America's Independence Day. This purposely humiliates the Americans. US officials are loath to admit it, but pride is a huge factor in how Washington makes policy toward North Korea: it's fundamentally *embarrassing* that this little basket case of a country has defied the United States for a quarter century and has developed nuclear weapons and ICBMs.

Pride has become a huge issue on both sides. As an expert on negotiating has written, "In some instances, protecting against loss of face becomes so central an issue that it 'swamps' the importance of the tangible issues at stake and generates intense conflicts that can impede progress toward agreement and increase substantially the costs of conflict resolution.[36]"

North Koreans can be extremely prideful, which is why they ask visitors to take pictures of only beautiful things. It is why they are reluctant to show us markets since they represent a failure of their system (to some in Pyongyang). It is why at this hotel in Pyongsong, I was standing in a circle of eight hotel staff and my guide, with mumbling voices, red faces, and a mood of shame hanging over us like a cloud.

I'd updated the wet Americans that this had turned into an issue and that I might ask them to apologize if necessary. One of them had become slightly enraged and that idea and especially that the Koreans floated the idea of asking him to pay for the hose. "What! Where I come from they would be upgrading me and giving me free meals and stuff!"

"Don't worry, it won't come to paying for the hose. Also, we're a long way from where you come from," I reminded him and then returned to the shame session downstairs.

While Ms. Ha took a hard line with the staff, telling them off for creating this unnecessary problem and berating them for having such thin skin, I played the good cop.

"Look," I said in the kindest and most avuncular tone I could muster, "Where we are from, when something bad happens, we try to laugh. We think it releases the tension so people don't have to feel bad. These guys didn't have any ill intent with their laughter. In fact, where they are from they would expect you now to give them something for free to say sorry for the inconvenience. I've told them not to expect that and they are trying to understand. I'm asking you to please also try to understand and not to ask them to pay for the hose. I will also ask them not to share the video or pictures."

This seemed to work and the meeting was adjourned. One of the videos ended up online anyway. I feel bad that I failed the hotel staff in that regard, but as they are not allowed internet access, they will never know.

Notes

1 Justin Corfield, *Historical Dictionary of Pyongyang* (London: Anthem Press, 2014), 146.

2 Adrian Buzo, *The Guerilla Dynasty* (Boulder: Westview Press, 1999), 1–2.

3 Sonia Ryang, "Visible and Vulnerable: The Predicament of Koreans in Japan," in *Diaspora without Homeland Being Korean in Japan*, eds. Sonia Ryang and John Lie (Berkeley, CA: UC Berkeley Press, 2009), 63–64.

4 Wada Haruki and Gavan McCormack, "The Strange Record of 15 Years of Japan–North Korea Negotiations," *Asia-Pacific Journal* 3, no. 9 (2005): 1.

5 Haruki and McCormack, "Strange Record," 5.

6 Ryang, "Visible and Vulnerable," 62.

7 Yaechan Lee, "Japan's North Korean Diaspora," *The Diplomat*, January 5, 2018.

8 Sonia Ryang, "The Rise and Fall of Chongryun—From Chōsenjin to Zainichi and Beyond," *Asia-Pacific Journal* 14, issue 15, no. 11 (August 1, 2016): 1.

9 Hong Ju Hwan, "홍주환. 권해효 "우리 민족 가르치는 조선학교, 일본 우익에겐 눈엣가시 같은 존재" [Kwon Hae-hyo: The existence of Choson Schools teaching our people is a thorn in the side of the Japanese right wing], 시사저널[Sisa journal], July 22, 2017, http://www.sisapress.com/journal/article/170463.

10 Ra Jong-il, 장성택의 길 [Jang Song Taek's road] (Seoul: Alma, 2015), 115–17.

11 David Mikkelson, "Jang Sung-taek Executed by Hungry Dogs?" Snopes, January 6, 2014, https://www.snopes.com/fact-check/howl-to-the-chief.

12 Eric Ellis, "Keeping Dear Leader's Score," *New York Times*, October 19, 1994.

13 Peter Simpson, "Playing the Capitalist Game Badly Where 'Dear Leader' Kim Excelled," *The Telegraph*, November 3, 2006, http://www.telegraph.co.uk/news/world news/1533198/Playing-the-capitalist-game-badly-where-Dear-Leader-Kim-excelled .html.

14 Jean H. Lee, "Kim Jong-il: Legendary Golfer and Mythical Powers Even in Death," *Christian Science Monitor*, December 22, 2011, http://www.csmonitor.com /World/Latest-News-Wires/2011/1222/Kim-Jong-il-Legendary-golfer-and-mythical -powers-even-in-death.

15 Kathryn Weathersby, "The Soviet Union," in *The Ashgate Research Companion to the Korean War*, eds. James I. Matray and Donald W. Boose (Burlington, VT: Ashgate, 2014), 89.

16 Weathersby, "Soviet Union," 86.

17 Mina Yoon, "Who Do North Koreans Think Started the Korean War?" NK News, January 8, 2014, https://www.nknews.org/2014/01/who-do-north-koreans-think -started-the-korean-war/.

18 Heritage Foundation, "Maintaining Focus on North Korea Human Rights Violations Panel 1," Youtube, April 29, 2015, https://www.youtube.com/watch?v =C-2HbYHFjf4.

19 I recognize this is true everywhere, but the intensity and continuing relevance of today's battles over historical narratives in Northeast Asia strike me as particularly intense.

20 Don Oberdorfer, *The Two Koreas: A Contemporary History* (New York: Basic, 2014), 5.

21 Donald W. Boose Jr., "Amphibious Warfare," in *The Ashgate Research Companion to the Korean War*, eds. James I. Matray and Donald W. Boose (Burlington, VT: Ashgate, 2014), 191.

22 Education Division, National Museum of the United States Air Force, *Korean War, 1950–1953, Teacher Resource Guide*, 17.

23 See Roger Dingman, "Atomic Diplomacy during the Korean War," *International Security* 3, no. 13 (Winter 1988–89): 50–91.

24 Wada Haruki, *The Korean War: An International History* (New York: Rowman and Littlefield, 2014), 287.

25 Fyodor Tertitskiy, "Exclusion as a Privilege: The Chinese Diaspora in North Korea," *Journal of Korean Studies* 20, no. 1 (Spring 2015): 180.

26 Tertitskiy, "Exclusion as a Privilege," 187.

27 Tony Ita Etim, "Nigeria: Govt Loses 500,000 Oil Barrels Daily—Akpana," Allafrica.com, August 18, 2005, https://allafrica.com/stories/200508180137.html.

28 Kevin J. Kelley, "Nigeria, North Korea Sign Co-operation Agreement on ICT, Education," Allafrica.com, May 6, 2014, https://allafrica.com/stories/201405070583.html.

29 Kevin J. Kelley, "Uganda: UN Probes Tanzania and Uganda Deals with North Korea," Allafrica.com, September 13, 2017, https://allafrica.com/stories/201709130792.html.

30 Guanhong Hu, "Mine Workers, Idyllic Landscapes, Tigers: North Korean Artists Have Made Tens of Millions of Dollars for Pyongyang," Quartz, November 14, 2017, https://qz.com/1113866/north-koreas-art-studio-mansudae-has-made-the-country-tens-of-millions-dollars-by-exporting-art.

31 Paul K. Kerr, Steven A. Hildreth, and Mary Beth D. Nikitin, *Iran-North Korea-Syria Ballistic Missile and Nuclear Cooperation*, Congressional Research Service Report 7-5700, February 26, 2016, i.

32 Josh Rogin, "Inside the 'New York Channel' between the United States and North Korea," *Washington Post*, August 11, 2017, https://www.washingtonpost.com/news/josh-rogin/wp/2017/08/11/inside-the-new-york-channel-between-the-united-states-and-north-korea.

33 Press conference by General Staff of the Korean People's Army, KCNA, April 18, 2009, quoted in Jihwan Hwang, "Face-Saving, Reference Point, and North Korea's Strategic Assessments," *Korean Journal of International Relations* 49, no. 6 (2009): 58.

34 James A. Kelly, "Assistant Secretary of State for East Asian and Pacific Affairs Remarks at the Woodrow Wilson Center," US Department of State, December 11, 2002, https://2001-2009.state.gov/p/eap/rls/rm/2002/15875.htm.

35 Leon Sigal, "Hand in Hand for Korea: A Peace Process and Denuclearization," *Asian Perspective* 32, no. 2 (2008): 10.

36 Bert Brown, "Face Saving and Face Restoration in Negotiation," in *Negotiations: Social-Psychological Perspectives*, ed. Daniel Druckman (Beverly Hills, CA: Sage, 1977), 275.

6

Propaganda

E ighty percent normal, 20 percent profoundly weird." This has become my short answer when people ask, "What's it like over there?" The weirdness is, in part, because of the intensity of the official messaging, the pervasiveness of the propaganda. It is relentless. And it can be effective, especially since there isn't much else for it to compete with.

I don't want to suggest we aren't exposed to propaganda in the West. The United States is probably the most overtly propagandist country in the developed world, in terms of nationalism. If you've ever watched American sports, you'll noticed flags and anthems hoisted and sung before each contest—not international competitions, but domestic ones, even on the local level. The Super Bowl, the pinnacle of sporting culture, began in the Cold War and served a role "not unlike the Soviet Union's May Day parade... operated as a primary site for the display of military nationalism."[1] Post-9/11, there have been pregame shows on aircraft carriers, readings of the Declaration of Independence, flyovers by military jets, and other overt displays of nationalism. Flags are everywhere. (Don't believe me? Do an image search for "America flag in gym," then "British flag in gym." You will find hundreds of the former, vs. nearly none of the latter. Do Americans need a flag to inspire their workouts, one wonders?)

Cartoons such as GI Joe and Teenage Mutant Ninja Turtles invariably reinforce national values. Advertisements train us to be good consumers and get excited first by toys, then fashion, then trucks and cars. Debates on television news talk shows present us with the range of socially acceptable opinions, though this mode of idea-shaping began undergoing real strain as of 2019.

The capitalist-democratic form of propagandizing is diffuse, however. It's handled by the private sector, largely, and targets different types of consumers, making us feel unique as we increasingly choose our preferred propaganda.

This is the exact opposite in North Korea where, as it happens, the word "propaganda" has no negative connotation. Using state-driven propaganda they have overtly built a monolith—they call it that—where everyone is supposed to fall in line with the Worker's Party's decisions. That imperative is built around the idea of *Juche*.

What is Juche? You know the Sinatra song, "My Way"? It's like that. In fact, if you ever have a night out in Pyongyang with your Korean guides that ends up at karaoke, that Sinatra hit will almost certainly come up at some point. It trumpets the auteur's independence, creativity, and uniqueness in the face of opposition. It's the perfectly North Korean pop song that happens to be American.

Juche is a mishmash of autarky, race-nationalism, and leader-centrism. Kim Il Sung first referred to it in 1955, vaguely. A decade later the term *Juche* was referred to as an ideology for the first time.[2] Kim wanted to ensure independence from the USSR and China. In a real sense North Korea's "never again" is the prospect of being beholden to or controlled by a foreign power.

In order to achieve that key goal, he and his propagandists, one of whom was eventually his son and heir, Kim Jong Il, built some other key elements into Juche. It means (partly) self-reliance, mostly but not entirely at the state level. I've heard local officials or factory managers reference it as they discuss solving their own localized problems of their own volition. Still, at the core of Juche is the idea that the whole of society should follow the will of the leader in order to be independent together.

Lest there be any doubt, a set of "Ten Principles for the Establishment of the Unitary-Ideology System" were announced in 1974, by Kim Jong Il.[3] They include injunctions such as "Make absolute the authority of the Great Leader Comrade Kim Il Sung." I'll let you look the rest of them up for yourself if you're interested, they're all pretty similar. Here's a summary: each principle is in some way about following, honoring, or obeying Kim Il Sung. Following Kim Jong Il's death in 2011, his writings and teachings were elevated, so what was once "Kimilsungism" is now called "Kimilsung-Kimjongilism." You will come across slogans such as, "Let's firmly arm ourselves with the ideology of Kimilsung-Kimjongilism." Or the even-more-awkward-to-translate, "Let's Kimilsung-Kimjongilism-ify this society"

Juche is sort of Marxism, but with much greater emphasis on ideology, rather than the material forces that Marx was concerned with. From the 1970s to the 1990s, references to Marxism-Leninism were gradually phased out as Pyongyang sought to emphasize that they really were doing things "their way." (Marx's portrait was finally removed from Kim Il Sung Square in 2012. Lenin's, too.)

Juche was used to consolidate Kim Il Sung's power in the postwar years. By elevating his ideas—for example, the need to prioritize heavy industry—into revolutionary ideology, he was able to claim that elites opposed to *him* were opposed to the Korean Revolution itself. It was also used to rebuff outsiders, primarily the USSR, who wanted Pyongyang not to focus on heavy industry, but rather supply raw materials to their own factories to make industrial products. Kim Il Sung essentially said—just as the South's Park Chung-hee later would—get stuffed, we're making steel, chemicals, and ships ourselves.

In a 1965 speech in Indonesia, Kim targeted both "revisionists and dogmatists" (i.e., anyone disagreeing with or challenging him) and the USSR, saying "their purpose, in the final analysis, was to prevent our country from building its economic foundations. . . . Of course, we could not follow their view."[4]

That speech was also a watershed in the DPRK's quest to export Juche. The DPRK was using it to elevate Kim Il Sung not only to the forefront of domestic society, but also to increase his prominence in the international community, and why not? After all, "Kim Il Sung thinks more deeply than others about the position of the socialist camp and the international communist movement," as one hagiographer bluntly put it.[5]

North Korea funded Juche study groups around the world, held conferences and workshops, as well as brought people to Korea to study the idea of the "peerless man." During the Cold War the idea that a small state must go its own way and not bend to the will of the great powers found resonance. These worldwide study groups were used in domestic media to show North Korea's citizens, "See? People around the world love and respect our leader. We are so, so lucky to have him." Some of those groups still exist (as we saw in the previous chapter) and, while there are far fewer international conferences to attend, will still pop up in Pyongyang from time to time. They come and do a tour, bearing names such as "Nigerian National Committee for the Study of Kimilsungism-Kimjongilism," "British Group for the Study of the Juche Idea," and even "'Sun of Juche' Association of Journalists and Men of Culture for the Study of Kimjongilism in Ukraine." One wonders if that name is satirical.

They are few in number these days: the world has largely moved on from Juche. When in Pyongyang, these "revolutionaries" are confronted by propaganda everywhere, but since the vast majority of them can't read Korean, they are largely oblivious to what's being said. Still, when they visit, they appear in newspapers and on TV, offered as proof of Juche's popularity abroad.

Some slogans call for "Independence, Self-Defense, Sovereignty," the three pillars of Juche. In 1982, Kim Jong Il submitted a paper to a huge Juche conference organized to celebrate his father's seventieth birthday. It was called "On the Juche Idea" and is considered a defining text in the DPRK canon. It set him apart as the sole interpreter of the philosophy and added a bit more focus on self-defense. Now, Juche's self-reliance means an independent economy, self-rule in politics, and the ability to defend oneself. (Funny story about the word for "self-defense" in Korea—I'll get to that in a minute.)

One popular set of slogans is "Resolve to die in defense (of the leadership)," "Single-hearted unity," and "Ideological attack." As well as these and other general slogans about "our-style socialism" or "the army, the party, and the people together," there are more policy specific slogans too. So sometimes these might read "all households—let's extensively raise goats," or "all efforts to build the economy" or "let's settle up with the US empire," depending on the needs of the day.

When relations are bad with the United States, more of the latter type appear. The lettering for "America" or "American Empire" is written in black. Nothing else ever is. Red and white are the most frequently used colors for slogans.

Not only is every billboard, mural, and banner dedicated in some way to the state or leadership, but citizens are regularly exposed to neighborhood-wide broadcasts by propaganda vans, small vehicles with megaphones attached to the roof. These drive through town blaring exhortations to implement certain policies and support the country. The Doppler shift means that the shouty voice, sometimes with a musical backing, raises into a whine as it drives by you, then distorts and drops pitch once it passes.

Television on the main channel in North Korea, Korea Central Television, is a varied experience, ranging from quite boring to catatonia-inducing boring. It shows a mix of news, movies, dramas, music videos, and what might only be called infotainment—without the "tainment." It seems like every day there is some turgid explanation of a mushroom farm, glass factory, or noodle research center. The channel also seems to broadcast a Kim-related documentary nearly every day. It's been doing so since 1963.[6] Sometimes you can see global content—I've watched Champions League or World Cup football on KCTV before, though in both cases weeks and weeks after the actual contests took place.

The most popular station is *Mansudae,* which since 1983 has broadcast a mix of light entertainment, documentaries, and movies, often foreign, and generally more entertaining than KCTV offerings. I've tuned in and watched the *Lion King* and Red Bull–sponsored extreme sports, for example.

Unfortunately for country folk, the channel seems to be quite hard to get outside of the Pyongyang area, though a friend did watch highlights of the 2019 Women's World Cup in a provincial capital.

Under Kim Jong Un, the selection of channels has expanded on weekends. There is now an educational channel and a sports channel that broadcast for six hours on weekends. In 2016, they also started a Netflix-like streaming service called *Manbang*. Manbang means ten thousand directions, or ten thousand broadcasts, but unfortunately in English it reads like a 1990s gay nightclub name. This has led to plenty of "Manbang and chill" jokes, referencing the twenty-first-century equivalent of asking someone up for a nightcap. Netflix themselves got in on the joke, briefly calling themselves a "Manbang knockoff."[7]

In all honesty, my favorite program is the weather forecast, which comes on each night a few minutes after nine o'clock. They show a dozen boxes on the screen and one-by-one reveal each city's next-day high and low temperatures. You can create, therefore, a gameshow-style guessing game with the temperatures, calling out your guess for each city before it's revealed and making bets with your friends. Sometimes you have to find entertainment where you can.

There are times, as a visitor, when the propagandizing becomes too much. The constant, monolithic, political messaging can feel exhausting.

For example, on KCTV there are frequent music videos. They don't seem pressured to fill every minute of airtime, so if a show is only twenty-five minutes instead of thirty, no problem: they just chuck a couple music videos in the space where elsewhere ads might fill the airtime. Once, after a number of days in-country, feeling a bit fatigued by everything, I popped on the TV just as a music video was coming on. The first few lines of this song, "My Mother's Voice," go:

> I feel warm whenever I hear my loving mother's voice,
> Whether I'm by her side or far away.

I thought, "Oh, that's nice. Something that isn't political for a moment. Something just about family." I smiled inside a little. About sixty seconds went by before the reveal:

> That voice is that of our party,
> Aaaa...a warm feeling.

The rest of the song is about the party's leadership of the familial nation. It made me physically slump on my seat and shake my head. I'd been so pleased to hear something apolitical for a minute and to have it wrenched away was deflating.

Another time I found myself watching a music video with a cheery tune, the first verse of which was "I love my hometown, I love my homeland," which seemed pleasant enough. The second verse, however, was "Hate the enemy for your hometown; the enemy is hatred." In the same cheery lilting tune as the first verse. Again, a real comedown.

The need for North Korean society to have a monolithic system with a maximal leader is also deeply embedded and reflexively expressed. As one North Korean told me in 2012: "Foreigners just don't understand the relationship we have with our leaders. They really do everything for us, and we do everything for them."[8] This was a sophisticated guy. He'd traveled abroad and was not naïve. I couldn't quite tell if he was saying it as part of a performance in front of my group or if he meant it. He also emphasized that "some countries don't have a strong sense of national identity" the way Koreans do, which helps with that very personal relationship.

He used the word "*minjok*" (national), but here he meant something along the lines of "racial." There is some ambiguity in the term "minjok." Race, ethnicity, nationality, people—minjok can have all of these meanings. And it appears everywhere. Slogans proclaim Koreans are "Kim Il Sung's minjok." A pop song about the DPRK's Computer Numerical Control technology proclaims the "pride of the minjok is high." And, of course, it is widely proclaimed that unification is an issue to be solved "by our minjok ourselves." If you read those back and substitute the word "race" for minjok, as a Westerner you might get a bit of a discomfiting feeling. North Koreans generally translate it as "people" in English-language propaganda, which triggers significantly less emotion for a foreign audience.

The idea is that—above the other solidarities the state promotes, with the working class or with "progressive" countries, for example—Koreans should be in solidarity with each other first. I've seen this displayed the couple times I've been in North Korea with ethnic Koreans: they really are treated like long-lost family, at least relative to the rest of us. This doesn't always work out in real life, of course.

Once, on the eve of the Pyongyang International Marathon, I was asked to translate the list of runners' nationalities for the tour company that was helping to organize the race. The spreadsheet was in Korean. I sat in the lobby of the Sosan Hotel, in the city's sports district, and went through the names: "Swiss... Australian... Dutch... Puppet?"

"This one just says 'puppet'," I said to the tour company representative. "Puppet" is what North Korean media tend to call the government in Seoul, which they portray as quislings of the American occupiers. The word here was beside the name of a South Korea–born Canadian, it turned out. I'm not exactly sure what transpired next, but thirty minutes later I saw that Canadian and a North Korean guide yelling at each other in the parking lot. I couldn't quite make out what they were saying, and I knew enough not to stick my nose into it. Regardless, it was clear there was a lack of racial solidarity going on.

Still, for North Koreans, their ideology *does* contain a heavy dose of race-nationalism. Socialist and Juche ideas intermingle with race to create a pretty powerful national narrative. And this is something that many Western observers miss about North Korea (and perhaps the potency of ethnic identity elsewhere, too). Yes, there is repression and extreme control over information in the DPRK, but there is at the heart of it all a national story that remains quite compelling. That story is that Koreans have long been set upon by a hostile world and that only they can look out for themselves, as a family. This resonates.

I grew up half-Armenian and 100 percent Seventh-day Adventist. Armenians have a strong ethnic identity and victimhood is also at the core of our shared experience, so I have a sense of how powerful it can be. Adventists believe that they are the only sect that has found the truth and will be oppressed for it by a hostile world. Such sentiments create a powerful sense of belonging and are difficult to shed, even when you grow up and see that there are mismatches between the doctrines you've been taught and the world you observe. Leaving a religion is not emotionally easy for many people, despite the massive cognitive dissonances that come with believing in dogmas that are contravened by science or observed experience.

If there is one thing I've observed, it is that North Koreans live with huge amounts of dissonance. Perhaps more than most of us. They are constantly juggling competing aspirations—the ones they've been told they should have—and their own far more personal and sometimes international aspirations. They have to tuck away a number of thoughts and not let them form fully, lest they cause too much frustration, depression, and social risk. It is simply too difficult to let yourself completely believe something that contradicts what you have been taught your whole life.

In one conversation our workshop leaders were having with a very bright young North Korean lady, we were discussing the differences between our two- or multi-party system and their one-party system. At one point, she stated of her leaders, "because they are not elected, it reflects the unanimous will of the broad masses." Of course, the "will" to do something implies an option to choose something else, which doesn't exist in DPRK politics. Her statement on the face of it makes little sense. This is something, given her keen intellect and often insightful comments on other matters, she must have known at some level. Or maybe not. Perhaps she had cognitively papered over it before she ever thought about it. The psyche has an incredible capacity to deal with things that don't make sense so that we can function.

I don't wish to imply that this is only a North Korean condition: it happens everywhere. As in all societies, the key to getting people to believe something is to instill it when they're young. One brisk spring morning at a collective farm we walked by a nursery, the kind for children, not plants. Tiny kids of about three or four years gathered in the courtyard, ruddy cheeked from the cold, colorful sweaters dusted with dirt from the farm. They were coaxed into singing a song and doing some accompanying hand motions and most of my group thought they were pretty adorable. I, however, could understand the lyrics:

"Leader Kim Jong Un is our parent, we want to see Kim Jong Un..."

There are a handful of well-equipped schools in the Pyongyang area that they are keen to show off to foreigners. This wasn't one of them—the kids were a bit too grubby and snotty. Usually when visitors are shown a school, the kids and buildings are immaculate. Most of the posters lining the rooms are about normal things such as the water cycle, human anatomy, or the countries of the world. But there are almost always posters with beady-eyed and hook-nosed Americans committing crimes against the minjok during the war.

Schoolkids sometimes perform for visiting delegations; the mini-concerts are usually of high quality. The lyrics are always about the leadership or the fatherland. Even without understanding the words, the school experience can really divide visitors. Half think, "My gosh, what talented kids!" This is what the state wants you think. The other half think, "My god, the state has press-ganged these kids into performing tricks for us." The state, I suspect, is also okay with this takeaway. The North Korean authorities know that most people disagree with how they've organized their society, but if they leave the place shaking their head about how repressive and unbreakable it is, that is fine by them.

Those children will grow up revering their state and the leaders who built it. They will see the portraits of Kim Il Sung and Kim Jong Il every day in their living rooms. If they live in Pyongyang, at various ages through to adulthood, they will have to take part in political parades or mass games—helping propagate messages to the rest of the country, and indeed, the world. When they get married, they and their families will go to the nearest statues of the leaders to bow and pay homage.

Before all that, elementary schoolchildren will already be learning about Juche, the genius philosophy thought up by their current leader's grandfather.

They will learn about the three pillars of having a Juche Fatherland, *jaju, jarip,* and *jawi*—political autonomy, an independent economy, and self-defense.

Once I was with the cheery Mr. Bae and I was feeling a bit cheeky. "What does the word *jawi* mean?" I asked as we drove by an installation atop an apartment building that spelled out the three words in front of a sculpture of Mount Paektu. It means self-defense, but it also means masturbation, though of course that usage has fallen out of use in North Korea. It would be like using Victorian-era terms like "self-abuse" or "onanism."

"Self-defense," he replied confidently.

"Are you sure?" I asked. "Because my dictionary says something else."

"No," he scrunched his face in a quizzical way. "It means self-defense."

"Are you sure it doesn't mean something else? Something you, um, do on your own?"

His face stayed scrunched for a second as he pondered that clue and then his eyes widened.

"Nooooooo!" he exclaimed, laughing. "Oh no!" He clapped his hand to his forehead. "You've ruined this beautiful idea for me!" he said as we laughed at my puerility. I later wondered if he told some of his friends about it and shared the joke. Or if he went the other way and solemnly brought it up at his next self-criticism session. I doubt he did that; that's generally not how it works.

Every week all North Korean adults engage in political study sessions that also include self-criticism and mutual-criticism sessions. These are conducted at your workplace or, if you don't work, through the Women's League or some other institution. (As noted earlier, every North Korean is required to be a member of a mass organization, starting at age twelve with the Young Pioneer Corps, then the Youth League when they turn fifteen or sixteen.) The political study aspect of these meetings sees party officials giving dry lectures on the latest party policies that people are expected to support or implement. Participants are expected to rote memorize a lot, sometimes whole tracts, and be able to later recite them. You see people studying all over the place: behind the check-in counter at hotels, while strolling through parks, or sometimes at night under a streetlamp, insects swirling above them in the beams that cut through the coal dust.

The criticism sessions you might imagine to be intense, as individuals jockey for political favor and try to take down rivals. This is generally not how they go. Instead, people often try to highlight the most anodyne, apolitical failings they can think of. Colleagues generally don't want to get each other in *real* trouble and people certainly wouldn't want to admit to any doubts about party policies in a group setting.

Instead, people will admit to minor failings, such as "I failed to faithfully do my road cleaning" or "I went to a friend's house and drank booze while I was supposed to be working."[9] These indictments allow for a political ritual to take place, but one devoid of actual, dangerous political content. Where you work can define how intense these sessions are, as can your level. University student sessions are mild compared to "adult" ones, I've heard.

This wasn't (and isn't) always true. In particular, during the revolution's earlier years, the criticism sessions were especially intense. One poet who was subject to humiliation for poems that were pro-communist but that did not cleave sufficiently to the party line later recalled, "It was all so self-important; no one could believe that just a few poems could cause such a fuss." In those days, people were taught to *love* criticism sessions, and films and books depicted characters as invigorated and rectified by them.[10]

By the 1980s, some of that began to wane as DPRK culture saw a rather pleasant thaw. That thaw saw much more relaxed fashion, films, and cultural events. Songs became lighter and breezier. Criticism sessions also loosened up.

Culture and criticism became more intense and militarized during the famine period and afterwards, as the state struggled to reassert its control. A further twisting of the screws happened in 2017 and 2019. As one frequent visitor to the country warned me before I went in for a trip in 2018: "Be especially careful not to talk about anything sensitive. Everyone is under so much pressure, rivalries and spats are getting worse. People are looking for reasons to get others into trouble." We surmised that under conditions of scarcity, people become more inclined to remove rivals that eat into a shrinking pie.

In periods of political instability or uncertainty at the top of society, pressure reverberates downwards through the system. So, following the collapse of the 2019 Hanoi summit, when sanctions were squeezing the country and the political direction was unclear, criticism sessions became more intense. Overall trust between people decreases as pressure to be ideologically pure increases: what might have once been overlooked can become an issue as people feel more compelled to catch each other out. "There are no real friends anymore," one North Korean confided to a friend of mine.

Koreans will freely tell you that these study and criticism sessions take place, but they will rarely, if ever, tell you about the topics discussed. This is, after all, how the most sensitive propaganda gets disseminated. DPRK authorities know that radio and TV are monitored outside the country and they know newspapers are read by foreigners. They certainly know that propaganda posters and other public displays are visible to the various outsiders who are in-country at any given time. So messages in those fora are crafted with an awareness that they will get out into the wider world. Content that is shared in weekly study sessions is tightly held and only generally leaks out through some of the defector media outlets that have networks in North Korea. And only rarely.

Amazingly, on that trip in 2018 our itinerary took us to the DMZ, to the truce village in Panmunjom. This was a little over two weeks before the Moon-Kim summit, where they would make the "Panmunjom Declaration for Peace, Prosperity and Unification of the Korean Peninsula." On the day we were there, across the dividing line, workers were power washing and painting buildings on the Southern side. "Oh," I said to one of the foreigners in my group, "that must be for the upcoming summit."

Out of nowhere a North Korean guide popped up. "What summit?" she asked. "Our leader with Donald Trump?"

"What?" I whispered back. "How do you know about that one? There isn't even a date or location chosen!" (It would end up happening in June, in Singapore.)

"This one is for Moon and Kim. In two weeks," I added. We wandered off from the group to discuss it further. It turns out rumors about the Kim-Trump summit were rife in Pyongyang. Trump had made a snap judgment to hold a meeting with Kim after South Koreans had briefed him in early March. The business community was particularly electrified, dreaming of an end to sanctions, an increase in investment opportunities, and, well, more electricity.

Later that year I got a glimpse of how some messaging remains largely hidden. It was September, so Kim Jong Un had met South Korean president Moon Jae-in twice and US president Donald Trump once. Talks weren't really progressing between the United States and North Korea, but the mood was still fairly positive. The Sinchon Massacre Museum was on our itinerary, but a couple days before we were told the visit was canceled.

"Because it doesn't fit in with the current atmosphere?" I asked. They didn't know or wouldn't say.

The Sinchon Massacre Museum, about an hour's drive south of Pyongyang, commemorates a place where some sort of massacre took place. The North Korean narrative blames an officer called "Harrison"—every North Korean knows this name—claiming that the "Yankees massacred 35,383 innocent Koreans, or a quarter of the population of Sinchon in 52 days" of occupation in 1950.[11] The historian Bruce Cumings believes the newsreel footage of the aftermath is real enough, though it doesn't show who carried out the killings.[12] It may well have been South Korean forces or militia, or something else entirely.

The main point is less what actually happened, however. What is more important is how the DPRK uses that location today—it is *the* set piece to demonstrate American evil and instill it into the hearts of DPRK citizens. It has visceral dioramas and paintings, all featuring defiant and brave Koreans being subjected to all manner of horrors by Americans with bug-eyes and hooked noses. There are all sorts of cruelty, including nails being hammered into heads, breasts being cut off, and babies ripped away from mothers to be killed.

It is the only place where I've seen something approaching graffiti by Koreans: the word "revenge" scratched into moss on the side of a pathway leading to a building where villagers were trapped and set alight. In fact, upon first arriving at the museum, a sign in the parking lot has arrows pointing to three crucial facilities: the parking lot, the toilets, and the "revenge-pledging place."

Anyway, we weren't supposed to see it, except that because of flooding in the South, our bus had to take a detour on the way back from Kaesong. The parking lot of this museum, supposedly closed, was absolutely packed with buses. Hundreds of students and adults were there, milling around or being organized into lines.

Anti-Americanism had disappeared from the propaganda channels visible to foreigners in 2018, but it was alive and well, still coursing through the internal organs of the state. Resident diplomats told me that around this time you could also find the black-lettered anti-American placards sometimes on side streets as well, just not in neighborhoods or towns where foreigners were usually allowed to go.

Notes

1 Christopher R. Martin and Jimmie L. Reeves, "The Whole World Isn't Watching (But We Thought They Were): The Super Bowl and U.S. Solipsism in Sport," *Society: Cultures, Commerce, Media, Politics* 4, no. 2 (2001): 222.

2 Kim Seok Hyang, *The Juche Ideology of North Korea: Sociopolitical Roots of Ideological Change* (Athens, GA: University of Georgia Press, 1993), 28.

3 "What Are the 'Ten Principles'?" *Daily NK*, August 9, 2013, https://www.dailynk .com/english/what-are-the-ten-principles.

4 Kim Il Sung, *On the Socialist Construction and the South Korean Revolution in the Democratic People's Republic of Korea* (Pyongyang: Foreign Languages Publishing House, 1968), 6.

5 Paik Bong, *Kim Il Sung: Premier of the Democratic People's Republic of Korea* (New York: Guardian, 1970), 590.

6 Andrei Lankov, *North of the DMZ: Essays on Daily Life in North Korea* (Jefferson, North Carolina: McFarland, 2007), 59.

7 "Netflix Jokes about N Korean Imitator Manbang in Twitter Bio," BBC News, August 26, 2016, https://www.bbc.com/news/world-asia-37192784.

8 In conversation with the author, September 2012. This individual appeared a little more cynical by 2017, for what its worth.

9 Roh Jong Min, "노정민 "북 생활총화 수첩 내용 들여다보니..."" [Looking into the contents of the criticism note book...], Radio Free Asia, April 13, 2015, https:// www.rfa.org/korean/weekly_program/radio-world/radioworld-04132015134544.html.

10 Tatiana Gabroussenko, "Socialism with a Human Face? North Korea's Brief, but Impactful, Cultural 'Thaw,'" NK News, January 28, 2019, https://www.nknews.org /2019/01/socialism-with-a-human-face-north-koreas-brief-but-impactful-cultural-thaw.

11 "Sinchon Simmering with Rage," KCNA, July 3, 1998, http://www.kcna.co.jp /item/1998/9807/news07/03.htm.

12 Bruce Cumings, *War and Television* (New York: Verso Books, 1992), 221.

7

Workshopping the New Economy

Don't worry, this chapter will be more fun than you think.

Politics is always economic in nature and economics is always political. Politics is fundamentally about distribution of limited resources for a community or country; political ideas justify how things are controlled and distributed. Immediately in politics, then, we're talking about economic rules. The prevailing ideas about how to develop and allocate wealth are what allows any political regime to exist. In fact, until the late nineteenth century, "economics" was not really a term in use: the discipline was called "political-economy," in recognition that there is no purely scientific approach to describing the social world. In trying to describe it, you actually create it. You either justify or undermine the prevailing order.

This is true everywhere. "A women's place is in the home" is a social idea: that a woman's natural role is to raise kids and maintain family life. It just happens to imbue men with greater economic and political power. The idea that some races are better suited to physical labor than intellectual work justified slavery. Many of the people who held these ideas are not overtly engaged in a political project: they genuinely thought they were describing obvious truths about the world. The political ramifications of social ideas can be hidden, often even from those who hold them. Today, for example, we hold it to be "natural," if regrettable, that there are billionaires and homeless in the same city. That is "just how it is" and the subtle, political ramifications of our hey-that's-how-it-is ideas are played out almost subconsciously.

In North Korea, things are more overtly political. Politics is deliberately infused into almost every aspect of life and the ideas promulgated by the system are constantly linked directly to North Koreans' daily routines. Your workplace is politicized, as it ostensibly takes instructions from the party. Slogans and charts remind of you this. With your work unit, you study the country's political line every Friday. Your children take state education that emphasizes the father-figure-like nature of the supreme leader. Your *living room* is political. Portraits of Kim Il Sung and Kim Jong Il sit on the wall of every household's main room, reminding you of the social order.

The economic development of the country is explicitly connected to the "unparalleled genius" of those two men and the country they built. Economics in North Korea is therefore *extremely* sensitive, because the ideas of the leadership are considered sacrosanct. Yet, fundamentally, every North Korean knows that their country is economically backward. There has been so much exposure to illegal foreign media content and so much interaction with China that everyone knows that in their Northeast Asian neighborhood, the DPRK has been left behind.

The running explanation for this is the "hostile anti-DPRK policy of the United States." Some people largely accept this position. But many know that locally made policy choices are at least partially responsible for the weak economy. And fundamentally, with Choson Exchange, we were going there to discuss policies and practices that would improve the economy and the skills that people would need in order to achieve economic success in the twenty-first century.

This was tricky because sometimes implicit criticisms of the North Korean way of doing things could be embedded in these discussions. We had to keep them from becoming explicit. Our volunteers had to tread extremely carefully. Before we took people to run workshops, we spent hours helping them craft their presentations so they could be substantive, but also inoffensive.

Once, for example, a workshop leader wished to discuss the economic relationship between China and North Korea. This was tricky – it is perhaps the most sensitive international relationship of all.

North Koreans hate the United States almost in an abstract way, as a distant, evil force set upon destroying the Korean people and way of life. But China is the country that historically has had the most impact on Korea and currently has the most influence over the DPRK. The modern influence grew after the fall of the Japanese Empire in 1945 and then the victory of the Chinese Communists led by Mao Zedong over the Nationalists in 1949.

Less than a year after that, the Korean War broke out. When the conflict encroached on Chinese interests, the young People's Republic of China intervened. This preserved North Korea as an entity, but relations between the two states have been tense as frequently as they have been positive. Even during the war, there were tensions over who was really leading the war effort. During China's Cultural Revolution (1966–76), North Korea came under withering criticism for its personality cult around Kim Il Sung. Pyongyang resented Beijing's normalization of relations with Washington in the mid-1970s, seeing it as a betrayal. Soon thereafter Pyongyang became suspicious of Beijing in the 1980s as the Chinese moved away from a planned economy.

Another moment of huge frustration for Pyongyang came when Beijing recognized South Korea in 1992: in their eyes, a bitter betrayal. At the time one writer noted that while the Chinese knew of Pyongyang's anger, "they reckon that Pyongyang cannot afford to break its ties with China, which is now North Korea's last ally and on which it has become more dependent for political, military, and economic support."[1]

That has largely come to pass, though the two are very much trapped by each other. China, if it wished, has the leverage to squeeze North Korea so hard it could induce regime collapse. But regime collapse—and Pyongyang is fully aware of this—could create so much chaos that it might threaten the stability and economic prosperity of East Asia. This represents a major threat in the eyes of the Chinese Communist Party, for which economic growth is the font of legitimacy. Moreover, a crisis and rebuilding of the regional order may or may not go in China's favor.

Meanwhile, North Korea has also become trapped in its economic relationship with China. Russia has basically disappeared, economically, certainly when compared to the days of the USSR. Inter-Korean trade, robust from the mid-2000s to 2013, dropped to basically zero after the inter-Korean industrial park in Kaesong was shuttered once in 2013 and again in 2016.[2] This meant that China became responsible for over 90 percent of North Korea's trade during the early Kim Jong Un years, a period when the relationship between the two governments was extremely poor.

Pyongyang has fumed at the Chinese as they signed on to every round of UN sanctions against the DPRK since 2006, with particularly stringent rounds of sanctions enacted in 2016 and 2017. In 2013 Xi Jinping was greeted to his first year in office as president with the execution of Jang Song Thaek and Pyongyang's third nuclear test; it is said that he personally loathed Kim Jong Un for these actions.

That very year, our workshop leader wanted to generate discussion among a handful of North Korean academics and officials on the North's economic relationship with China. After some deliberations, we decided that this was too tricky to navigate, but we *could* discuss relations between Big Island and Small Island. He introduced these fictional places and let the audience fill in the gaps: Big Island represented China and Small Island was North Korea. Had he just said, "Now we're going to discuss the relationship between China and North Korea," he'd have elicited no discussion at all.

I can clearly imagine the classroom atmosphere if he'd taken that approach. The participants were not authorized to speak on such a topic; they would have sat there silently trying to figure out what they *could* say. There would have been a long silence. Maybe a cough. At the most, after an awkward, lengthy wait, someone might have stood up and said something trite like "Our countries have a very close, fraternal relationship, forged in blood," or "Of course there are difficulties in relations between countries, but our leaders are pushing ahead with the correct policies to improve the relationship." Such comments would be safe: none of the other participants would note and report such anodyne statements.

One feature of North Korean society I was finding increasingly troubling was the mental self-regulation that constantly takes place there. You can almost see people's minds whirring when the topic becomes sensitive, figuring out what they can and cannot say. Moreover, they are constantly on guard and aware when a conversation moves from safe toward risky. It is a form of self-regulation and emotional tension endemic to North Korean society that most of us in the West breeze through life never having to even consider.

In a way, this became even more troubling to me than the idea of the North Korean prison system, which of course I have not seen. But I can imagine the brute misery of such places. An understanding and fear of privation and overt suffering is baked into our DNA as humans. One can *sort of* imagine what it might be like to be in pain, tired, hungry, thirsty, and lonely in the extreme. Prior to working in North Korea, however, I could not really understand what it meant to constantly self-censor, to be mentally on guard, to be persistently in fear of one's own ideas and acquaintances. It is draining.

Imagine what it's like to always be considering how to stay rhetorically safe; to avoid thinking—or at least expressing—your own thoughts, lest they be dangerous. Or if you cannot suppress reservations about a policy or some other aspect of society, to try to figure out whom you can trust in order to discuss it. Or perhaps having no one and feeling absolutely isolated with your thoughts.

We sat there in our coats in the large conference room in the Grand People's Study House, wondering if people would pipe up. Someone cleared his throat. But nothing. Then someone stood up and began talking about the smaller economy needing to develop industries to supply the big island, but also other economies. The "island economies" our workshop leader confected had unlocked the freedom to speak out. People started popping up, framed by the room's circular, Dr. Strangelovian lighting design, their ideas flowing freely. Our workshop leader then decided to ask what would happen if the small island faced an economic crisis. He later wrote about the experience himself, in *The Economist*:

People were divided into groups, and told to sort the island's problems out. They then had to nominate a spokesman to explain, in English if possible, what should be done.

Their responses would have made the IMF proud. The first spokeswoman suggested privatization of the state-owned companies, to raise hard currency, and to foster competition to improve efficiency. Her group proposed raising interest rates to attract inward investment. It argued for time, to mitigate the consequences of austerity on the work force. Another group suggested adding value to the raw materials, by turning them into desirable finished products. A third suggested bringing in multilateral institutions to help tide people through the austerity drive. I could hardly believe what I was hearing. Not least, I was shocked at how freely and easily they were speaking out. One young man approached me afterwards, and joked: "I never realized how much I would enjoy running my own country." Such interactions serve as a stunning reminder of how valuable, and under-exploited, people-to-people exchanges with pariah states like North Korea can be.[3]

Heated debate on policy even broke out, though not hot enough to actually warm up the frigid room. The workshop leader had a space heater under his desk. Everyone else, as it is in the unheated winter offices of Pyongyang, was bundled up in coats and scarves, shivering.

Once, after a different winter workshop, our volunteers did a day of tourism and fun to decompress, as we usually do. This time the circus was on the agenda, but inside the concrete building it was even colder than outside. Clowns kept dropping their batons. Breath plumed out of acrobats as they rubbed their hands together. The skimpily clad trapeze artist fell so many times the ringmaster cut her performance early. It was a disaster.

Of course, all the performers and audience had been through a real economic disaster just three years earlier. Then, North Korea was facing down a genuine economic crisis, due to a misguided currency reform. On November 30, 2009, the DPRK executed an immediate and unannounced reform, under which people had to exchange their old *won* (the name of the currency) for new *won* with a maximum cash conversion of about $200. About double that could be deposited into banks, more if legitimate means of accumulation could be proven.

This caused chaos. The sudden change had the effect of "wiping out considerable household savings and the working capital of many private entrepreneurs."[4] It was less a currency reform in the traditional sense, when a state is signaling a break with a past regime or era. This was more of a straight confiscation of wealth. If families were holding on to Korean won instead of Chinese yuan or commodities, they stood to lose almost everything.

A friend who has interviewed hundreds of North Korean defectors over the years once told me that for many of them this was a watershed moment. Many realized for the first time that the authorities were *not* looking out for them, or were incompetent, or both. In fact, at the time, I presumed that the leadership must have prepared a store of foodstuffs and other essentials, as well as flashy prizes for loyal citizens, to roll out after the fact.[5] If they had, this would have not only punished moneymakers but would have effectively rewarded loyal citizens who had not been as good at adjusting to the new reality. They hadn't. They didn't really have a plan. They didn't know what they were doing.

The new currency immediately began tumbling in value and didn't stop dropping until 2013. Nobody wanted it: everyone wanted Chinese yuan or assets that couldn't be disappeared overnight. Something they could trust. The new won was supposed to be about 100 to a US dollar. Nearly every month it slid in value until early 2013, when the authorities arrested the decline at about 8,000 won to the dollar.

I can't prove it, but conversations I've had in-country lead me to believe that around this time, the DPRK Central Bank began actively restricting the availability of won by buying it up and making it scarcer. I also suspect that Beijing played (and is playing) an active role, both in providing advice as well as perhaps supplying the yuan necessary to buy won out of the markets. The value of the won has been essentially stable since 2013, something that seems impossible without state intervention in the market.

Meanwhile, people kept learning how to run companies, small and large, better and better. People at all social strata were learning first how to survive, but in many cases how to thrive as well. We wanted to support these people who were helping rewrite North Korea's social contract. That didn't mean, however, that we'd shy away from breaking their hearts sometimes. I often told workshop leaders the balance of content should be 80 percent applicable, 20 percent bad news: that some things would not be possible without the internet, without abandoning the minder system and other rules that separate North Koreans from the outside world.

One workshop leader was having a conversation with a group of North Koreans from a software company, who were doing international business and carried themselves as such. There was a spring in their step, a strut in their stride. When they explained that they were working on parts of simple code for a Chinese app developer, the workshop leader, Colin, felt he had to tell them, "Look, guys, this is at the very bottom of the value chain. It's the least amount of money you can be making in this business." It was the stuff that the Chinese company thought wasn't worth the time of even their cheapest engineers. The guys from the company looked crestfallen. Implicit was the fact that because they didn't have full internet access, they couldn't see what markets would bear, they couldn't make their own competitive products, and they couldn't compete for better outsourcing projects.

Colin also delivered some bad news to a company developing optical character recognition software, which they described to us and of which they seemed quite proud. He whipped out his iPad and showed them an app that gracefully changed English letters to Cyrillic as he pointed it at a printed document. "Is it something like this?" he asked.

"Ah," said the manager as he furrowed his brow. "This is more advanced than we expected."

"It's been out for at least a year, maybe two."

A bit of a quiet descended on the group as they pondered this app, which was clearly better than what they were working on.

"Well," the manager sighed. "You've saved us a lot of time." He raised his eyebrows in a way that signaled disappointment but also genuine gratitude that his team could move on to something else.

Indeed, even if they'd finished the app, their go-to-market strategy was painfully obsolete. They hadn't heard of and didn't fully grasp the Google Play store or Apple's App Store. Their plan was to license the app to hotels, who would then sell it or perhaps provide it to guests so that they could more easily get around town. It was the sort of thing that made you want to laugh at how absurd it was, but also made you extremely sympathetic. These were decent people, trying to run a software company in a system that simply made it nearly impossible to be successful.

After all, as noted earlier, North Koreans app stores are physical places, and you must have apps installed while you wait. Smartphones in 2014 were still quite rare in Pyongyang, but by 2018 were fairly common.

This software company just had no idea how to compete with the outside world. They had technical talent, but no skills in market research, product design, marketing, or strategic talent. This is a direct result of how isolated the country's leaders have kept their citizens. It wasn't a new problem: at the end of the day, North Korean industrial products have never really had to compete in the world. During the Cold War, the Koreans were frustrated that socialist European trading partners were not interested in purchasing lower-quality Korean-made versions of machines that they could and did produce themselves.[6]

By 1980, even the vaunted Taean Electrical Factory, the paragon and exemplar of North Korean industry, was only exporting about 20 percent of its generators abroad, and only to friendly countries such as China, Yugoslavia, and Hungary, where competition was also not a primary concern.[7] If company managers competed, it was to exceed state-set quotas by exhorting their workers to follow the party line better.

In 1972, the vice rector of the University of the People's Economy in Pyongyang could proudly pronounce: "I never sent anyone to learn management in other countries. Of course, we read outside publications but we got nothing important from them."[8] Political studies took up about half the curriculum back then, although a good portion of their studies were about the "Taean Work System."

This system was rolled out in 1961 and was (of course) conceived of by Kim Il Sung. It combined industrial managers and workers into committees that ran factories. This was a move away from the Stalinist one-man management system, creating buy-in from laborers and allowing for more feedback from skilled workers with expertise. It also made sure the committees were taking the party line properly. It *did* make things more democratic, which was one of Kim's goals. But it didn't fix the problems that plagued planned economies throughout the twentieth century: individual units "underestimating production capabilities in order to get lower production quotas, while exaggerating material and manpower needs to guarantee sufficient supplies."[9]

Indeed, the 1960s were a period in which the North Korean economy was beginning to stagnate. The DPRK rebuilt the country with two extremely successful economic plans of three years (1954–56) and five years (1957–61). These plans focused on heavy industry and mostly hit their targets ahead of schedule. North Korea's model did a great job of exhorting its citizens to build-build-build after the Korean War, but then started running out of steam.

In 1961, alongside the Taean Work System, Kim Il Sung introduced a seven-year economic plan that focused on light industry and the production of consumer goods. This was aimed at improving quality of life after the post-war years of privation and sacrifice as North Korea rebuilt its heavy industries.

The plan faltered. Military expenditures ballooned during this period and there were ongoing problems of efficiency that the Taean Work System could not fix. The economic plan had to be extended to 1970. It was the first sign that North Korea would not be the economic powerhouse it initially seemed it could be. The Taean Work System is something about which all North Koreans are taught. They can recite tidbits on demand: "It is the best management system because it ensures the masses work closely with managers to accurately understand working conditions," I once heard a tour guide say. In reality, this system no longer reflects how things actually are.

Our participants—who generally were pragmatic, smart people—of course knew this. We were pleased to have members of the Economic Research Institute, linked to the cabinet, increasingly participating in our workshops. They had been an influential think tank until about 2007, when the country began moving away from a series of reforms the institute advocated in 2002. These reluctantly undertaken reforms were a response to the facts that the central distribution system was broken and that the gap between the official price index and market prices, as well as that between the official exchange rate and unofficial rate, were eroding the relevance of the planned economy.[10]

The reforms did a few key things: they limited the rationing scheme, which wasn't working anyway, and simultaneously allowed for street markets, which were operating illegally anyway. If you've watched the 2004 documentary *A State of Mind,* the main character's grandfather is involved in building one of these new official markets in the early 2000s. He seems thoroughly confused by this new reality in which the authorities are telling the people to go shopping, but on camera, he is nonetheless supportive of the policy.

The state also increased wages and introduced incentives and pay grades or bonuses to employees of state-owned enterprises. They also experimented with allowing factories to set their own prices, even as the state continued to fix some prices according to a central plan. Or as the pro-North Tokyo-based *Chosun Shinbo* newspaper put it, "bottom-up efforts are being made to resolve the lack of raw materials and to correctly implement an autonomous accounting system."[11]

Official prices jumped overnight, coming close to the market prices for things. In July 2002, "bus fares in Pyongyang increased from 2 won to 10 won, and the price tag on rice rose from 0.8 won per kilogram to 44 won."[12]

The reforms caused inflation. This spooked the leadership: inflation has, after all, destabilized and caused the collapse of more than one government in modern times. So, as the 2000s progressed, conservatives pushed back against the reformers, sidelining them. The Economic Research Institute sort of disappeared.

The fact that they were back by 2014 was encouraging. They were exactly the sorts of people Choson Exchange wanted to bolster and encourage. The head of the institute was a matronly but immaculately put-together lady of about sixty years of age. She dressed sort of like a church-going aunt. She was extremely appreciative of what we were trying to do. She not only tried to advise us on how to run successful trainings in her country, but she also tried to take care of us. Once, as we sat in the adjacent room to our workshop, she noticed that I was scratching some dried-out skin on my shin.

"Oh, I have something for that," she said and pulled out a plastic bottle that once held mineral water. She poured a bit of the liquid into the cap.

"Put that on your leg and rub it in."

"Thanks very much!" I said. She poured another capful.

"Now drink this."

I paused. It smelled vinegary.

"Drink it? It's not for putting on the skin?"

"It's for both."

I had a tremendous amount of respect for her; that she'd kept studying various economic theories and managed to keep her organization alive during a politically challenging few years. She was a better economist and administrator than a doctor, however. I drank the liquid. It tasted vinegary. It might just have been vinegar. I still have the skin condition five years later, Western and Eastern medicine both failing me.[13]

The volunteers we brought as workshop leaders varied in their backgrounds. Some were quite young and just curious about the DPRK. Others were older and wanted to get a better sense of where North Korea was heading as an economy and a market. Many just wanted to visit but thought that tourism to such a repressive place was ethically dubious or that the experience would be insufficiently free to be worth their time. "I didn't want to go see the same monuments and take the same pictures as everyone else," one volunteer told me. Many thought that tourism was just handing money over to the state, while taking part in education was giving back in a positive way.

Many, particularly Westerners who'd worked in government, journalism, or South Korea, could be a bit nervous. I would, I'm not proud to say, pick on these people a little bit. In-country I found it necessary to joke as much as I could, in order to alleviate tension (often my own) and of the group as a whole. It is, after all, outside of most people's experience to be unable to move on one's own and be constantly monitored for a week. If you don't laugh, it can become a bit much. So, if someone had a Samsung phone or any South Korean brand of camera, I would feign distress: "Oh my god, they're going to take that from you if they see it. Can you scratch the brand off? Let me get you a coin."

The North Koreans actually didn't care about your phone brand, though there was enough truth in such jokes that they worked. North Koreans will still tape over or scratch off pictures of foreigners on the packaging of imported products. So if there is a Malaysian baby on a pack of diapers or a Chinese model on the box of a TV set, they get removed, pretty crudely. What they think they are doing, I can't quite fathom.

Another would be an excessive-bowing gag. There are places in North Korea where you are expected to line up and give a respectful bow: the statues of Kim Il Sung and Kim Jong Il at Mansudae, the mausoleum, and a handful of other places. I would sometimes, with self-conscious guests in tow, just bow at all kinds of things—pictures, plaques, flags—then see who caught on first that we were the only ones doing it. I'd get a laugh as the group figured it out.

My absolute favorite, however, is "the photo gag." Here, usually with Ms. Choe, my quick-witted and bubbly partner in crime, we'd wait for one of the nervy volunteers to take a picture of something innocuous, say, a tree or an apartment building. Then we'd both simultaneously shout, "What are you doing!?" "Kevin, no!" or something to that effect. The volunteer workshop leader would inevitably jump out of their skin, sputter, and apologize profusely. "I didn't know! It seemed fine! I'm sorry! It's just a tree!"

We'd only let it go a few seconds before letting them know it was a joke and watching them exhale in relief. I promise you this was funny, though as I read this back it seems monumentally cruel.

One morning, Kevin was late for our departure to the workshop venue. He'd left the other half-dozen of us sitting in the van, engine idling for nearly ten minutes. As he rushed out of the lobby, across the parking lot, still hauling his jacket on and trying to straighten his hair, I suggested to Ms. Choe that we should give him a hard time for delaying us. He jumped on board and plopped in a seat in the back, apologizing profusely. Ms. Choe affected a tone that made her seem unmoved by his excuses as she turned back to face him.

"Being on time is very serious here," she scolded, "You should never be late again or you never know what might happen to you in this place." My eyes widened. My god. That was intense. Kevin sat in the back, suddenly ashen-faced and silent. Ms. Choe only let it linger a few seconds, but it felt like time stood still. *Was that a literal gulp I heard from the back?*

"Just kidding!" She exclaimed, her half-imp, half-cherubic expression returning. "Did I go too far?" She asked. Poor Kevin. Poor, traumatized Kevin.

I'd also try to joke with the Koreans, though very cautiously when it came to anything approaching politics. The safest was to proclaim that any creative solution or improvisation was the manifestation of Juche ideology. If we rigged a projector screen out of sheets of paper—"Hey, that's the spirit of Juche!" would elicit chuckles.

If I knew the person a little bit, I'd sometimes point to a picture of Kim Il Sung and ask, "Who's that?" They might answer, "That is our eternal President Kim Il... wait a minute... you know who that is!" Once I did that with Miss Choe and she snapped, "Don't point! You should understand the feelings of the Korean people and use an open hand to gesture toward such pictures." She wasn't joking this time. I mumbled an apology, chastened. I brought this up with her years later: "Do you remember when you told me off in the Grand People's Study House?" She didn't. It had clearly stuck with me more than her.

If I was personally pushing people out of their comfort zone through top-notch hilarious cultural commentary and sophisticated bilingual masturbation humor (see prior chapter), as an organization we also tried to push the workshop participants outside their comfort zone in more productive ways, not least of which was through interactive pedagogy.

One of our key volunteers (and then later employee) was Nils Weisensee, a data-privacy-obsessive coffee entrepreneur from near Hamburg (or somewhere, he wouldn't tell me as I wrote this book, for privacy reasons). He had a passion for all things tech and for the thoroughness for which Germans are so rightly stereotyped.

He wanted to do a session on mind mapping, which is a way to create a visual chart to help groups brainstorm or pursue ideas, making sure everyone can actually see how concepts are developing and linking to other aspects of a project. Rather than just do them on paper, however, he wanted to show how mind maps could be used across locations, for teams spread across separate departments, offices, or even countries.

So what we did was bring cheap Chinese tablets and a little Wi-Fi box that ran a simple program that everyone could connect to. Groups could throw their ideas onto the box and then the other teams could access them wirelessly. This would have been the first wireless connection anyone in the room had ever used, except perhaps for the few who had traveled abroad.

Another workshop leader wanted to talk about the value of crowdsourcing, something that the North Korean audience would have no experience with. Crowdsourcing's fundamental principle is that the aggregation of information in groups often results in decisions that are better than could have been made by any single member of the group: you ask large groups for answers on things, like on Wikipedia, or on threadless.com, which uses user feedback to decide what designs get turned into products. Now, this concept could be problematic if framed incorrectly: if it were proposed that a single wise leader is less desirable than a mechanism that draws in multiple voices. This is basically the point of crowdsourcing. Nils had to emphasize aspects of crowdfunding that challenged North Korean thinking, but in a way that was inoffensive.

This meant focusing on corporate management. So, as he talked about the need for diversity, he emphasized that successful *companies* have that quality. In North Korea politics is a monolith and everyone must follow the party line, but the corporate space allowed for less authoritarian decision-making. (Curiously, we may have the reverse in Western societies, where we like democracy in politics but are basically fine with authoritarianism in the corporate world.) He also talked about the need for decentralization to take advantage of local knowledge and cooperation and some means of turning private judgments into a collective decision. This was all language that *could* be understood by people accustomed to hearing about the Taean Work System or mass participation, even if the process we were championing was radically different.

He even discussed the need to flatten one's organizational structure and avoid groupthink in order make the best decisions. Again, these ideas are anathema to North Korean political culture, in which everything flows down from a wise leader and one *must* engage in groupthink as proscribed by the Korean Worker's Party. But by continually using the word "company" or "corporate," he kept these risky ideas in a safe space.

Overall, the workshop or small-conference format allowed much greater interaction with a wider range of North Koreans than most foreigners get to experience. Diplomats are largely confined to their foreign ministry interlocuters. Aid workers and tourism agents are generally stuck with working with a single partner organization. We, by contrast, got to interact with officials from various ministries, people from companies small and large, and academics from a range of institutions.

We also got out to the provinces through our special economic zone (SEZ) development program, holding workshops in Wonsan that gathered participants from all over the country. It was easier to hold them there than it was to get permission for everyone to come to Pyongyang. Wonsan was also the hub for a new policy under Kim Jong Un.

If under Kim Jong Il there was deep ambivalence about economic reforms, Kim Jong Un has been much more focused on development. He understood that while his family background might buy him some time, legitimacy was ultimately going to come from economic development. Geoffrey and I began perceiving this trend in 2010 and 2011 as the political classes came to grips with their disastrous currency reform and the raw fact that marketization and more economic freedoms were necessary solutions to the country's problems. Rigid military-first politics and state planning were on the way out.[14]

Moreover, the famine and distance in time from the revolutionary foun-dation of the DPRK had caused a relative erosion of ideology. People were looking for more pragmatism, more twenty-first-century thinking. The era of *Songun*—"military first"—politics coincided with a period of great hard-ship, but also a successful nuclear weapons program. Kim Jong Un's new narrative was essentially this: "We had to suffer to get our nuclear deterrent, but now that we have it, I will help you live better."

He made that promise during his first major speech as leader, in April 2012, the hundredth anniversary of his grandfather's birth and just five months after his father's death. He vowed to build the military, boasting that top military technologies—i.e., nukes—were "no longer monopolized by imperialists," but he also promised that his citizens would "never have to tighten their belts again."

A few months later, as we strolled through the humid streets of Pyong-yang, I asked a North Korean if he thought the economy would improve. He said, "Kim Il Sung made us ideologically strong. Kim Jong Il made us militarily strong. Because of this, Kim Jong Un can make us economically strong. We *expect* this."

Kim, for his part, set about making some important changes. He passed what in the outside world we call the "June 28 measures" in 2012, followed by the "May 30 measures" of 2014. These were the biggest *intentional* steps away from state planning that the country has ever taken. The details have never been publicly announced, but roughly we know that farmers got to keep more of their produce—perhaps 60 percent—to sell in markets, and they also got to work in smaller groups. Factories and state-owned compa-nies were given more autonomy. Under the new system, they had to decide their own inputs and outputs while paying workers' wages. In the past, they would mostly be given raw materials by the state and give their products to the state for distribution. Now they were becoming market driven.

Then Kim created over a dozen SEZs in 2013, followed by a second new group announced in 2014. Most of these zones would go nowhere—no one is going to invest in a high-tech business zone on the east coast that has no roads, electricity or ... anything. But some were in promising locations and perhaps more importantly, the policy signaled a willingness to explore economic development more proactively than under Kim Jong Il. SEZs are places where heterodox policy experiments can take place, tweaking the rules on sensitive issues such as internet access, ownership rights, or immigration procedures. Still, this would not be easy, given plenty of stodgy, bureaucratic thinking, the ongoing sanctions Pyongyang faced over its nukes, not to mention the incredible controls over information and interaction with the outside world.

That wall of North Korea was frequently evident even when we were within the walls of the workshop venue, so to speak. We were, for example, not allowed to eat lunch with participants. Every so often our partners would ask if we would pay to have lunch provided: "It is inconvenient for them to go out to find lunch and come back on time," they'd argue.

"Sure, as long as we can have lunch together." This always ended the conversation. It wasn't even a huge amount of money they asked for, something like five dollars per head; we just thought there was a principle at stake. Similarly, on tourist trips the Korean guides are never allowed to eat meals with the guests. Even if it is at some small hotel in the country with a single dining room, the guides will eat at a separate table. The authorities must see lunch as a dangerous opportunity for counter-revolutionary propaganda.

This is such a curious rule, given that during the conferences, workshops, and consultations we've organized, real, sensitive conversations happen all the time. In 2016, one group of young businesspeople were going through a business proposal for a line of makeup with a couple of our workshop leaders. They had a pretty good pitch, with some nice visual graphs, some well-identified challenges, and some estimates of the market.

"How'd you come up with those figures?" one of the foreigners asked.

"Well, to be honest," came the response, "We can't really do market research here. So these are kind of guesses from talking to people and observing as best we can." Everyone nodded in sympathy. No one needed to say this was because collecting or spreading information outside state control hurt their attempts to run a business. It was understood.

Indeed, communication for business is extremely hampered. No sort of surveying is allowed in North Korea. Advertising is basically limited to signboards at sporting events or A4-sized flyers in stores, and even those are relatively new. Knowing or shaping what customers want is difficult, but the fact that this team understood that foreigners expected to see that in a business plan and were trying their best was heartening.

Other times, the non-lunch-hour conversations could be quite personal. Once, in 2012, for example, we held a workshop that was mainly targeted at bankers and included one mid-twenties functionary at the Foreign Trade Bank, a Mr. Goh, who asked one of our workshop leaders for advice. He didn't make much eye contact, looking down, his shoulders hunched a little in his Western suit jacket.

This was a new job and the workshop with foreign consultants was a new environment for him—he projected a fear of what he'd gotten himself into.

"Listen," he said, clearing his throat, "I studied the works of Tolstoy at Kim Il Sung University"—the country's top school—"but now I'm supposed to help manage the bank's foreign currency reserves. I don't know if I should be putting our money into dollars, RMB, Euros ... what should I do?" This was a technical question, by a young man working at the country's most important bank, but also a personal one: here was a guy whose silver spoon had served up something he couldn't quite digest.

"I don't know," replied our highly qualified workshop leader. "Diversify, that's all I can tell you." He tried to emphasize that nobody knows the future, no one knows what the Fed and European Central Bank are going to do, and you just have to get as much information as you can and hedge your bets.

Six months after this conversation, the Foreign Trade Bank was sanctioned by the United States and we stopped inviting their staff to workshops. As such, we never got a chance to see Mr. Goh again. I wonder if he figured out how to manage his basket of currencies or if he returned to the literary arts as a career. Either way, I hope he's doing okay, even if he never got enough training or information to do his job.

We kept plugging along with workshops and other programs for entities we could still invite. Two of our more enduring programs ended up focusing on construction and design, crucial industries in a marketizing economy that needed to plan cities to facilitate business, and women's issues, something long overlooked in North Korea.

Notes

1 Hong Liu, "The Sino-South Korean Normalization: A Triangular Explanation," *Asian Survey* 33, no. 11 (1993): 1086.

2 Leo Byrne, "Trade Figures between Two Koreas Drop by over 99 Percent," NK News, June 15, 2016, https://www.nknews.org/2016/06/trade-figures-between-two -koreas-drop-by-over-99-percent.

3 "Cheeseburger in Paradise Island," *The Economist,* June 13, 2013, https://www .economist.com/banyan/2013/06/20/cheeseburger-in-paradise-island.

4 Marcus Noland, "North Korea's Failed Currency Reform," BBC Online, February 5, 2010, https://piie.com/commentary/op-eds/north-koreas-failed-currency-reform.

5 Andray Abrahamian, "North Korea's 2009 Currency Reform in the Context of National Narrative," *North Korean Review* 7, no. 1 (2011): 64–77.

6 Bala'zs Szalontai and Changyong Choi, "China's Controversial Role in North Korea's Economic Transformation: The Dilemmas of Dependency," *Asian Survey* 53, no. 2 (2013): 272.

7 C. I. Eugene Kim, "Introduction: A Long Journey," in *Journey to North Korea: Personal Perceptions*, eds. C. I. Eugene Kim and B. C. Koh (Berkeley, CA: Institute of East Asian Studies, 1983), 13.

8 John M. Lee, "North Korean Leaders Get Basic Economic Education," *New York Times*, May 29, 1972.

9 Edward W. Kloth, "The Korean Path to Socialism: The Taean Industrial Management System," *Occasional Papers on Korea*, no. 3 (June 1975): 37.

10 Bernhard Seliger, "The July 2002 Reforms in North Korea: Liberman-style Reforms or Road to Transformation?" *North Korean Review* 1, no. 1 (Fall 2005): 9.

11 Hong Ihk-pyo, "A Shift toward Capitalism? Recent Economic Reforms in North Korea," *East Asian Review* 14, no. 4 (Winter 2002): 97.

12 Hong, Ihk-pyo, "Shift toward Capitalism," 94.

13 Please write to me with your remedies for dry skin/eczema/psoriasis. Coconut oil, cold packs, acupuncture, cortisone, kombucha...everyone has one and they are all amazing and really useful.

14 Geoffrey K. See and Andray Abrahamian, "Economic Performance and Legitimacy in North Korea," East Asia Forum, November 26, 2011, http://www.eastasiaforum.org /2011/11/26/economic-performance-and-legitimacy-in-north-korea.

8

Run the World

In 2013, we got funding for and began running programs tailored toward women. We turned this into what we called our "Women in Business" (WIB) program. Our goal was to have a series of workshops that would culminate with the founding of a DPRK Women's Business Association. We wanted to create an institution and culture in which female entrepreneurship could flourish.

First, we had to convince our partners that it was necessary.

"Really?" the wiry Mr. Kim asked, "Just for women? Why?" It had never occurred to him that the barriers facing women in the business world were an issue.

Perhaps this was because he came of age in an era when women were economically empowered as the famine pushed so many of them into money-making roles: women must have seemed in charge of many families' finances anyway. Or perhaps he was just a traditional, Korean man, steeped in generations, centuries, millennia of patriarchy.

"Not *just* women," we said. "But we need over 50 percent for our workshops in Korea. And over 60 percent for our programs abroad."

Again: "why?"

"Well, we got funding from an organization that focuses on women's issues. So we have to do it. Or give the money back." We had tempered the donor's expectations, however: from the beginning we thought that asking for 100 percent female participation wouldn't work in the DPRK: the gatekeeping men at various organizations could possibly cause problems if there weren't at least some opportunities for their male colleagues. But we did insist on majorities.

"Okay," said Mr. Kim, "We can do this."

Three months later we held our first workshop in a large, very groovy room in the diplomatic club on the banks of the Taedong River. It was an event/karaoke space, with colored lights and a bar at the back. It had the positive effect of relaxing the group, I thought, given the informality of the environment. We would later be told we couldn't have workshops there again because "the space was inappropriate."

"Because it's not a classroom?" I asked. "We thought that made it very effective."

"No, not that. There aren't any portraits of the leaders at the front."

"Ah." End of conversation.

Still, at that first WIB workshop, I kicked off the event by telling the group of roughly thirty people that we were inviting ten to twelve women to come to Singapore for a two-week study trip later in the year. I let them know that I would be conducting interviews to choose who would go and any female participants were welcome to come chat with me.

One handsome chap, a recent Kim Il Sung University graduate who spoke perfect English, sidled up to me. KISU is the Harvard of the DPRK. He said, "You should take me," with a grin. I said, sorry, this was to help business-*women*. He said, "Sure, sure, but at some point if you want to get anything done in this country, you need to speak to a man."

"This is exactly why we're running this program," I replied. He harangued me a little bit more in a way that was sort of jokey, but also sort of like, "I'm mostly used to getting my way". Eventually I tired of him and walked away. I also put him on our sanctions list. Or at least *my* sanctions list. As an organization we provided our partners with an updated US and UN sanctions list every time we visited to make sure they didn't invite any sanctioned entities to our workshops.[1] I didn't put him on that list, obviously, but he was annoying and privileged and didn't need our help.

I started to interview women for our WIB program. These interviews could be awkward: this was a really alien process for North Koreans. Still, we felt it was important. In the West, a job or college entrance interview really means hyping up your personal accomplishments and individual strengths. This sort of self-congratulatory immodesty isn't socially acceptable in the same way in Asia in general, and in North Korea in particular. I thought about this for a while and decided that part of what we were looking for were participants who could intuit the characteristics I, as a Westerner, was looking for, and respond to them. This was useful because if we invested in bringing them to Singapore, we wanted them to be able to impress the Singaporeans and expats they interacted with. We needed them to not be too shy in new situations, to be intuitive and adaptable.

I also thought about the fact that I, as a male, was acting as the gatekeeper for women who were trying to get ahead in the world. We couldn't really fix that, given that we were a small organization with an all-male staff of two.

I would at least preface the interviews by saying, "I understand this will be a new and maybe difficult experience for you. This is a very Western concept, this kind of interview—relax and don't stress about it!"

Some of the interviewees were really great. One young woman said she came up with a "new way of accounting" that helped save her company lots of money. This may have amounted to hiding revenues so that when the authorities came by looking for contributions, there was little or nothing available. I didn't push her on it. Another wanted to open a chocolate shop. She'd been abroad once and had been blown away by the selection and quality of chocolate. "There are enough people here who would pay for nice chocolate and would visit a special shop as a treat or for gifts," she said. "Also, I love it."

Others struggled with the interview process. To the question, "What accomplishment are you most proud of?", designed to draw out their individuality, one young lady said it was swimming in front of Kim Jong Il at an athletic event when she was in school. I tried to redirect. "Is there anything at your work that you've done well, like a challenge you've overcome or a problem you've solved?"

"No, there isn't."

The interviews were time-consuming and tiring. An interview would take 15–25 minutes, then I'd chat about the person with our partners Mr. Jang or Mr. Kim, whomever was helping out that day. So, the interview process could be as slow as one person per thirty minutes. Once, in between interviews, which are always sort of performative, Mr. Jang put on a little performance of his own.

He began recounting a story of the Korean War, when a lieutenant in a desperate—but brave—retreat, had lost all his equipment, including his shoes. He still rushed to give General Kim Il Sung himself an update. "General Kim," said Mr. Jang, "saw that the man had no shoes and took off his own..." he interrupted himself with a sniff and muted sob. *He was crying.* "...his own shoes," he managed to continue, "and gave them to his soldier." Tears welled in his eyes and ran down his cheeks. "He was such a great man," he said as he dabbed his face with a handkerchief. Geoffrey and I glanced at each other, both of us silently asking each other: "Is this really happening?" It was the only time I'd seen crying in North Korea, other than at Kim Jong Il's mausoleum in 2012, the year after his death. Then, you could easily hear and see weeping and sniffling.

Emotional interludes aside, the interview method was quickly becoming too burdensome. If from 2011 to 2013 we were getting around twenty-five people, by 2014 we were started to get over fifty in our workshops. (This later swelled to over a hundred per event.) We could no longer interview people one by one to choose who we'd support for a study trip to Singapore; we had to think of a different way to try to identify the individuals we wanted to involve.

We decided to have focus groups or group consultations with our workshop leaders. So, while a presentation or exercise was going on, we'd devote a corner to individuals or teams who wanted to chat to our volunteers. This was also kind of a filter because it took a bit of bravery or initiative to initiate a conversation with a foreigner. That was part of what we were looking for.

Sometimes we would find incredibly bright people, like the woman who wanted to know how shops in Singapore were organized, "because here they mostly look the same so customers can't feel any distinction between them." We'd also find creative people who were constantly on the lookout for gaps in their system that they could fill. Like, for example, "no one is running a convenience store that is open late for when people need things at night." Or, from the same guy: "People here look at foreign products as more desirable...so I want to make handbags and accessories here but brand them like they're from Hong Kong. When we build a customer base here, we can then start to send them to other markets." His first concept he managed to get off the ground; the second idea not yet, as far as I know.

In spite of a nuclear test in February 2013, things were going well. We were hearing rumors of economic reform and that the rules for starting companies were easing up. We heard that private banking was becoming more important. Our reputation was growing and our brand was good, evidenced by increasing numbers at every workshop.

Then at the end of 2013, a real blow was struck. Kim Jong Un's uncle, Jang Song Thaek, was purged, and in dramatic fashion. In early December, he was arrested and charged with a number of crimes. He was humiliated at an expanded politburo session on December 8. Diplomats and journalists in Beijing, where I was living, were abuzz. Chinese government bureaucrats don't generally liaise with foreigners, but there is an academic community that is something like a proxy for official positions. During this week, they were generally saying, "Don't worry, it will be fine. This is natural in their system."

On December 12 Jang was taken before a military tribunal, where he was labeled "a traitor to the nation for all ages who perpetrated anti-party, counter-revolutionary factional acts in a bid to overthrow the leadership of our party and state and the socialist system."[2] He was executed immediately.

The Chinese academics stopped answering their phones. Beijing was shocked. The world was shocked. My friends and I who focus on North Korea began worrying. What does this mean? Is this the end for economic reform? Jang was seen as something of a pro-economy pragmatist by some. Others saw him as merely pro-economy in the sense that he was building a business empire for himself. A North Korean once suggested to me in a frank moment, "He is so powerful. Because of him, many people have been killed."

Then, suddenly, as we kicked off programs in 2014, our main guy was no longer around. Mr. Kim was, according to various accounts, "in a different job," "recovering his health in the countryside," or "taking care of his mother in the countryside." Everyone had a different explanation.

"Can we get in touch with him?"

"No."

Was he dead? Was he in the gulag? It was here that the system truly enraged me. It forces mistrust. People that I'd previously trusted to be basically truthful were now clearly lying to me. But they *had* to. They weren't allowed to tell me what had happened to Mr. Kim. I also started to feel guiltier about the little lies I would tell also, or at least the slight gaps I'd leave, particularly about my citizenship.

"I'm British," I'd say. But if pressed about my accent, I'd say, "Ah, my mother is American and my wife is too," and leave it at that. I wouldn't mention that I also have a US passport, having been born in Chicago, the greatest city on earth in the Midwest. If asked about how I learned Korean, I'd say I took two terms of classes in South Korea, which is true. But I wouldn't say that I'd lived there for years. As I saw it, the fewer people putting that stuff in the daily reports they had to write about our activities in-country, the better. But it was still deceitful.

As much as these little things could be stressful, I became more tense following the removal of Mr. Kim. I found myself clenching my jaw more when in Pyongyang. I also found myself snapping more when something absurd happened. For example, once we were discussing opportunity costs and the trade-offs decision-makers have to make:

"We can't say that the government would trade off more road deaths by raising the speed limit," said Mr. Jang.

"But it's a choice all governments have to make!" Higher speed limits mean more productivity, but inevitably, more road deaths.

"It isn't appropriate," he said, frowning. He couldn't abide by the idea that we'd suggest his government would make decisions that would cause its citizens to die.

I lost it. "This is ridiculous! Every government makes this choice!" I barked and stormed away. Usually I had the patience for such nonsense. (Eventually we agreed we'd frame it as a government choosing to *lower* the speed limit to save lives, but at some economic cost. That was good enough for Mr. Jang.)

I would sometimes sit, tired after a long day of workshops, and stare at the wall, wondering where Mr. Kim was and under what conditions he was living. Or if he was alive at all.

Finally, at some point in the summer, one of our interlocuters cracked as we asked for the umpteenth time about Mr. Kim.

"Look," he whispered. "He's okay. He was fired and sent out of Pyong-yang. But he'll be back. He's okay."

This took a load off and I instantly felt better. I trusted this guy and could tell he hadn't been happy about having to lie to us, either. As more time went by a few more hints were dropped. It appeared this wasn't directly connected to Jang's purge. Rather, it seemed as if the irascible Mr. Kim had picked too many bureaucratic battles of his own and bitten off more than he could chew.

There were other disappointments, of course. For example, we had two awesome repeat students, who always sat at the front of the classroom, soaking in as much in as possible. One was a former singer, tall and beautiful, who was enjoying a second career as a restaurant manager and hoped to open her own place once she found the capital. The other woman was also in the restaurant business and was a few years older. They both asked incisive questions of the lecturers and during coffee breaks would mingle as much as possible with the visiting foreigners. They were really the perfect students.

They also joined in group activities without coercion. By "coercion" here, I mean that Western-style participatory pedagogy is mostly absent in North Korea (as well as many other parts of Asia). We'd try to build in group activities, but sometimes I'd literally have to pull chairs out from under people to get them to stand up and to form groups and begin chatting or gaming something out. Not these two.

They were the ideal candidates to join us on a study trip to Singapore, or so we thought. State Security disagreed. The older one had "too many relatives in Japan" and the younger one came from "an inappropriate career background." They were denied exit visas. These workshop participants were the only two people we'd ever had rejected for a trip abroad. They would have been perfect.

Two of the WIB groups we took down to Singapore in this period crack-led with energy. You could feel the difference between these groups and the groups of predominantly men that would often make up other delegations. The women were more lively, happier to be there, and less conservative with their questions, not just about the workshop topics, but also about dating, families, and lifestyles.

"Is it common for a man and woman to have a drink together without anyone else?" I was asked as we passed a lively bar.

"Yes, unless they come from a very conservative or religious home," I answered. "I got together with my wife with the help of some drinks," I offered.

"And after drinking together ... ?" She grinned, slyly: North Koreans love sexual innuendo and sex jokes. A lot. Much more than you'd think, lest you judge me for my *jawi* joke from a couple chapters ago.

"That depends on the couple," I answered, pretending to clear my throat in embarrassment.

We also learned from seeing our participants engage with the city they were visiting. It was clear that in-classroom experiences were important, but the "free time," ranging around Singapore, checking out things of interest, whether retail outlets, tourist destinations, or urban infrastructure, was just as important. Seeing how retailers discount certain products, for example, was useful for shop managers from North Korea but beyond that, exposure to the lived experiences in a different society helped participants to see possibilities in their country's future *and* their personal lives. It had impact. They would often begin forming impressions immediately.

"Whoa, what's that building?" one of the them asked when we arrived, marveling at the red-lit, metal-clad Crowne Plaza.

"That's an airport hotel," I answered. "Wait 'til we get downtown."

There were of course unexpected challenges during this period: the biggest was North Korea's Ebola quarantine. In late October 2014, a 21-day quarantine was announced by Pyongyang as an Ebola countermeasure. This amounted to a travel ban and sealed North Korea off more than it would any other country faced with a similar decision: in a more open system, businesses could try to cope with the quarantine by switching to telecommunications as much as possible. This was, of course, impossible in North Korea.[3] The policy saw mixed enforcement at first, but soon all foreigners *and* returning Koreans were forced to do the quarantine in a hotel room, without visitation allowed.

As best we could piece together from the various rumors we heard, the Ministry of Public Health went to the cabinet and requested more funds, in case Ebola popped up in the region. Some hardliners took the opportunity to push for a full shutdown, arguing that the DPRK's public health infrastructure would not be able to cope if the disease reared its head. Kim Jong Un created a committee to deal with the issue, in which control-first and economy-first politicians fought it out for several months. The ban was lifted in February 2015. There had been no Ebola cases reported anywhere in Asia.

Our last workshops under the WIB brand took place in 2015: after that, discrete funding ran out, though we did keep insisting on female participation in our other programs. It did seem to have an effect: we saw more women taking part after our WIB programs than before. It speaks to the idea that you can socialize ideas in North Korea, even if the various constraints there make it more resistant to outside ideas than most countries.

For me, the very last WIB workshop was emotionally powerful. This was not necessarily because of the content itself, though it was particularly good this time. One of the workshop leaders who came made the case for female network-building, illustrating her talk with how female entrepreneurs in other countries supported each other to help overcome institutional and cultural barriers to success. One workshop leader walked through the steps an entrepreneur goes through when starting a business. These included identifying a realistic idea, testing products or services through customer trials, then finding the right suppliers and distributors. How to build a successful team was also highlighted, along with a warning to expect suffering through a period when one is investing lots of time, effort, and money before making a profit.

Another volunteer made the case for informal lending circles between women. In fact, this was an old Korean idea, a *kye*. This is a lending circle concept that goes back centuries, but has mostly been forgotten under seventy years of socialist rule. Essentially, over many months or years, each person in the *kye* contributes a set amount, with one person taking the month's pool at each meeting. This allows them to put the money to productive use when it's their turn. The audience lapped it up.

Mostly though, it seemed to me that this last Women in Business workshop, above all others, cut through the robust barriers of culture, politics, and suspicion that unavoidably divide the Western workshop leaders and the Korean participants. It's hard to describe, but the women in the audience and the female workshop leaders just seemed to . . . *click*. It was profoundly moving to see that as different as the Koreans were from us, as dissimilar as our lived experiences were, commonalities could be found and built upon.

Choson Exchange staff and volunteers have kept in touch as best we can with these businesswomen, or at least tried to inquire about how they're doing. It isn't easy, of course. Founding the DPRK Women's Business

Association—which would have been a non-governmental organization—proved impossible, but we have heard that a number of our participants stay in touch and meet for dinners or coffee now and then and try to help each other out. The program remains one of the things I'm most proud about and I lament its demise several years later due to lack of funding.

It's trite to say, but whatever the future holds for the DPRK and whatever interactions we have with the country in trying to shape that future, the role of women should be given more attention and resources.

Notes

1 The United States and other countries maintain lists of North Korean individuals and companies with whom trade is illegal. Most are connected to the military or other security services.

2 "(4th LD) N. Korea Executes Leader's Uncle for 'Treason': KCNA," Yonhap News Agency, December 13, 2013, https://en.yna.co.kr/view/AEN20131213002451315.

3 The coronavirus outbreak in 2020 also illustrates the difficulties in adapting to a pandemic in a relatively closed society. South Korea switched to remote work and all-online education in late February 2020. North Korea doesn't have those options. It can only rely on stricter restriction of movement—something in which it has considerable expertise.

9

If You Build It...

That folksy, vinegary medicine given to me by the head of the Economic Research Institute made me twitch in my green plush chair, which had long flat arms with cushioned armrests. It looked like the kind of chair in which *Mad Men*'s Don Draper would lean back and light up a cigarette. Indeed, in front of me there were white ceramic ashtrays in case one got the urge to spark up. The ashtrays sat on long, light beige wooden coffee tables. The aesthetic was sort of modern, but also sort of from the past. Familiar, but not.

Imagine when Europeans discovered marsupials for the first time. It wasn't like finding a dinosaur, some alien creatures from a vastly different evolutionary pathway. It was like finding creatures we knew or remembered, just a little bit...weird. That's what North Korean interiors are like. They sort of seem like 1970s kitsch, but they also aren't quite from *our* 1970s. They can sometimes seem like an alternate reality of our own design history or a Wes Anderson movie.

Other times, especially in new buildings, the designs can seem extremely modern, but again, not really *our* modernity. Pastels or bright, popping fuchsias and aquamarines are common. Abstraction is not much in display. For example, when you visit the zoo, the centerpiece is a gigantic tiger head you walk through to enter the park. Though perhaps the real attractions might be the smoking chimpanzee or the actual tigers.

One of the tigers still in captivity there features relatively heavily in the personal life of a North Korean colleague of mine, Bok Soon. In her rendering:

> I was about four or five and there was a baby tiger the other side of the
> bars that was so cute. I was trying to play with it and my parents and aunt

were standing nearby. The mother tiger casually walked over and then, while quite far away, turned around and shot a huge jet of pee, completely soaking me. "Piss off!" she was saying. My family still laugh about it.

This was long before the tiger-head entrance appeared at the revamped zoo in 2016. Actual tigers and urine-soaked infants aside, compare the literalist design of the zoo entrance to, say, the Panda Breeding Center in Chengdu, China, where the logo is a series of circles that evokes a panda. Or Sea World, whose logo is a sort of whoosh that evokes a manta ray or cruelty to orcas.

It's partly this literalism that makes Korean design just feel different to ours. Choson Exchange has conducted a number of workshops focused on urban planning, including two abroad. This was important to us because, fundamentally, you need to be designing to meet your political goals and if your political goals are a better economy, that needs to be reflected and enhanced by how you organize your built spaces. It also helped that we had a passionate point man for these programs, Calvin Chua, a slender London-trained Singaporean architect who dresses like a Brooklyn barista. He, too, is fascinated by this literalism: "If you ask them to design something that evokes a rose, you'll get a rose," he once told me.

There's a reason for this, as one of the chief planners from the State Design Commission told Calvin: "Abstraction is something that doesn't fit here, it's totally different to the Western world." DPRK values, he said, dictate that "architecture shouldn't be abstracted, because it should be for the people—ordinary people should be able to understand it and approach it. It's important for the public to understand what the buildings are." So the shape of the tallest building at Mirae Future Scientists Street is very literally that of an atom, as is the entire science-technology center, which sits nearby.

North Koreans tend not to be nostalgic for older buildings, either. One Choson Exchange student, traveling abroad, was being shown a disused factory that had been converted to a coworking space and innovation center (to use two buzzwords about which history will no doubt be unkind). He was puzzled: "What is the point of keeping old buildings," he asked, "when their functions have been lost?" In developed or postindustrial societies we tend to love when old structures are repurposed because they can no longer accommodate modern production, logistics, or even sporting venues. North Koreans don't really see the point.

This is for a few reasons. First, socialist cultures tend to be obsessed with building modernity. Second, not many buildings survived the Korean War, so there really isn't much early twentieth-century stuff to repurpose. Finally, the first modern buildings were built under Japanese rule, a bitter reminder of Korea's backwardness and subjugation. There is no love lost for those buildings nor the period they represent. North Korea does take care of the few very old buildings that remain, as these temples and pavilions link back to the "five-thousand-year" history of the Korean nation that they like to promulgate. This premodern heritage thus becomes a source of pride.

As with everything, heritage sites are imbued value by being recognized by the Kims. Mountains have quotes from Kim Il Sung or Kim Jong Il splashed across them in giant lettering. For example, "Mount Myohyang is the most celebrated under heaven," according to Kim Jong Il. This is carved in two-meter-high letters on a cliffside. Politics intrudes even on natural beauty.

Ancient temples also prominently feature Kim quotations about their value to the Korean people. Each one will have a sign about how many times a Kim visited and the "monk" who guides you around will have as many facts about the Kims' visits as other historical tidbits. I write "monk" in scare quotes because though they have shaved heads and don robes, they seem more like custodians than practicing monks. They're there to explain to local and foreign visitors alike the depth of Korean history. I've visited temples perhaps a dozen times and I've never seen devotees nor smelled the tart fragrance of incense the way one does at temple sites elsewhere across Asia. Still, it is positive that ancient buildings or rebuilt versions of them are being preserved.

It isn't unique to North Korea that colonial-era sites get lost while trying to race for the future. Even Lee Kwan Yew, who built a modern Singapore that now features erstwhile industrial sites repurposed into hip spaces that confuse North Korean visitors, copped to "making our share of mistakes." Too late he realized that many of his island state's signature buildings were being torn down and that "we were destroying a valuable part of our cultural heritage, that we were demolishing what tourists found attractive and unique about Singapore."[1]

Still, North Korean workshop participants are generally impressed with the planning in Singapore, as are most people. Space is at a premium—the country is only 719 square kilometers—and so every bit of land has to be used efficiently. It is so valuable. Calvin has noted that the new urban developments in Pyongyang are more tightly packed together, stacking people upward so they have easier access to retail, services, and transportation.

Old neighborhoods, such as Gwangbok (Liberation) and Tongil (Unification) streets are dominated by massive edifices, apartment blocks so huge, wide, and set back from the main road that residents can be some distance from the nearest tram stop. Retail spaces can be so far back from the gigantic boulevards you can't even see them from the other side. This is the case with the showroom for Pyonghwa Motors, for example.[2]

Packing residences together and upward may reflect new trends in aesthetics but could also flow from a keener grasp of real estate value. Real estate, as such, didn't exist when the monster apartment blocks of Gwangbok and Tongil went up in the 1970s and 1980s. These days it does. And it is simultaneously one of the most sensitive yet mundane issues in North Korea today. There are no property rights in the DPRK; if you're visiting for the first time and ask your guide about it, they will likely tell you "the state provides housing for everyone," and leave it at that. Over time, you might get the truth, which is that in North Korea you're not allowed to own, rent, or sell a residence, and yet it is common practice.

How does this work? Every neighborhood has a broker or two. That broker keeps his or her ears to the ground for families that are looking to move. Maybe you are a family with a big apartment, and you think you can make some money by selling it and moving somewhere smaller. Maybe you've come into some money and you want to live somewhere larger or with better access to shopping and the tram line. You would then list the residence with the broker, who matches you with buyers, whenever they come along.

When a deal is reached, the broker takes the residence certificate of the selling family down to the housing office of the local People's Committee—the equivalent of a city or district council—and says, "These families have agreed to switch residences," or, "The Lees are willing to give their apartment to the Choes."

And then, "Oh, and here's a little something in an envelope to expedite the paperwork, thanks very much." The broker also has to make sure the local security agency staff are taken care of, and perhaps the head of the *inminban*—the neighborhood organization—in whose area the sale is taking place. In fact, many of these brokers are the heads of neighborhood associations: they are specifically tasked by the party with knowing every coming and going in their area, so are often the best positioned to match buyers and sellers.[3]

Sometimes this happens at scale, when authorities want something constructed but don't have the funds. They can ask—or sometimes force—wealthy people or semi-private companies to chip in to build apartments or other facilities. If it's apartment blocks, the state will then distribute some of the units and the financiers are also allowed to "distribute" some. They, of course, distribute their share in exchange for cash, either renting or selling units.

New, large apartments in the most desirable neighborhoods of Pyongyang can go for over $150,000. East of the railway line and Chollima Street is very desirable as it's close to many offices, the Taedong River, restaurants, and hotels. Older residences on, say, Tongil or Gwangbok streets, can be as cheap as $3,000. Apartments get cheaper the higher up you go, too, because Pyongyang's aching electrical grid means elevators and water pumps often don't work. Neighborhoods near urban factories located south of the river can also be quite cheap.

Private investment takes place outside of Pyongyang, also. One example: when Sunchon Thermal Power Plant built swimming pools and bathhouses to make use of otherwise wasted steam power, it was reported that all the money came from private investors. Bathers would pay a fee to use the bathing complex and the state and funders would split the profits fifty-fifty.[4] This strategy is a good solution for getting things built in this extremely gray area: the state gets what it wants but can't provide on its own; rich people get richer. And the state wants to build stuff. Boy, does it want to build.

In 2014, Kim Jong Un published a tract with the cracking title "Let Us Usher in a Great Golden Age of Construction by Thoroughly Applying the Party's Juche-Oriented Idea on Architecture." We were soon hearing North Koreans quoting lines about this "golden age" to us. As for what "Juche-Oriented" means here: something like "whatever we make will be called Juchified."

In Pyongyang, three major urban developments have come to fruition under Kim Jong Un. The first was Changgon (Foundation) Street, which runs from the river past the Supreme People's Assembly, just down the hill from the gigantic Kim statues. Eighteen curvy blue-tiled towers stretch up to forty-seven stories, with views of the river and access to new shops and restaurants, including an import grocery store that wouldn't be out of place in the foreigner-heavy neighborhoods of Shanghai, Geneva, or Qatar. They sell things like root beer, granola, and Gouda cheese. Changgon was finished in 2012, the centenary of Kim Il Sung's birth.

Mirae (Future) Scientists Street was finished in 2015, the seventieth anniversary of the Korean Workers Party, and features that atom-shaped building. It has skyscrapers of harvest orange and field green that run along the Taedong River. The best pizza restaurant between Seoul and Beijing moved there from down the road and features imported meats and cheese, as well as a delightful waitress who will happily crush a version of "My Heart Will Go On" on the piano.

Ryomyong New Town was the final of these developments and has Pyongyang's tallest functioning tower, at over 70 stories. When the street opened in March 2017 it also featured North Korea's first-ever international retail outlet, a Miniso. Miniso is a Japanese-Chinese low-cost retail brand store. Media found out about it, Miniso headquarters freaked out about possibly violating sanctions, and then the "Miniso" sign disappeared a few months later.[5] In 2019 the shop was still there, selling all the same stuff, but with a different name over the door.

That aside, at its opening ceremony Premier Pak Pong Ju boasted that "the construction of Ryomyong Street is truly a significant, great event." He said, "It shows the potential of socialist Korea, and that is scarier than the explosion of hundreds of nuclear bombs above the enemies' heads."[6]

I agree with Pak that these developments are scary, but probably not for the reasons he suggested, and obviously not as scary as nuclear explosions. (I mean, obviously.) First, they were built super-fast; all of these complexes were completed in about a year. Second, none of them feature steel structures—they are all concrete and rebar. A seventy-story skyscraper without steel or advanced concrete techniques is basically unimaginable almost anywhere else in the world.

North Korean cement is notoriously lumpy and uneven. You can hear boats grinding away gathering rock for concrete in the Taedong River in the summer. With their poor-quality materials and a commitment to speed over quality, construction sites look shoddier than in any other country I've traveled in, even quite poor places. The work is done by soldier-builders, who billet in tents nearby the neighborhoods they are creating, and who certainly work hard, kicking up dust and noise, but may not be working effectively. On the structures they build, lines are often clearly not straight from say, one window to the next, and many elements seem guessed at rather than measured. One stair to the next can be different heights, for example. (This can be a tricky proposition after several shots of soju.) By late 2018, you could see tiles were chipping or falling off some bits of Ryomyong's towers, while water was leaking and staining other parts.

Construction quality is something to keep an eye on, given that in May 2014 an apartment building in Pyongyang's Pyongchon district collapsed, almost certainly causing some fatalities. This prompted a rare apology from authorities, but cleanup of the site took just four days—one wonders if this hurt search and rescue operations, or if any were even conducted.[7] Even in getting rid of buildings, North Koreans seem to prioritize speed over carefulness.

Of course, most people in North Korea don't live in new towers. They live in modest single-story homes in small towns. I've visited one of these once. It had a TV, but no bed or sofa: in the traditional Korean fashion, sleeping and dining is done on the floor. Pictures of Kim Il Sung and Kim Jong Il hung on the wall in the living room. It had a simple well outside for water. Above the door, a sign read "Model Household." The urban apartments I've been shown also have such a sign. In most of them, you will find a picture of the head of the household at his place of employ, from a day when one of the Kim family was visiting. They all had televisions and fridges.

These are not show homes, however. Actual families live in these model homes. I've always felt a bit awkward being part of a government-approved delegation poking around a real, if privileged, home. There's nothing like being in a group of foreigners taking pictures like at a zoo exhibit of "Koreans in their natural habitat" as the bemused residents graciously offer tangerines or tea. In other countries I've visited, if you're invited into a home, there is a degree of personal hospitality. The intermediation of the state in these in-home interactions always feels slightly surreal.

I've not visited the home of any North Korean colleagues, nor have I heard of it ever happening. I suspect it is not "illegal" in a formal sense. It is, like so many things, just "not possible."

At least a tourist resort is honest in its isolation. Wherever you are in the world, if you're staying in a resort you're kind of nowhere near whatever culture is nearby. And if you've chosen a resort holiday, you probably don't care. The city of Wonsan could someday cater to this sort of tourism. Choson Exchange programs on urban planning and special economic zone management took us to Wonsan a few times. Wonsan is on the east coast, a pleasant beach city of slightly over 300,000 people.

Here the North Koreans have long been planning a large tourist zone, which also features some curious design and planning features. The most pristine beach, they'd decided, should have a utility building every thirty meters or so, to rent deck chairs, provide showers, and sell drinks. This creates an odd repetition that distracts from some of the natural beauty; it is unlike any tourist beach I've ever seen. That main beach is on the Kalma Peninsula, which juts out from the city of Wonsan.

Kalma used to be exclusively for high officials and the Kim family, and has a large guesthouse at its tip. That was completely refurbished to house tourists at hefty fees starting at $150 per night. They'd refurbished it as if it were 1980, however, with radios built into bed stands and lace curtains that evoke Victorian-era shawls. Running alongside the beach is an airport, refurbished and renamed Wonsan Kalma International Airport in 2015. It seems as if no one involved in planning for the Wonsan Special Tourist Zone stopped to wonder if jet fumes and take-off noise are what sunbathers are looking for. Or, perhaps more likely, it did occur to someone, but they didn't want to take the risk of sending that feedback upwards.

The new tourist zone stretches down south to Kumgangsan, a stunning mountain that hosted millions of South Korean tourists from 1998 to 2008, until a middle-aged visitor wandered into a military area and was shot and killed. That event pretty much brought North-South tourism cooperation to a close. The zone also reaches west about an hour from Wonsan to Masikryong Ski Resort. It makes sense to have this be a tourism hub: stunning scenery, lovely beaches, a ski resort.

Masikryong was built in just ten months in 2012, mostly by KPA soldiers. It was part of Kim Jong Un's drive to create a "Civilized Socialist Country"—in other words, having the nice things that other countries have. It birthed the term "Masikryong speed," yet another slogan calling on citizens to be proud of just how damn fast something can be built. North Koreans almost always say, "We built this in 12 months," or "We built this for the people to enjoy," in reference to these projects. It is framed as a collective, national effort. I once feigned surprise when the erstwhile tiger adversary Ms. Bok Soon used "we" to describe a construction project, saying "Oh, I didn't know you helped build this!"

She raised an eyebrow and smiled, gesturing vaguely at the world around her. "'We'," she said, "means, 'we Koreans'." The commitment to collective life is baked in early and deeply.

Unfortunately, like the rapidly built construction projects in Pyongyang, this commitment to speed comes at a cost: quality. When we stayed at Masikryong in 2013, tiles were already chipping and falling off the outer wall, and some areas inside had a mildewy smell. Still, the lighting was nice, common areas were spacious, and you could get a decent espresso. Most uniquely for a hotel in the DPRK, you could also get internet access in a computer room and check your email, in case you think logging into your email on a computer in North Korea is a good idea.

The "Golden Age of Construction" also encompasses a stage of urban renewal connected to sports that Kim Jong Un kicked off in 2013. In the DPRK, as most places, sports serve as an outlet for patriotism at the national level, tribalism or regionalism at a domestic professional level, and as a form of discipline for youths and recreation for adults. It has always had a place in North Korean life, but Kim Jong Un's promotion of sports has been uniquely intense and comprehensive.

By 2015 they had created a sports TV channel and began talking in the media about the hot wind of sports, which sounds funny in English but works in Korean: "hot wind," meaning passion or trend. As part of this hot wind, Kim Jong Un invited Dennis Rodman, the greatest rebounder of all time, to visit on multiple occasions. The state tried to get more people involved in sports, which in turn contributed to a degree of urban renewal mostly but not entirely in Pyongyang. Riversides were developed to have more volleyball, basketball, and tennis courts. Another hot wind—rollerblading—inspired the creation of skateparks in various cities. Swimming pools and gyms were built or refurbished across the country.

Kim also directed investment in elite athletes and facilities to encourage mass participation in athletics.[8] This meant that in the west of Pyongyang, the "sports district" that was built for the 1989 World Festival of Youth and Students got refurbished. This massive boulevard features stadia for each sport—a taekwondo hall, weightlifting gym, badminton center, etc. Naturally, the badminton building is shaped like a shuttlecock. Elite athletes train in this district year-round, so visiting is often interesting as you can see sportspeople running around hither and thither. Foreigners can also visit a shooting range where one can shoot Olympic rifles, handguns, and even a pheasant in a cage. The range's restaurant will then cook it up for you. There was no vegetarian option for people like me, though I do like the idea of blasting a head of broccoli from a hundred yards and then having it gently sautéed.

Improving elite sports seems to have paid off at the 2016 summer Olympics in Rio, where the DPRK won seven medals, its most ever. Even more important, supporting winter athletes and winter sports through Masikryong Ski Resort and other new facilities contributed to the remarkable political breakthrough in early 2018.

The year prior was an extremely tense one. In 2017 North Korea launched dozens of missiles, including a massive intercontinental ballistic missile in November. That one, the Hwasong 15, was capable of reaching nearly the entire United States mainland. In September they tested a nuclear weapon that was by far their biggest. The United States and the UN Security Council piled on more sanctions. Donald Trump's belligerent rhetoric included the insult "Rocketman" applied to Kim Jong Un and a warning that North Korea would be met with "fire and fury" if it threatened America. North Korea called Trump a "dotard," introducing a defunct term back into the lexicon. It means old and infirm.

The US military was more prepared than in decades for the prospect of war. "People don't know how close we were," a Department of Defense–connected researcher told me in 2019. "We were," as he put it, "ready to go." The mood was so dire, many wondered if the South Korean Pyongchang Winter Olympics, to be held in February 2018, would be a success. Athletes and coaches wondered in the media if they should attend.

Then it all changed. Kim Jong Un, having declared his nuclear force completed after the November 28, 2017, missile test, pivoted to peace overtures on January 1, saying "North Korea's participation in the Winter Games will be a good opportunity to showcase the national pride and we wish the

Games will be a success."[9] South Korean president Moon Jae-in seized the opportunity to invite a northern delegation and athletes to come participate. This framed the subsequent year as a period of mostly cautious cooperation and rapprochement.

Following this, there was hope in Seoul that it might lead to a breakthrough with the United States, which holds the key to most of the sanctions facing the DPRK. If the two Koreas could cooperate on a range of projects, including infrastructure, it could be a huge win for North Korea and potentially for South Korea, too. An infusion of technical expertise and resources could help transform cities, making them safer, more efficient, and more livable. Should that breakthrough occur and major cooperation begin someday, I hope they retain at least some of their unique style aesthetic. Although much about North Korea needs to come in line with international standards, it would be a shame if the pastels disappeared and Pyongyang ended up looking like a generic South Korean or Chinese city. There are already plenty of them.

Regardless, we will have to see some peace-building before we get to cooperation on actual buildings.

Notes

1 Jose B. Collazo and Curtis S. Chin, "Building the Future while Saving the Past," *Straits Times*, November 5, 2015, https://www.straitstimes.com/opinion/building-the-future-while-saving-the-past.

2 "Oh, Did You Want to Buy a DPRK-Made Car?", Choson Exchange, October 18, 2015, https://www.chosonexchange.org/our-blog/2015/10/12/oh-did-you-want-to-buy-a-dprk-made-car.

3 정영 [Jong Yong], "북한 부동산 중개 수수료" [North Korea's real estate brokerage fees], Radio Free Asia, April 30, 2018, https://www.rfa.org/korean/weekly_program/c27dac8c-d480c5b4bcf4b294-bd81d55c-bb3cac00/priceindex-04302018102325.html.

4 "'Donju' Step In on State Construction," *Daily NK*, March 16, 2015, https://www.dailynk.com/english/donju-step-in-on-state-constructio.

5 Damin Jung and Kosuke Takahashi, "Miniso Japan Claimed Last Week that Operations in Pyongyang Had Ended," NK News, July 18, 2017, https://www.nknews.org/2017/07/japanese-lifestyle-retailer-miniso-still-running-pyongyang-branch-sources.

6 Saša Petricic, "Why Pyongyang Is Using Gleaming Skyscrapers to Show 'Potential of Socialist Korea'," CBC News, April 13, 2017, https://www.cbc.ca/news/world/cbc-north-korea-ryomyong-street-opening-1.4069982.

7 Chad O'Carroll, "Exclusive: Photos Confirm Date of North Korea Building Collapse: Four Day Search, Rescue and Clean-Up Operation May Have Come at Risk to Survivors," NK News, July 3, 2014, https://www.nknews.org/2014/07/exclusive-photos-confirm-date-of-north-korea-building-collapse/?c=1547523440350.

8 Andray Abrahamian, "Sports!", 38 North, September 19, 2013, https://www.38north.org/2013/09/aabrahamian091813.

9 Heekyong Yang and Josh Smith, "North Korea's Kim 'Open to Dialogue' with South Korea, Will Only Use Nukes If Threatened," Reuters, December 31, 2017, https://reut.rs/2lEkzTl.

10

All You Need

Three gigantic stone fists hold a brush, hammer, and sickle, casting over us a shadow of respite from the summer sun. The stones were also providing shelter from the group of tourists we'd been shuttling about: they were around the corner, listening to a guide in traditional dress drone on about which stones symbolized what exactly and on what auspicious date this Party Foundation Monument was completed. Behind the monument stand two apartment buildings, crimson red, and tapering upward. They suggest the image of a gigantic flag, fluttering and framing the political monument.

It was the end of a long trip, and the guide, Bok Soon, and I had grown quite close. Over hundreds of kilometers of bumpy roads, we had mediated cultural misunderstandings, but also had intimate conversations—we'd chatted about dating, marriage, freedom, travel, peace, and politics. We had sore feet and bags under our eyes, though hers were hidden by imported makeup and a pair of sunglasses.

"What are you doing round here?" I asked, stepping further into the shadow. She wasn't checking her phone or reading anything, just standing.

"Taking a minute," she said. Minutes alone were rare and tomorrow she'd be sending me and the others off before picking up another group. We looked down, just the hum of cicadas and the distant explanations about the monument filling the air. The crackle and grind of a street tram in the distance. I hesitated, trying to weigh up the value of leaving things unsaid.

"It's so hard saying goodbye here," I decided on. "Because in this place...you have to assume it's forever."

She brought her left hand up to her mouth, her whole face now concealed. Was she overcome by the notion of missing me or was it the countless forever goodbyes she'd said before? Someone specific she was remembering? Or something else entirely? Or nothing at all? I couldn't tell because she'd hidden her face. For five or six seconds the neighborhood grew quieter, the gray of the monument grayer, her yellow jacket, sunnier. Then she took her hand away. Her expression was calm, neutral.

She and I would not be able to write one another; not be able to share the poems and articles we'd written on social media; nor share pictures of birthdays or food items that had become our in-jokes.

Unlike in the old USSR, intellectuals are included in the Korean Worker's Party symbol, hence the gigantic brush alongside the more familiar hammer and sickle. And under this monument to political ideology, I felt at the same time as close to and as distant as I ever had to a North Korean. The monument's 216 blocks and its 42-meter diameter symbolize Kim Jong Il's official birth date (February 16, 1942). The seventy-meter outer platform symbolizes the seventy-year history of the party. I'm not sure how much it weighs, but in that moment, it could not have been heavier.

In another world with different rules I could have been really close to this woman; we could have been fast friends. In this life, however, not only does North Korea impose rules that separate us, but I'm also happily married and far too uxorious to start a tragi-romance with a North Korean several years my junior. Not all who visit North Korea have such fetters, however.

I have heard several tales of dalliances in stairwells between Koreans and foreigners. These I suppose are not profound connections between people so much as explosions of sexual curiosity; the kind that all people have all over the world and that take complex social structures to properly repress. (I'm looking at you, religion!) Even in this country, where the consequences for a cheeky kiss with a foreigner would be severe—job loss at the least—that curiosity can't be fully stamped out.

I tended to dismiss most of the stories as male bragging until I'd finally heard enough of them to think that libidinous encounters did sometimes take place. A North Korean once told me, largely unprompted, that between Koreans cheating happens "in stairwells and toilets... because then you know no one is watching."

He also said, "I think maybe my wife is cheating on me," exhaling a cloud of cigarette smoke. "But that's okay," his mouth pulling up into a cheeky smile, "because me too, when I get the chance." This segued into the facts about stairwells and toilets.

Flings with tourists would also end up in those illustrious venues, from what I've heard, but would begin like this: flirting over several days of a delegation or tourist trip; increasing physical contact, touching shoulders and arms in conversation; the decision to drink together in a group; and then a brief, awkward smooch and perhaps adolescent groping in a musty stairwell. Then a goodbye at the airport. The foreigner has a story to boast about; the Korean will never speak of it to anyone for the rest of her life.

The Korean participant, of course, had perhaps only seen at most a kiss or two on illegal foreign DVDs or USBs; there is nothing of the sort on North Korean television. Kissing rarely if ever takes place among dating couples in Pyongyang. In fact, the slang term for dating among young Koreans is *sanbo*—strolling—because that's the extent to which intimacy can take place before marriage.[1] The quick holding of hands would be *an absolute maximum* of touching. In such a prudish environment then, the result of these illicit kisses with foreigners is predictably uncoordinated, like teenagers bumping teeth and smashing noses.

Sometimes things can go further. There is the story, for example, of a tipsy female tourist dragging a male guide into a bathroom and performing oral sex for him. The guide, who like all other North Koreans, would have had basically zero sex education, couldn't contain himself and rushed out to pull his foreign colleague aside: "I have to tell you what I just experienced!"

The tour guides, particularly the women, have been chosen for the job not only for their language skills, but because of their personalities, looks, or both. They are often very charming and flirtatious in a Christian summer camp kind of way. Tourists develop crushes on them all the time. They are the ultimate forbidden fruit.

Romantic interactions can also sometimes go deeper and be less salacious. Marko, a friend of mine from Serbia, was a visitor to the Pyongyang Spring Trade Fair a few years ago. One evening, his group stumbled upon a small restaurant near the Potonggang Hotel, where they were staying. It was a beige-tiled two-story building just next to the river but wasn't on the normal hard-currency-foreigners-welcome circuit of restaurants.

They nonetheless poked their heads in and asked if a foreign delegation could dine there. The middle-aged manager assured them it was fine, though the menu was priced in local currency and the décor was noticeably less plush than most places they'd been. But the food was excellent. They found themselves sitting around a large, pink, Chinese-style round table, the only diners in the place. A waitress brought out course after course of fresh seafood and side dishes.

My friend was mesmerized by the waitress. The way she floated around in her traditional dress; the way she nodded and smiled upon requests from the guests. He went to bed thinking about her.

The next morning his group was scheduled to depart but overnight heavy snow, unseasonably late in the year, had dropped on the city. A thousand kilometers away, in Beijing, Air China canceled its flight due to the weather. (The Beijing-Pyongyang route is not a moneymaker for Air China. It exists for political purposes and gets canceled on any pretext.) Marko and his team were scheduled to leave but suddenly couldn't. An attempt to get on the sold-out Air Koryo flight the next day failed and Sunday there were no flights scheduled. They were stuck over the weekend.

Moreover, their local hosts had scheduled use of their van for another project over the weekend. This meant that they could potentially take taxis (accompanied by their hosts, of course) to locations outside the hotel or would have to stay within walking distance. That suited Marko. "We'll just relax in the hotel or walk to that little restaurant nearby," he helpfully suggested.

So they went back. Marco and the waitress kept looking at each other, making and holding eye contact. They went back again. And again. Finally, after several meals, hours of gazing at one another, and the odd bit of snatched conversation at the group's table, he downed a couple glasses of beer for courage and slightly red-faced handed her a plate and said in Korean, "This is dirty, please change it."

She looked at him quizzically. It didn't look dirty. And why was he holding it in such a weird way? She found out when she took it. He was pinning a $100 bill to the bottom. She felt it as he passed her the plate, but she couldn't see it. She tilted her head and she scurried away toward the bar to look at it. When she saw the value, her expression froze, and she dashed out the door.

Marko's heart sank. Had he shamed her somehow? He mumbled an excuse to his companions about smoking a cigarette and went out to the restaurant entrance, a gray stairwell with a lit Christmas Tree for decoration. She was at the bottom of the stairs speaking in a panicked whisper into her phone. Was she reporting him? Did he get the whole group into trouble? At one point, though, she laughed and he breathed out. He slinked back to the table. Later he went back to the hotel, then back to Europe, and got on with his life.

When his organization decided to go back to the fair the following year, however, all he could think of while buying airplane tickets, getting visas, while on the plane, going through security, checking in at the hotel, at the welcome dinner, the first day of the trade fair... was getting back to the riverside restaurant.

When he finally did, she was there. Her face lit up.

"You remember me, right?"

She nodded: "Of course I do."

The group ate and this time Marko seemed to need to smoke a lot more often. He did so in a European fashion, stepping outside, even though of course you can smoke indoors in Pyongyang. She would come into the foyer where he was lingering, make small talk and stick around as long as she felt safe—they couldn't be seen to be having a private conversation, after all.

Back at the table he found she was brushing against his arm when placing dishes on the table; subtly touching his shoulder as she poured Pyongyang Soju, a 30 percent clear grain alcohol of surprisingly high quality. (Soju is traditionally a more northern drink—part of why it remains so much better than in South Korea.)

Toward the end of the meal he held a plate up in a slightly weird way and called for her to change it. She smiled and took it. The others at the table kept munching away and pouring shots; they didn't notice. On the way out, Marko made sure he was the last in the group and leaned in as he walked passed her. "Let's promise to meet each other next year," he whispered. They locked eyes for a second. She nodded.

The following year's trade fair came, Marko attended again and this time it was unseasonably warm. She wasn't wearing a traditional dress this time, with its long bright top and huge, rustling, flowing lower half. She was wearing a smart, elegant blue dress, her hair back, more like a flight attendant. But not a manager's suit. Still a waitress, these years on.

This time, during a cigarette-dependent snatched conversation, he asked her, "Do you like your job? What would you be, if you could be something else?" Her answer was quick: "I hate it. I want to do business, to trade."

For a nominally socialist country, North Koreans are awfully into entrepreneurship. As we've seen, the famine of the mid-1990s shattered the previous relationship of the state to the individual. Prior, most citizens could expect the state to take care of everything for them. Provided you worked hard, had a decent family, and gave the party unquestioning and unquestioned loyalty, the state would provide your housing, clothing, food, education, and career. You had little choice in the matter, but it was stable.

Once the state's public distribution system collapsed, a key pillar of the social contract—provision of food—disappeared. People had to learn to fend for themselves, to be able to buy food. This meant entrepreneurship learned from scratch. This meant money. In the old system, money was not important. Now money was the key first to food, then to comfort, then to social advancement. Marko knew all this.

"I tried to help you a bit last time I saw you," Marko said, glancing around. "Can I help you again this year?" To this question she looked away and didn't answer at all. A few seconds later they heard footsteps on the stairs and so quickly moved apart. The restaurant manager walked past him and gave a polite smile. Had she seen? Did she know? That could be trouble. He went back to the table worried.

A couple shots of soju allowed him to put that fear out of his mind. And toward the end of the meal this time he offered her the plate but also settled the bill for the group. He gave her twice as much as the year before. He thought maybe her hand trembled a bit after she'd realized how much he was overpaying.

He went back to his group's table and sat down and a minute later she came and sat down next to him. She'd brought a bottle of Pyongyang Soju and said to the group, "Thank you for coming to our restaurant every year." She poured liberally and the group quickly got drunk. They bought another bottle. Singing broke out. Cheeks crimsoned and ties loosened, even amongst the Korean minders. Fruit was ordered. More soju. Singing. Sloppiness.

Nearly the whole time they held hands under the table, stealing private sentences when the singing or cheering got loud enough that it was just the two of them. Multiple power cuts created moments of darkness that gave them the occasional chance to even touch each other on the back or the hip.

The next day, she turned up at their booth at the trade fair, with a friend. This was new. She walked past the booth and he knew to follow her, but not too closely. When she stopped at another booth to look, he would come alongside her and they would snatch conversation, touching hands as they passed products back and forth. Sometimes he would break off to another booth and then she would catch up with him. The friend stood nearby, scanning to see if anyone was paying undue attention to the foreigner talking to a Korean girl. A good friend.

At one point, when perhaps they'd lingered too long and were too obviously chatting to each other, they noticed people were looking at them. They quickly drifted apart. A few minutes later he returned to the same area but couldn't find her. She'd disappeared. He thought of nothing else, imagining the proper goodbye they never had, for days afterwards. But he soon slipped into his normal life, thinking about her less often. No doubt she did the same. He'd begin thinking about her again as his annual trip to the DPRK approached.

The next year Marko returned to the restaurant with his group. She was gone. There were two waitresses he didn't recognize behind the bar. Still, his Croatian colleague, who by now also knew about this restrained romance, asked if they could eat. The manager said no. But she then quickly added: "Only because there was a problem with the distributor today. Please come tomorrow and I'll make sure everything is ready for you."

So they did. And then there she was. Dressed in a splendid Korean dress, pouring drinks, bringing dishes, stepping outside when she could to chat to Marko, who was again suddenly smoking more than usual.

"I don't work here anymore," she told him. "I'm not a waitress. I don't know the dishes well. I'm sorry for your group." The other two waitresses were off doing other tasks and the manager also made herself scarce, not helping bring dishes or open drinks. Marko realized they were in on it. *They were freaking in on it.* The manager had told his group to come back and then had brought in her old employee.

"So what are you doing now that you're not working here anymore?" he asked.

"Business. I'm in the seafood business."

"Is it going well?"

She shrugged. Not really, her expression said, but she wasn't a waitress. She was doing something more interesting, more fulfilling, something with prospects. Marko was sure he'd contributed. He'd put in the seed money, probably equivalent to four or five months' wages. He lent in and kissed her on the cheek. Or, rather, she'd moved a bit and it ended up being sort of her hair and ear.

"I'll see you tomorrow," she said, before ducking off to pretend to be a waitress again.

The next day, there was more pretending when she showed up at the trade fair. They wandered around together, pretending to look at various products and booths, but really just looking at each other, brushing hands when possible, locking eyes for the briefest of moments. At one point, they ran into a group of people she knew and Marko had to sort of drift away.

He stood at a distance, pretending to read leaflets, but really watching as she talked to her acquaintances. She appeared to finish chatting and seemed to be alone again, standing in the middle of the exhibition hall, clutching her silver-laced parasol and handbag. He sensed this was his moment to approach her and bid farewell. As he walked up toward her to say goodbye, he noticed she'd moved her things to her right hand. Her left hand was down by her waist, her wrist subtly moving back and forth as if brushing a speck of dust off something. She was waiving him off.

So Marko kept walking, forcing himself to stare elsewhere as he moved past her.

Perhaps they will meet again. Perhaps not. Every goodbye in that place might as well be forever.

Notes

1 A friend of mine who knows many people in the defector community thinks much more salacious, scandalous, and freaky activity is taking place among the youth of the DPRK. This may reflect the fact that we've interacted mostly with North Koreans from different regions and social classes. Pyongyang is more cosmopolitan, but in many ways also more conservative and uptight than other regions.

11

Yanji

Go, and Sin No More

To get to the Rason Special Economic Zone by road you usually have to go through Yanbian, China. You can also take the far less traveled route through Khasan, Russia, on the train.

It is a strange region, this so-called Tumen Triangle, named after the river that separates China from North Korea. It is a region where all three countries used to send internal troublemakers to be as far as possible from their political heartlands: a nexus of exile. It is still a place that feels remote.

The Russian Far East has been depopulating since the end of the Cold War. Fewer than seven million people now live in a region that is about twice the size of India, well over half the size of the United States. North Korea is famously closed, even if Rason is more open than most areas. And Yanbian Korean Autonomous Prefecture is about as far east as China goes.

In Yanbian summers, because China absurdly only has one single time zone, the sun rises before four in the morning. The prefecture has one main city, Yanji, and two smaller towns, Tumen and Hunchun, and several dozen villages. Hunchun sits right on the border with Russia and the DPRK, something of a dusty shopping and trading outpost for Chinese products going to the east and for seafood coming into China from North Korea and Russia. Tumen is about an hour's drive west, on its eponymous river and a border crossing with North Korea. Yanji is another hour away. Into the early 2000s, Tumen and Hunchun had no traffic lights. (Those are the prefecture's second- and third-largest towns.) People still washed their clothes in the river and didn't really wash them much at all in the winter, since temperatures could and still can get down to −40 Celsius.

Though we are now accustomed to stories of North Koreans escaping across the river, it is a region from which Chinese people fled the famine caused by the Great Leap Forward in 1958, *into North Korea*. As one elderly Tumen resident put it, "in 1959 they came up to Namyang," the DPRK's border town that sits across a bridge from Tumen. "They [North Koreans] threw up these five- or six-story buildings in just a few weeks. I'd never seen anything like it."[1] He'd considered trying to defect. Now of course, behind where the old man sat in Tumen's modern tourist pavilion, featuring an espresso shop and performance space, are dozens of much taller, more modern buildings. The feats of construction he once marveled at across the water still stand as the tallest buildings in Namyang, moldering and quiet.

In the 2000s, as Chinese coastal cities continued to boom, Beijing took steps to encourage development in other regions. In 2007 the central government began conceiving of the Changjitu plan, in part to link Changchun and Jilin—the region's biggest cities—to Russia and North Korea. Now there are pristine highways and gleaming high-speed rail lines. In places, the high-speed rail tracks are within a couple hundred meters of the North Korean border.

Yanji today is full of fairly nondescript apartment towers and office blocks. But some parts of the city look like imitations of Gangnam, in Seoul, with bright signage stacked up and up. The downtown is brightly lit in orange and rainbow lights at night, a display that straddles an abstruse line between impressive and tacky. The city has developed immensely but still doesn't come close to providing the opportunities that China's top-tier cities do.

Not only that, but in the 1990s, ethnic Korean Chinese citizens from Yanbian began going to South Korea to work. The Korean population in the prefecture has dropped from 1.83 million in 2010 to just 1.6 million in 2015, as working-age residents continued to leave to find employment elsewhere.[2] The decline is important for Yanbian: the ethnic Korean population comprises 36 percent of the overall population, just six percentage points higher than the 30 percent required to maintain its status as an autonomous prefecture, or so it is commonly said around town.

Still, these ethnic Koreans, or *Joson-jok,* with *"jok"* meaning "ethnicity" and *"Joson"* being the last dynasty of precolonial Korea, return from South Korea with some savings. Many have set up successful businesses and some have become quite wealthy. The city is globalized far beyond similarly remote, small cities elsewhere in China (small by Chinese standards: still about 650,000 people). In Yanji there are fancy coffee shops that will draw a picture of a bear in your latte and Western-style restaurants that serve you a burger that so flirts with authenticity, you'll be reminded what a real one tastes like back home. Kids run around with K-pop haircuts, watch foreign media, drink craft beer, and use Kakao Talk for messages, just like youths in Seoul or LA.

In Yanbian you find local Joson-jok, who in conversation strongly insist on their Chinese-ness though are clearly caught in between Chinese and Korean identities.[3] They look down on the Joson-jok outside of Yanbian, whom they see as less cosmopolitan, apparently. There are North Koreans there running businesses. Then there are North Koreans there illegally, blending in with ethnic Koreans and hiding out from North Korean agents and Chinese authorities. Then there are South Korean tourists, who've come to hike the Chinese side of Mount Paekdu—the mythical mountain where President Moon Jae-in and Kim Jong Un took a hike in September 2018. Then there are South Korean missionaries, compelled to save their ethnic brethren and in many cases, help refugees. Then there are several hundred Westerners—again, far more than in comparable cities elsewhere in China—many there because they were called by God.

It makes for a curious social scene if you go out to a bar in the city, these people who are somehow drawn to a place that was once considered punishment for those exiled there.

At a bar you might find the restauranteur, Mike, who had been working at a Christian university in the southern United States, when one day he felt the Holy Spirit tell him he needed to go help North Koreans. So, having never been to China, or possibly anywhere, he up and moved his family to Yanji to help in any way he could. Other, less divine motives meant you could find him at the bar. He did like a beer or two. He also, it seems, liked a Chinese girl or two. His family left him over this, I heard later.

There was chubby Canadian Chris, who was keen on pontificating about a range of topics with complete authority. He was middle-aged, but his face would get animated and boyish as he'd confidently make outlandish claims such as: science has proven a man can survive three days in a whale's stomach; Canada designs stealth jets for the United States; or Singapore is under sharia law.

Another such barfly was an antipodean gentleman who one night was loudly complaining that a rural landlord had kicked his group of North Koreans out of a refugee safe house where they were in hiding. He was tipsily swaying back and forth and periodically raising his arms in exasperation as he bellowed about a situation in which people's lives genuinely hung in the balance. I looked around nervously, amazed at the level of indiscretion.

The majority of North Korean refugees cross into this region. Partly because it is vast and smuggling networks exist, and partly because they can blend in more easily than elsewhere along the border, where there are fewer ethnic Koreans. Chinese authorities, if they catch them, repatriate them to North Korea, where they suffer a range of punishments depending on how long they were gone for and with whom they may have had contact. Being in touch with Christians or South Koreans is the most severe transgression. Lengthy sentences in work camps, beatings, and other forms of torture have been documented for repatriated refugees.[4]

Blending in is relatively easy in Yanbian, though escapees usually need some coaching in how to dress and comport themselves. But to be truly safe, they need to get out of China, which means taking trains or buses to Mongolia or Southeast Asia and declaring themselves to South Korean authorities: South Korea automatically recognizes them as citizens and these third-party countries facilitate their transportation to South Korea, unlike China. China wants to continue discouraging refugee-defectors, so sends them back.

This whole process of defection has become tougher lately: not only have both China and the DPRK stepped up security at the border, but China is now implementing all sorts of high-tech security measures across the country, including facial recognition systems. Those already run in major cities and at rail hubs. If they ever deploy them in Yanji, they could conceivably choke off the flow of illegal migrants almost entirely.

There are North Koreans living with permission in Yanbian, also. Some run the sorts of DPRK restaurants you find all across Asia, featuring pricey food and waitresses who double as musical performers. Others are studying at the university in Yanji, while others are running small businesses or branches of businesses in North Korea. Those who are not on show at restaurants seem to shed their North Korean identifiers as easily as they slip out of shoes into slippers when entering a home. Their accents blend with those of Seoul and Yanbian—less Pyongyang. Their haircuts and styles adjust somewhat. They—or one of them, at least—exchange racy pictures of women with other male friends on chat apps. Generally, they seem to enjoy the comforts and relative quiet of a city like Yanji. There's more autonomy to life than in Beijing, where there are many more North Koreans.

Back in the nearly separate world of the Yanbian expat social scene, other Westerners were less Christian and seemed instead to be lost souls, who'd found themselves somehow running small businesses in Yanji. Poorly. They'd perhaps come to the ends of the earth to find themselves but ended up mostly just drinking with the other assortment of folks who'd ended up in a strange place and who liked a tipple.

Not everyone did, of course. There were the intense believers living pure lives; the sort who not only didn't drink, but also didn't listen to rock music and were sending their kids who'd grown up in Yanji off to Liberty University, the evangelical school in Virginia founded by TV evangelist and blamer-of-homosexuality-for-9/11 Jerry Falwell.

That Christian community also included people such as Kim Dong Chul, Kim Sang-duk, and Kenneth Bae. You may have heard of them. They were all arrested and detained for years in North Korea for various infractions. Kim Sang-duk was a professor who worked between the evangelical sister universities set up in Yanji and Pyongyang—Yanbian University of Science and Technology, and Pyongyang University of Science and Technology.[5] (Yes, there is a Christian-run university just outside Pyongyang.) Kim Dong Chul lived in Yanji for many years, running a business in Rason.[6] Kenneth Bae was a pastor who ran tours and perhaps other businesses in North Korea. He also, it appears, was something of a covert missionary in China. He left some incautious videos on the internet about his hopes for opening up North Korea.[7] Bae was arrested in 2012 and released in 2014. The other two were arrested in 2015 and 2017, respectively, and released in 2018 when the United States and North Korea were exploring the idea of a summit.

There were also much more careful members of this community, who followed the rules of the countries in which they were operating businesses in and sought merely to "show an example of how to run a clean business" and live with grace.[8] Over the years, people like this have carried out many noble projects in North Korea. These include a small "stand-alone" or island four-turbine wind power plant, a soy-milk factory to supply protein to kids, and a trading company that would intentionally import rice to help depress prices when they'd periodically begin to rise. But also, this community would bring groups of tourists in, recruited through church networks, touting the right to pray together in groups. They'd follow the country's rules for the most part: only one bible allowed per person was a key one.

Still, the arrests of the American missionaries, along with a handful of tourists and careless journalists in the 2000s, became a problem for the United States. American detainees were being used as pawns in Pyongyang's political dealings with Washington. Essentially, they'd be held until a US dignitary was dispatched to Pyongyang to retrieve them. This allowed Pyongyang a small propaganda win and a face-to-face encounter with a US official or former official they wouldn't usually get. Ex-president Bill Clinton went in 2009 to get two journalists, and in 2010 former president Jimmy Carter visited Pyongyang and helped secure another American who had committed "hostile acts."

American tourists were at risk of detention too, though all had to *do* something to get in trouble: Jeffrey Fowle left a bible in a restroom while on a tour in 2014; a month earlier Matthew Miller tore up his visa and demanded asylum; in 2013, eighty-five-year-old Merrill Newman began talking about his covert operations during the Korean War while on a tour in Pyongyang. They were all imprisoned but released between two to seven months after their detentions.

One young man was not so fortunate. In January 2016, Otto Warmbier was arrested for the crime of attempting to steal a sign with a political slogan after an evening of drinking in the Yanggakdo Hotel. Some North Koreans, expecting the situation they'd seen before, where a tourist was held for a few months then released, would jokingly call him "Onebeer," because "that's all it took for him to lose his mind."

During his trial, a grainy video was shown in the courtroom of Warmbier—or someone—taking down the sign from a staff area of his hotel. Surely a problematic stunt to try in a country such as North Korea, but even by North Korea's standards, Warmbier's sentence of fifteen years of prison and hard labor, handed down in March 2016, was harsh.

The jokes among North Koreans stopped.

A friend of mine had a DPRK foreign ministry interlocuter who confided to him that there was something much more disrespectful that wasn't shown in the video. "You'll never find out what he did," the official said, though. "Because we can't say it out loud. Saying it would put that information out there and it would get back . . . and we can't have that." One is therefore left to only imagine what something so disrespectful might have been.

Regardless, in early June 2017, North Korean officials told the US State Department that Warmbier was in a coma. Perhaps most shockingly, he had fallen into the coma just weeks after the trial, some fifteen months earlier. The Koreans said he had contracted botulism and had become comatose after taking a sleeping pill.

Special Representative Joseph Yun flew to Pyongyang to repatriate Warmbier and returned to the United States on June 13, 2017. He died six days later. Warmbier's family claimed he'd been tortured. "His bottom teeth look like they had taken a pair of pliers and rearranged them," Warmbier's father claimed in an interview, prompting the coroner to publicly contradict that statement, and noted that "the teeth are natural and in good repair" in his report.[9]

It seems, tragically, that an attempted suicide was the most likely cause of Warmbier's condition.[10] Even if this is true, this does not absolve the North Koreans: had they allowed consular access, perhaps Warmbier could have been reassured that he wouldn't do fifteen years; that he would be freed much sooner. Instead, this young man had been kept alone, afraid and confused.

His death had a profound, emotional effect in US policymaking circles, "changing the entire atmosphere. . . . Washington began to churn out criticism."[11] It provided a rallying point for lawmakers and those in the young

Trump administration eager to take a harder line against North Korea. It contributed to the Countering America's Adversaries through Sanctions Act, passed on August 2, 2017, and President Trump's Executive Order 13810 of September 20, 2017, both of which tightened sanctions on North Korea.

A travel ban for US citizens, long pondered by the State Department, was then implemented on September 1, 2017. Then the Warmbier family were used as an instrumental set piece in the State of the Union address in January 2018 as President Trump made the moral case for pressure, perhaps war, against North Korea. Expanded US Treasury sanctions came into effect in March of the same year. It isn't an exaggeration to say Warmbier's case led directly to greater pressure against the DPRK and contributed to an extremely tense 2017, as North Korea tested its biggest nuclear bomb by far and its most powerful long-range missile.

The travel ban requires (as of time of writing) a US passport holder to apply for and get a temporary single-use passport for every visit to North Korea, provided it is deemed to be in the US national interest. It has cut US tourism to North Korea from 1,500–2,000 people a year to zero. It has also meant delays and problems for American NGOs working on issues such as tuberculosis, agriculture, and water supplies. Indeed, for about a year, the US government was denying most applications, seeming to weaponize humanitarian aid in negotiations with the DPRK.[12] The system for applying for special passports improved subsequently, but as of 2020 it continues to reduce US-DPRK interactions.

The travel ban was in part designed to limit the in-country work of the other high-risk group, the missionaries, though clearly some of that Yanji community has not taken the ban too seriously. I met one American woman in Rason in 2018, who was working in textiles and was extremely evasive when we asked if she was on her special single-use passport. She may have been thinking along the lines of Peter and the Apostles when they claimed "we must obey God rather than human beings!"[13]

For Christians, North Korea today, as it was for the missionaries of the nineteenth and early twentieth centuries, is a dream target. Then, Korea was the ultimate blank slate for missionary work: it was seen as "civilized," yet without religion; less devoted to native superstitions than other Asian countries; easier, then, to convince of the truth of the Gospel.

In the twenty-first century, the north has somehow become more fertile ground: more than one author has noted that Kimilsungism seems like a religion.[14] The North Korean people live in a totalizing ideological system. A system that purports to explain everything. From a missionary's perspective, if you could just strip Koreans of the one they've got and replace it with another, one that promises eternal paradise instead of mere temporal utopia...how great would that be?

In Yanji, a handful make plans for evangelizing after the eventual fall of North Korea. Some help refugees as they hide out, some in safe houses, some in plain sight, while Chinese and North Korean intelligence agents prowl the city. All of this bubbles just below the surface while wayward expats share a drink or two in a South Korean–styled bar on any given evening.

Notes

1 In conversation with residents, 2015.

2 Lee Jun-sam, "시진핑, 북중접경 연변 조선족자치주 첫 방문(종합)."[Xi Jinping visits North Korean border Yanbian Autonomous Province (general)], 연변뉴스 [Yonhap news], June 7, 2015, https://www.yna.co.kr/view/AKR20150717019551083.

3 Eddie Park, "Too Different to Be Chinese, Not Good Enough to Be Korean," Korea Exposé, September 20, 2018, https://www.koreaexpose.com/too-different-to-be -chinese-not-good-enough-to-be-korean.

4 "China's Repatriation of North Korean Refugees," Testimony before the Congressional-Executive Commission on China by T. Kumar, International Advocacy Director, Amnesty International, March 5, 2012, 5, https://www.cecc.gov/sites/chinaco mmission.house.gov/files/documents/hearings/2012/CECC%20Hearing%20Testi mony%20-%20T.%20Kumar%20-%203.5.12.pdf.

5 James Pearson, "North Korea Detains Third U.S. Citizen," Reuters, April 22, 2017, http://reut.rs/2oUSnyq.

6 Tim Schwarz, Will Ripley, and James Griffiths, "Exclusive: North Korea Reveals Alleged U.S. Prisoner to CNN in Pyongyang," CNN, January 20, 2016, https://edition .cnn.com/2016/01/11/asia/north-korea-alleged-us-detainee/index.html.

7 James Pearson, "Kenneth Bae Was Arrested for Plotting 'Operation Jericho'," NK News, May 10, 2013, https://www.nknews.org/2013/05/north-korea-lists-propaganda -materials-hidden-by-bae.

8 In conversation, August 2011.

9 Michael Nedelman, "Coroner Found No Obvious Signs of Torture on Otto Warmbier," CNN, September 29, 2017, https://edition.cnn.com/2017/09/27/health/otto -warmbier-coroner-report/index.html.

10 Doug Bock Clark, "The Untold Story of Otto Warmbier, American Hostage," GQ, July 23, 2018, https://www.gq.com/story/otto-warmbier-north-korea-american -hostage-true-story.

11 Email interview with US Track II practitioner, January 2018.

12 Jonathan Cheng, "U.S. Blocks Aid Workers from North Korea," Wall Street Journal, October 11, 2018, https://www.wsj.com/articles/u-s-blocks-aid-workers-from -north-korea-1539288182.

13 Acts 5:29.

14 Philo Kim, "An Analysis of Religious Forms of Juche Ideology in Comparison with Christianity," International Journal of Korean Unification Studies 11, no.1 (2002): 127–44.

12

Frontier Psychiatrists

Rason is an amalgamation of two cities, Rajin and Sonbong, which together make a special economic zone that abuts Russia and China in the very northeast of the DPRK. It borders Yanbian and is literally as far as you can get from Pyongyang. In August 2011, I was going there with a German foundation to explore the possibility of conducting economic training for officials and businesspeople in the SEZ.

After clearing Chinese customs, our group crossed over a one-lane bridge on an old Japanese bus, whose gears wretched and whose windshield had a large crack running down it.

Customs on the Korean side, at Wonjong, are burdensome. Border guards insist on going through your computer, opening movie files, clicking through them. It's not clear what they think they will find. Porn? K-pop? A philosophical take-down of the Juche Idea? At one point, one of them just seemed to be interested in a movie he'd found on the hard drive. He was basically watching an action scene. They have no idea how invasive this feels to Westerners. I don't want anyone to know I have the complete *Fast and Furious* series on my hard drive.[1]

One of our delegation, a piqued German businessman with a gray mustache, leaned over close to the mouse-clicking border guard and said, "If you're trying to show me this is a good place to invest, why are you treating us like this? This is a terrible welcome!"

I rendered the phrase into Korean and the guard's languid eyes looked up for a second, past the brim of his oversized hat. He clicked one or two more things and then closed the laptop, moving on to a tablet. It wasn't his job to attract investment.

Once through, we met our three middle-aged guides, Mr. Kim Soo Hoon and Mr. Kim Yong Man from the Rason Economic Cooperation Bureau, and their colleague Mr. Lee, who introduced himself as being from the Ministry of Foreign Affairs, Rason office. They ushered us into a Chinese-made van. Kim Soo Hoon wore a tired-looking Mao suit, draped over his wiry, sun-beaten frame. The other two were in Western suits, Mr. Lee's looking newer and quite literally shinier.

North Korean men have three sorts of suits. There is what we call the Mao suit, a gray button-up jacket with a rounded collar, emphasizing uniformity and sartorial humility. There is the Western suit, which North Koreans tend to have made with slightly flared trousers. Then there is the "summer suit," a unique take on formal wear for hot weather: this is a short-sleeve suit jacket, with a low neckline and wide collar. It is worn without a shirt underneath. Decadent Western jeans are never worn. Shorts are worn only for athletic endeavors.

Mr. Lee stayed in the road and confidently halted traffic, palm deployed as if casting a spell, while the driver, Mr. Gu, maneuvered the van out of the parking space and into the road. Lee swung around and hopped in as the driver put it into gear and started up the hill. "Let's go," said Mr. Lee, unnecessarily.

We rumbled up the slope, dust streaming from the wheels. The road to the combined city of Rajin Sonbong was being paved and hundreds of people toiled in the heat, heads and faces covered in bandanas in an attempt to keep the dust away. There were a couple of tent cities, where Chinese crews would sleep when they weren't working on the road.

The road was just over forty kilometers from the border to Rason Special Economic Zone, even though Rason had been created as an SEZ back in 1991. Illustrating North Korea's ambivalence toward economic reform, they never finished the road. It just wasn't a priority. It was a three-and-a-half-hour trip, longer if it was rainy season.

As we bumped and lurched along, a crimson Humvee barreled past, its high-tech suspension dancing on the road like fingers on a piano. It left a trail of dust clouds as it shrank into the distance, so we snapped our bus windows shut, until the still air quickly got too hot and we had to open them again. The Humvees were owned by the Emperor Casino and Hotel, which lies in a cove overlooking the ocean, nestled between lush green mountains and crystal waters.

It is now called the Imperial Hotel; since the road to Rason was finished in 2013, Humvees have no been longer necessary. Chinese businessmen and officials go there to gamble away mostly ill-gotten gains at the Hong

Kong–linked resort, while also enjoying seafood buffets, a spa, and Russian prostitutes. North Koreans are generally not allowed in the building. If they were, they probably would have been as surprised as I was once to see someone checking in holding two plastic shopping bags just filled to the brim with ¥100 *renminbi* notes. It must have been $200,000 worth of bills.

We stopped by Mr. Lee's office so he could grab something, and he leapt out. Kim Yong Man leaned in toward me and said, "You know he's security, right?" nodding toward the building where Mr. Lee just dashed in. "They've added him to our group because they see you're from a sensitive country and don't know who you are." His voice was hushed so even other people in the van couldn't hear. It was an airy whisper. He lit a cigarette inside the van. Then, as if remembering Western norms, he turned to the group and asked, "Sorry, is it okay?" It grudgingly was.

Mr. Kim's revelation put me slightly on edge; as Mr. Lee strode back to the van and jumped in, yelping "Let's go!" I smiled at him, but it must have looked fake.

After checking in to a fairly clean if musty hotel, we went for dinner at an outdoor restaurant in the town square. A big screen played dramas and as the sun set and night became cool, a crowd of maybe 150 or so bought snacks and watched the shows. The screen was new that year. Indeed, along with the new road, new rail line to Russia, and new screen, there was new management in the city and a new buzz about the place.

The recently appointed vice mayor in Rason was called Hwang Chol Nam. He had lived in both Sweden and China and gave off an air of relaxed cosmopolitanism. The trade fair that we'd come to check out was his idea: it was the first in Rason's history. Infrastructure was being built under his oversight. He even accompanied a group of 120 journalists on a pretty crappy boat to demonstrate a trial run for a potential cruise. The "cruise ship" was a boat that used to run people and goods between Japan and North Korea, before Japan severed trade with the DPRK after the 2002 admission that Pyongyang was behind the abductions of Japanese citizens in the 1970s and '80s.

The boat was widely derided for its austere conditions, lacking some of the luxuries you'd expect, like running water. And beds. But still, it showed an independence and creativity that had long been lacking in Rason.

Indeed, by all accounts, including our conversation with the vice mayor, Rason had more autonomy than ever. The SEZ had been given a joint management committee – administered with officials from China's neighboring Jilin Province. It could now issue travel permits in just a day—without involving the cumbersome bureaucracies in Pyongyang. It had a slick promotional video, envisioning Rason as a Singapore or Hong Kong of the North. Ambitious.

This future hub still faced very real impediments standing between its position in 2011 and becoming the next Singapore. Those impediments came from being in North Korea. In the joint management building, there was a main workspace where the Chinese would sit on one side, while the North Koreans sat on the other. The Chinese computers were all connected to the internet; the North Korean ones weren't. We heard the Koreans never asked to use the Chinese computers. Still, Rason was the first part of North Korea outside Pyongyang to get mobile phone coverage, courtesy of a Thai company. Internet access was, according the vice mayor, "coming soon."

At our al fresco dinner of meat skewers and noodles, we were waited on by a lovely server with a cherubic face and a dress that was conservative in a retro way—you could imagine a 1950s Minnie Mouse wearing it. North Koreans have developed a unique way of pouring beer, to show off the skill of the waitress: they rest the lip of the bottle on the glass and then just using the bottle, pull the glass slightly to an angle while slooooowly dribbling the beer down the side. Halfway, they nudge the bottle forward and finish the dribble-pour off into an upright glass. It is, like so much in North Korea, unique, impressive, and prizes form over function.

The waitress was chatting to us, very interested in a Western barbarian who could speak Korean, her accent trained to be sing-songy, as in Pyongyang, not like the rough Northeast, where she was from. Northeast DPRK and Yanbian accents are very much like Southeast South Korean accents, a region where I'd lived. Under Japanese rule there had been huge migrations from the South to the new industrial belt the colonial overlords constructed in the 1920s and '30s. After a couple minutes of my chatting with this Northeastern girl affecting a Pyongyang accent, Mr. Lee felt this was enough unauthorized liaising with foreigners and shooed her away with a flick of his wrist. He was the classic minder-as-enforcer: there to impede. (Not all minders are like that; nor are all with the state security.)

In the morning, the trade fair kicked off, but not before a turgid, speech-heavy opening ceremony. It featured a variety of dignitaries and perhaps a thousand people in neat lines, pretending to listen attentively. This is very North Korean: organize people into a grid and have them listen to monotone speechifying. The Koreans always seem surprised at how poor Western adults are at forming neat lines.

The fair was hosted by the Sonbong Cultural Center, a socialist classicist concrete box, with wide hallways, exhibition rooms filled with stalls, an auditorium for a presentation, and other side rooms for meetings. In the summer heat, there was a damp scent lingering around. There were maybe a hundred booths in total, mostly North Korean companies or companies from the neighboring provinces in China. Medicines, real estate developments, tobacco.

The North Koreans were pretty keen to pop back to the hotel, in keeping with their tradition of siesta, so we went back to rest up. On the way in a bellboy was playing a first-person shooter on the lobby computer, under a seventies-era wall-sized clock that incorrectly displayed the times for London, Moscow, and Beijing. The game caught Mr. Lee's attention. When I came back down, he was playing and the bellboy was watching.

In the afternoon, back at the trade fair, I noticed a computer numerical control (CNC) producer, Ryonha, was there. Their booth was staffed by a corporate vice president and attracted lots of attention from the locals in attendance, given that they'd been singing about CNC technology for nearly two years. I mean that quite literally: the most popular song from 2010 to 2012 was "Break Through the Cutting Edge," an upbeat ditty that extolled CNC technology, which is used to cut shapes with extreme precision. The technology, not the song.

It is a genuinely catchy tune, and Ryonha's exhibition was like a celebrity zone, with people clamoring for a glimpse, though instead of some preening movie star, the attention was for seventies-era industrial technology. Ryonha, as it turns out, is a subsidiary of the Korea Ryonbong General Corporation, which is under UN sanctions as a proliferator of weapons of mass destruction.

Still, the president claimed annual exports of €30 million to Europe, South America, and Southeast Asia, and imports of €10 million worth of parts, mostly from Europe, such as control units and electronic relays made by Siemens and Arno. He also said their main CNC factory is 40,000 square meters and the "biggest in the world"; they have one in Pyongyang and one in Jagang with 12,000 employees in total. CNC technology has been crucial in missile and nuclear weapons programs: you need to be able to build things with a CNC-level of precision in order to accurately shoot them thousands of miles.

Jagang Province is de facto closed to Westerners. This is probably because it hosts a number of factories and facilities run by the military, producing weapons and other strategic goods.[2] There is one town foreigners are allowed to visit in Jagang: Huichon, which is home to the world-famous-in-North-Korea Huichon Machine Tool Factory and hydropower plant. Foreigners are only allowed to see a hotel that Kim Jong Il visited in the 1990s (he gifted a Japanese fridge that sits in the largest suite) and leave, however. They don't want prying eyes around there.

Mr. Lee didn't appear to want my prying eyes in the trade fair. We had a group of a few people, and at one point I told him I would look around the exhibitions on my own for a bit. Mr. Lee said he'd accompany me. "Why?" I asked. He shrugged. I already didn't like his penchant for bossing people around, so I pushed back. "Isn't this event supposed to show things off to foreigners like me?" I mean, come on: a trade fair is literally designed for people to see things.

"Sure, but I can help you."

"Help me what? I'm just going to look around."

"I'm coming with you."

"Why?"

"Let's go," he gestured. Shaking my head, we went and looked around together, him minding me. And like a petulant child being babysat, every time he stopped to talk to someone or look at a product, I moved on so that he had to follow me. If he was going to treat me like a child, I thought, I'd play the part; I became the infant and he the domineering parent in a degrading psychodrama of the state's making.

Mr. Lee's power trips aside, the discussions we had come here to have were about the prospect of a Choson Exchange workshop to be conducted in cooperation with the German group we'd teamed up with. The locals seemed receptive, if noncommittal, to the idea. They weren't sure about the concept, but gave the impression they could be persuaded. Follow-up communication with Rason was infuriating. Emails would go unanswered. Phone calls, at nearly $2 per minute, would result in lengthy holds and then eventually end with the information that "Mr. Kim is out," or that "Mr. Kim is on a business trip."

We returned the following year to check out the trade fair again and see what had happened. There seemed to be a lack of focus. No one had ever really offered training in Rason: they weren't sure what to make of it. We pitched all over again and made plans to come back in the new year.

Finally, three years after making the first proposal, we got something off the ground. We recruited two Singaporeans to come up and talk about how to organize trade fairs better. We spent months planning it and in late spring I went up to Yanji a day early to make final preparations.

As my Air China flight pushed back from the gate, I received a phone call:

"Mr. Andray?" the voice said after I'd picked up.

"Yes, this is Andray."

"Hello. This is Kim. From Rason."

"Hello Mr. Kim! How are you?"

A flight attendant strode over to me.

"You must turn off your phone now," she curtly informed me. I gestured that I would.

"We need to postpone the workshop until next week," said Kim.

"WHAT!?" I yelled.

"Sir. Please turn off phone."

I tried to show her the panic on my face.

"We can't do that, Mr. Kim! I'm on a plane! I'm on the way!"

"The border is closed Monday for a holiday, so we can't get you."

"Sir. Turn off phone!"

"Mr. Kim, I have four people coming, they're all taking time off work."

"Can they change time off?"

"Phone off, sir!"

"Not really, it's not that easy, they all have flights booked."

"Sir, we are taking off!"

"Kim, we are taking off!"

"Okay."

"I'll call you when I arrive!"

I sat there stewing on the plane until I could get to Yanji and buy an international phone card to call Kim Yong Man. Of course, he wasn't in his office. I decided to tell the volunteers to come anyway and we'd work it out. When I reached him the next day, he seemed to understand that it was too late to cancel. We agreed to shift the program by a day. The workshop leaders adjusted. We crossed the border a day late, in that same minivan with a windshield still cracked, gears still grinding.

That detail may have remained the same (and did so for a few more years) but something had changed in Rason. This was, it seemed, related to the execution of Jang Song Thaek. He'd been closely associated with the Rason SEZ specifically and China trade relations generally. The vice mayor who'd brought in a wave of energy in 2011 seemed to be gone.

Over kimchi pancakes and grilled duck, I carefully asked Mr. Kim about it.

"Is Vice Mayor Hwang still around?"

"No. He is gone," he quietly replied.

"Will he be back?"

Kim shrugged his reply.

"Have operations in Rason been affected by the situation with Jang Song Thaek?"

"Jang was just one man. We're still implementing the party's policy on development, the same as before." The lines on his dark, wrinkled skin grew as he pinched his expression.

"But personal relationships matter," I said. "He and his people had good relationships with a lot of Chinese businesspeople. Are enough of his team still working to keep investment coming?"

"I can't say," he answered. I tilted my head, wondering if he meant the ambiguity in that phrase.

"You don't know?" I asked. "Or you can't say." I pointed to myself, meaning "say to me."

"I can't say." He seemed to have a resigned smile on his face.

In that moment I wanted to hug him. Not only because I was imagining how stressful it must have been to see Rason's management disappear and wonder if you were safe. Not only because the political study sessions after the purge must have been so fraught and upsetting. But because he'd just been honest with me. He'd communicated to me that he was not allowed to discuss it with me and for that much, I was immensely grateful. Being in the midst of a serious purge must have been terrifying and the mental gymnastics it must take to adjust to a new reality must be exhausting.

Those moments of honesty are treasured when working with North Koreans. An American friend who in the first decade of the twenty-first century worked with an NGO in the DPRK recalls having such moments with one particular official he was paired with. The American asked him, while rumbling along to do some fieldwork, "If Kim Jong Il dies, who would be the next leader?"

His partner paused and said, "I understand your curiosity, but here that's not something that you should normally ask people. It's not okay to ask questions that presume the death of the leader." He was being helpful, giving friendly advice. The two had a good working relationship, to the extent that when the American went abroad for R&R, he'd always try to bring back items his partner requested: economics journals, toys, porn...that kind of thing. (Seriously.)

The Korean went on: "Since you've asked, I can tell you everyone thinks they know who the next leader will be through media and reporting. But I can't tell you names." He was, in retrospect, probably talking about Jang Song Thaek. This was several years before the name Kim Jong Un was known to anybody.

Back in Rason, in 2014, the workshop went incredibly smoothly, the panic of an attempted postponement well behind us. There were about twenty participants who were engaged and full of questions. They were livelier than Pyongyang crowds usually were. We closed the first day, celebrated at the Russian restaurant in town, and then retired early.

In the morning, I got up to enjoy a run in the clean air and mild summer temperature, happy to be out of the sweltering smog of Beijing.

"I'm going for a run on the little hill behind the hotel," I announced to the cheerful lady who manned the lobby shop in our musty hotel. The hotel sat along the northern side of Rajin Bay, with beautiful views across the water.

"Why not run on the road in front of the hotel," she kindly suggested.

"I prefer running on hills," I said.

"I think the road is better," she replied.

"Well," I thought, "thanks for the advice, but I'll just do the hill."

It was a few minutes later, when a soldier was grasping his rifle and yelling at me, that I'd realized I'd run myself into a cultural misunderstanding. She'd not wanted to firmly tell me not to go around the back of the hotel, and I was too stupid to realize she was telling me not to go around the back of the hotel. Silly person. Now I was facing a man wielding an assault rifle with a bayonet affixed to it.

The soldier was young, maybe twenty years old. He was scrawny and it looked as if his uniform had been bought for him to grow into. This helped make him a bit less scary.

"Where you from?" he asked in English.

"England," I replied, through heavy breaths.

"Here...no!" he told me, with a finger wag. I saw behind him there was some kind of gate and a long tree-lined driveway leading around a hill.

"Passport." His hand was out now, it was a demand.

"I don't exercise with my passport," I said, indicating my running clothes. He glared at me. I decided to switch to Korean and instantly his eyes widened with surprise. A smile briefly invaded and occupied his face.

"I'm so very sorry," I apologized. "I was just running."

"What are you doing here?" he asked. I explained about the workshops.

For a few seconds we chatted about the weather, how he'd learned some English and, again, how sorry I was for taking his time. I sensed he was about to let me go.

Then, from behind a little ridge, a second soldier appeared, slightly older, also with a bayoneted rifle. "Ah, shit," I thought.

The first soldier put his authoritative voice back on and switched to English.

"Where is passport!?" he demanded. I sensed it was better to just speak English at this point.

"Hotel," I answered, pointing at the hotel, which was about a hundred meters away.

The two conferred for a second. They had me write my name on a piece of paper.

"Wait," said the first soldier. They had to radio back the important discovery of some giant, hairy Armenian near their facility, loping around like a yeti in Lululemons. I stretched a bit, to emphasize I was all about the exercise and not spying on military facilities. As the minutes passed, I sighed, to show a bit of annoyance. I pantomimed a watch to show I was busy. Was the right move to act indignant and make a fuss, I wondered? After about ten minutes a verdict was reached.

"Okay, go," said the first soldier, who'd sufficiently demonstrated to his superior that he was tough *and* that he could be tough in English. His boss looked happy, so I thought this had all worked out quite well for the first soldier.

"Thank you, thank you!" I smiled and bowed gratuitously. I then turned and ran down the dirt road toward the main also-dirt road that would take me back to my hotel room for an inevitably cold shower. When I was about fifty meters down the path, I heard a voice call out after me.

"Let's be friends forever!" it rang out.

I turned and waved, a real smile irresistibly crossing my face. As I ran away, I laughed and laughed at this outburst, this phrase he'd learned from some book, this aspiration that could never be.

As with so many North Koreans I've met, I sometimes think of him, my imaginary friend forever, and wonder where he is. What's his name? Is he still in the army? Did he get married and have kids? Was he eating less after sanctions got stronger? He certainly wasn't earning any money at that job. I've stayed at that hotel since. Was he still there, just over that hill? I couldn't check. I suspect he remembers me from time to time too. I'm sure he can't imagine my life, either.

By 2014 the road to the city had been completed. Russian investors had refurbished a pier and some other construction was underway to expand the market. The buzz that had accompanied the 2011 trade fair was dampened, though. Then, there was an exuberance, a feeling that things were changing. A couple years later, the locals realized that development was going to come slowly.

Still, we decided to hold a second workshop the next year. We managed to recruit someone from the world's top consulting company and someone from the world's top investment bank to come discuss investment attraction strategies.

This time we set up in the meeting room of our favorite hotel, the one with the forbidden hills behind it. It was a cream color, with the sort of plush armchairs popular in Asian rooms where negotiations and important meetings take place. It was a bit of a squeeze with the projector screen and all the participants, but we managed.

The consultant began talking about the Vietnamese experience in going from a closed economy to a foreign-direct-investment–driven export economy.

Something was off. The participants seemed quiet, bordering on surly. Sparking discussion was difficult. Questions were few and far between. I thought maybe they felt patronized by some of the basics the lecturer was laying down.

We broke for lunch—just as in Pyongyang we were not allowed to have lunch with the participants—and reconvened. The discussion was just as morose. The next presenter, Amy, also struggled to get the participants to discuss investment-attraction strategies. Why were they not as energized as the workshop the previous year?

When we arrived the next morning at the venue, things got worse. There was no one there. We milled about while Mr. Kim got on the phone. One of the participants, a tall gentleman in his late thirties, arrived.

"What's going on?" he asked.

Mr. Kim returned from his phone call.

"Today's workshop has been canceled," he said, without contrition. "The officials have all been mobilized to go rice-planting."

"What?" We'd had these two experts travel thousands of miles to come share their knowledge with Rason. "How can this be?"

"It just is," Mr. Kim said with a shrug. We'd come in the month of May, when office workers are sent out to the fields to help plant rice. In the fall they are sent out to help harvest. At other times of the year, they are sometimes sent to help with construction or other projects when the state engages in "speed battles" to accomplish various tasks. One imagines that early in the DPRK's history this was a great way to build solidarity among different classes. Now, everyone hates it. The office workers don't like manual labor and farmers don't especially relish city slickers with no expertise bumbling about their farms. They'd prefer tractors, if it were a choice.

Usually, however, if there is some important work, such as having to host a delegation from abroad, such mobilizations can be avoided. But not this time. I chided Mr. Kim.

"How embarrassing for Rason," I said. "We've got people from two of the most important companies in the world here and you had a chance to really impress them. And instead... this." I waved vaguely toward the situation. The tall gentlemen seemed extremely embarrassed. He'd lived abroad before and understood how this looked. Mr. Kim appeared blasé.

"What can I do?" he asked. This attitude—resignation—is not uncommon in North Korea. The system sets up barrier after barrier and if you have to live and work in it, you can't let yourself be constantly disappointed and frustrated. He wasn't.

I turned to the lecturers. "I'm so sorry. I can't believe it. I'm so sorry."

"Not at all," said the consultant, smiling. "This is *fascinating*." In a sense, they were coming to learn as much as to teach. And this was a particularly acute lesson in the rules and mindsets limiting development in North Korea.

The tall man excused himself and went off to plant rice with his colleagues. He'd not gotten the message beforehand, so would have to make an excuse for being late.

We suddenly found ourselves with some time to kill, so Mr. Kim helpfully arranged for us to go for a walk in the mountains above Rajin city. Along our path were some "revolutionary slogan trees." These trees, according to North Korean lore, had slogans carved into them by loyal followers of Kim Il Sung during his days as a guerrilla fighter. They praise Kim, the revolution, and patriotism. Several were found at Mount Paekdu by a fifteen-year-old Kim Jong Il and his classmates on a school trip in 1956.[3] What good fortune that Kim Il Sung's own son and future leader of the DPRK was the one to find them.

North Korean media didn't begin talking about the trees until 1986, however, when most of the discoveries began. There are over two hundred at various sites now protected by plastic casing and vinyl sleeves.[4]

Seeing them in the context of the canceled workshop felt like the country was trying to prove to our esteemed guests that it prioritized myth-making and Kimilsungist ideology over twenty-first-century neoliberal economics, where cross-border trade and investment are priorities. There has been a real tension in the Kim Jong Un era between the country recognizing the need to attract investment and improve productivity, and the perceived need to keep running the country's political system largely unchanged. On this day, the trade and investment people lost out. Still, up on the mountain the pine forest was quiet and cool, so it wasn't a total loss.

In a couple days we'd be grinding our way back over the old bridge, built in 1938 by the Japanese. In a few years a new, wider bridge would open and the Koreans would get a new bus with an uncracked windscreen, replacing the Japanese one.

Notes

1   Not really. I have some dignity.

2 Fyodor Tertitskiy, "Why Foreign NGOs and Tourists Can't Visit North Korea's Jagang Province," *NK Pro,* December 10, 2017, https://www.nknews.org/pro/why -foreign-ngos-and-tourists-cant-visit-north-koreas-jagang-province.

3 Korean Central News Agency, "Revolutionary Spirit of Mt. Paektu, Eternal Spirit of Korea," June 25, 2009.

4 한국민족대백과사전 [Encyclopedia of Korean culture], "구호나무(口護一)" [Relief tree], http://encykorea.aks.ac.kr/Contents/Item/E0070136.

13

It's a Wild World

The badge becomes an issue the instant a North Korean goes abroad. At home, everyone wears a badge featuring the face of Kim Il Sung, Kim Jong Il, or both, over their heart. Outside the home they are never taken off, unless it is during a type of work or recreation where it could get damaged. From the moment of touchdown at Beijing's antiquated Terminal 2, the badge might as well be a gigantic placard reading "I AM NORTH KOREAN."

Regardless, for younger North Koreans going abroad for the first time, this is the first time they have viewed this item of ritual through the eyes of others. And, to be honest, it looks kind of weird. There is leader-worship in other countries, but no one is wearing Lee Kuan Yew badges on the streets of Singapore. Mao badges are now worn ironically or by tourists.

Can you remember the first time you went abroad? Perhaps you were young. Perhaps not. Either way, no doubt some important ideas were generated on that first trip. It is, after all, only once you're somewhere else that you start to question the things you take for granted as normal back home. A British child might think: "Why do we drive on this side rather than the other? Why do we wear school uniforms? Why do we have a separate tap for hot and cold water in the bathroom sink?"

It is only when you go elsewhere that you recognize aspects of your own society that you may have taken for granted as "normal" or universal practices. You may even think that some things from your home country, such as the vexing British insistence on two separate taps, just don't make any sense at all. Seriously. Every other country has figured out that mixing the water *in the tap itself* is manifestly superior. How, you begin to wonder, can this still be a thing? Things you take for granted as normal or standard get called into question.

One important writer on pre-twentieth-century Korea, Percival Lowell, perceived the power of interaction better than most of the condescending imperialists of his day. He wrote that Westerns thought Easterners to be "irrationally odd":

> For any people to write backwards, to talk backwards, to sit upon their feet, to take off not their hats but their shoes on entering a house, and in countless other ways to conform to what seems more like a photographic negative of our own civilization than a companion picture...

> However, it was only through encountering those differences that both sides could be provided with the opportunity to reflect on their own societies:

> It is because the far-East holds up the mirror to our own civilization,—a mirror that like all mirrors gives us back left for right,—because by her very oddities, as they strike us at first, we learn truly to criticize, examine, and realize our own way of doing things, that she is so very interesting.[1]

Such was Lowell's commitment to bridging these worlds, he ended up taking time out from his career as an astronomer to serve as foreign secretary and counselor for a Korean diplomatic mission to the United States. It wasn't always easy. "Korea is not China; it is not Japan. This may seem an unnecessary remark," he laments in one passage, "I assure the reader it is not."[2]

Part of Korea still struggles to understand the outside world and we, it.

Certainly, North Korea has been a mirror for me and forced me to ponder my own "civilization." As I've witnessed the starkness of their propaganda, I've thought more about how propaganda works where I'm from, shaping my views on everything from marriage to war to tofu. (HAHA real men drive trucks and eat BURGERS #amiright?) Seeing a Korean society hampered by mid-twentieth-century ideologies has let me see more clearly how ideology creates negative outcomes where I'm from. This is particularly true in the United States, where commitments to eighteenth-century ideals about the individual's relationship to the state and the need for an armed citizenry cripple policymaking today. I've been forced to think about where the balance is between North Korea's version of leader-worship and the mass cynicism toward political leadership in the West. I've come to see the year-month-day way of writing dates as superior.

Traveling outside your hometown, your region, your country is revelatory. The most rewarding point of working with North Koreans has been bringing them out for study trips abroad. Many of our participants had never been abroad. Still more had only been to China and maybe only once or twice. Only a few were seasoned travelers. Watching the first-timers wide-eyed as they saw Beijing, then Singapore, was always entertaining and often heartwarming.

Choson Exchange is a Singaporean NGO, so most of our international programs were held in Singapore, three thousand miles southwest of Pyongyang. But in almost all cases, schedules required passing through Beijing. We'd sometimes build in layovers in order to facilitate dialogues or lectures for participants there also.

For first-timers, Beijing invariably provokes a reaction of disgust. Remember, for North Koreans, a capital city is a showpiece; an organized, tidy manifestation of state ideology. They touch down in Beijing and it's chaos. Beijing is a beast. Along with its neighboring port city, it holds as many people as California, Washington, and Oregon combined. The air is often an apocalyptic haze. People are pushy—everything in a public space, whether it's queuing for a movie ticket or boarding a train, is a battle. It is loud and dirty.

One North Korean once said to me, "*This? This* is the capital city of the most powerful country in the world?" His face looked like he had stepped in dog poo.

At the end of 2012, we had a group of two men and three women passing through on their way to Singapore for an internship at an incubator, to help them understand how tiny companies try to make the leap to small companies. I was a few weeks away from moving to Beijing, so couldn't meet them to escort them around, but my white American wife was there studying Chinese. She offered to step in and graciously met them at the airport, helped them to their hotel, and then ushered them to their appointments for a couple days.

At one point she took them to our favorite dumpling place, very local—real Beijing. It was too real for the Koreans. One of them unfolded a napkin and put it down on her chair before she sat down. They looked scornfully at the cigarette butts and peanut shells decorating the floor.

This was during the height of an anti-Japanese outburst that the Communist Party was allowing to develop in China. In another restaurant my wife led them to, the waiter accusingly asked her, "Are these people Japanese?" He wore an expression of disdain and looked ready to kick them out.

"No," she answered. "They're from *Chaoxian*—North Korea."

His expression tilted toward the quizzical. "Well, where are you from?"

"I'm from the United States!"

This was too hilarious and he broke out into a howl of laughter. "Hey!" he shouted to his colleagues. "Get a load of these guys! Americans and North Koreans eating together!" He seemed to enjoy the bridging of cultures, so long as the Japanese were excluded.

North Koreans generally have pretty complicated feelings when it comes to China. The DPRK as a country is committed to Juche and yet by 2017 over 90 percent of its trade was with a single partner, China. This strategic over-reliance on their giant neighbor causes deep unease among political elites. But DPRK relations have always been up and down with China.

This began in the 1950s with disagreements over how to prosecute the Korean War. Then, in 1956, Kim Il Sung purged a Soviet and a Chinese faction within his party, causing grave concern in China. A joint ministerial level delegation from Beijing and Moscow then visited Kim in Pyongyang to tell him off, "a major insult."[3] In 1966, Chairman Mao Zedong unleashed a wave of instability with his Cultural Revolution. His impassioned revolutionaries denounced Kim Il Sung and North Korea. The DPRK leadership felt China could no longer be counted on.[4]

There were also tensions as China embarked upon its program of "reform and opening" in the 1980s. From the skeptical North Korean perspective, China was giving up on socialism. Today the line is that China is able to become wealthy because it is secure in a way that North Korea is not. "We have our own circumstances, we have to spend so much on the military because of the Americans," one chap once explained to me. The authorities don't try to hide how wealthy their giant neighbors have become. Indeed, there is so much interaction with China now that any such attempt would fail.

This interaction opens up new tensions, however. For ordinary people who might be engaged in trade or some other cooperation with Chinese people, things can be fraught. Chinese generally look down upon the Koreans, seeing them as backward, poor, and unsophisticated. China and Chinese people generally see Korea as the "little brother." And if there is one thing that is anathema to North Korean culture it's being condescended to by outsiders.

Compounding that, North Koreans tend to think of their own culture as more sophisticated and see the Chinese as boorish. Chinese tourists are not allowed to visit Kim Il Sung's mausoleum, for example. North Koreans generally also resent the fact that they are being trapped into basically having no partners other than the Chinese, due to sanctions and their own government's policies.

I once asked a security officer in Rason what he thought of the Chinese. "They're our brothers!" He proclaimed with a wide grin. "Really?" I asked as I scrunched my face with skepticism. He dropped his smile, shrugged and turned around. I guess, like family, you can't choose whom you get nor how much you like them.

Back in Beijing, the day after the dirty dumpling restaurant, my wife helped the interns check in for their flight and off they went to Singapore, glad to have China behind them.

Singapore, especially for North Koreans who have just experienced Beijing, feels like paradise. Not only is it clean and organized, but there is no historical baggage with the island state, the way there is with China or the DPRK's other neighbors. Singaporeans can deliver messages that are seen as non-judgmental: "Oh, you don't have property rights? Well, that's your choice, but call us when you get them and we can make money together!" There are not the implicit criticisms that Chinese have when they suggest reforms (copy what we did!) nor when Westerners give advice (organize society the way we do!)

Once, at a logistics company, the Singaporean chairman highlighted—without judgment—that North Korea's immigration policy was one problem with its business environment; Singapore has made it very stress-free for people to come and go, to facilitate business. Fairly daringly, one of the North Koreans agreed that "Yes, passport-issuing policy is a problem." These were businesspeople, after all: they wanted it to be as easy as possible to make money and seeing how easy it was in Singapore could be frustrating.

At another meeting, one North Korean asked, "How long does it take to register a business in Singapore?"

"A couple hours filling out information on the government portal," came the reply, "and then the response is usually within twenty-four hours." The group literally gasped. They couldn't believe how easy and fair it was. Again, this was delivered without judgment.

Back at the logistics company, the chairman beamed at our group and said, "We're waiting for your country to open for us to do business, invest, enjoy!" Everyone smiled back. When an American, Chinese, or South Korean says, "We're waiting for your country to open," there is more misgiving and resentment on the part of a North Korean.

In general, there is much about Singapore that North Koreans can grasp and feel positive about.⁵ A single party—the People's Action Party (PAP)—has been in charge of government since before independence, despite having regular elections. The state has a heavy hand in the economy, though it relies on market principles to deliver results. For example, it has a mandatory savings scheme that is used along with subsidies to provide healthcare for all, but "streams" patients according to how much they are paying themselves. About 80 percent of Singapore residents live in a state-subsidized home.⁶ Citizens can rent-to-own, linked to the national pension program, and home ownership is above 90 percent.⁷ This is the highest rate in the world and demonstrates state-guided market forces being harnessed to achieve fundamentally socialist goals.

Singapore also has a semi-official ideology akin to "rugged independence…
under the enlightened leadership of the PAP," with the country's founder
Lee Kuan Yew as "the ideological capstone of the system."[8] There has even
been a father-son power handoff: the current prime minister is Lee Kuan
Yew's son. All that stuff feels familiar to a North Korean.

We had assigned the group of interns a research project, but some of them
struggled a little bit with the unstructured nature of a self-study mode of
learning. We learned from this and adjusted future programs to be a bit more
mapped out, while also trying to leave space for autonomy and exploration.
This was our first long program abroad—nearly five weeks in total.

We took them around to top accounting firms, banks, law firms, and
incubators to see how a functioning business ecosystem works. The group
were mostly in their mid-thirties; it was the first time abroad for two of them
and the longest stretch outside their country for all of them. One lady, the
youngest, was a little shy. The other two were outgoing, while the men were
both fairly reserved, yet could be engaging in social settings, knowing that
they were representing their country to people who'd never met a North
Korean before.

One common misconception is that when North Korean delegations go
abroad there is a minder or a "security guy" there to oversee everything. It
doesn't usually work like that. Instead, there is a delegation head, who is
most responsible for the group's actions. Underneath the delegation head
everyone else is also considered responsible for each other. Every week they
are abroad, the group (or part of it) is supposed to go to the embassy to brief
the staff on their activities, as well as check in on the political messaging
for the week. When they return to Pyongyang, everyone is given a security
debriefing. If the State Security officers find any discrepancies or other red
flags, there could be trouble.

The North Koreans would never really talk about this process in any
detail; it was clearly something foreigners are not supposed to know much
about, and I didn't ask much about it after having my questions dismissed
a couple times.

"How long does it last?"

"Not long."

"Like a few hours?"

"It depends."

It clearly included a thorough search of materials and products. More
than once after doing a bunch of research, a participant would ask if we
could bring in the economics PDFs and downloaded web pages they had
downloaded the next time we visited, "because it will be easier for you than

for me." This mutual monitoring system turns everyone into a "security guy." In some ways this is far more insidious, with everyone invigilating against each other.

We started to suspect this was the case from Choson Exchange's very first program abroad, in 2011. We had a group of seven people, with different areas of expertise. From day one, we were trying to guess who the security officer was. As the ten-day trip progressed, we covered a range of diverse topics at a variety of ministries, agencies, and companies. A couple of the guys didn't talk much. "They must be security," we decided. "Definitely one of those two."

But then when meetings at agencies relevant to their work took place, they'd pipe up and become much more active. The last quiet, probably-he's-the-se-curity-guy finally led a discussion about managing public utilities a few days into the trip . It was then we realized there was no security guy. Instead, they were all responsible for security.

Going off on one's own is not common. If a group breaks up at all, it is almost always into pairs or threes. This can lead to some tensions. The group of interns was supposed to spend a whole day at a social-enterprise incubator, but after lunch the delegation head declared he was tired and said everyone had to head home. The women lobbied to stay, which failed, then lobbied to go shopping as they didn't want to go home and rest. They were overruled.

"The guys are so authoritative," one of them, Ms. Ri, complained. "There is nothing we can do."

This was a pretty forthright complaint. The delegation head was also stopping the group from splitting into different teams to work on projects at the incubator, slowing the learning process we had planned. Still, we didn't really try to intervene in their group dynamic. It was an early program abroad and we weren't sure if we should push more for separate activities or just let the Koreans work it out for themselves.

We generally choose the latter, though after that experience we tried to build in more optionality in order to provide encouragement for those participants looking for a bit of autonomy. We'd encourage individual or small-group learning projects. We'd also try to encourage a bit of explo-ration, saying things like, "We'll take one group to the mall and one group to the museum." In an unfortunate affirmation of stereotyping, the women almost always chose the mall.

One quiet afternoon during a two-week study trip to Singapore, we decided to visit the national museum, a lovely neo-renaissance building, blissfully air-conditioned down to 18 degrees Celsius. They happened to be having an exhibition of post-modern paintings, with abstract figures, non-realistic color schemes, and fantastic landscapes. As we wandered, the Mr. Jo, the delegation head, stopped in front of one that depicted a man of sorts, engaged in perhaps a yell. Or was he singing? Crying?

"What does this mean?" he asked, smiling. Like most North Koreans, he'd only been exposed to realist art and design.

"Well," I opined, "It means whatever you want it to mean." Feeling pleased with myself already, I went on: "The artist has one idea in mind, but when you look at it you'll have a different idea, and that's good. Finding the meaning together is kind of the relationship between the artist and the viewer."

"Well I'll be . . ." he mused, broadly smiling and shaking his head. He was a curious man and was soaking up everything he could.

Some of the delegation were less enthralled by the weird art. "Where can we go to smoke a cigarette?" one asked. Outside, under the blazing sun wrapped in a blanket of humidity, was the disappointing answer.

He may not have been so frank as to say, "This is boring," but I could tell that's what he meant. Overall, North Koreans are much freer to voice opinions when abroad than at home, for obvious reasons, but there are still often ambiguities.

Another once told me, as we stared out over a Beijing vista of skyscrapers and lights, "Twenty years ago, no one imagined this would be such a cosmopolitan city. Soon, Pyongyang will be too."

This comment was emblematic of the way North Koreans verbally dance around sensitive subjects. They often speak in a sort of code that hints at hopes or dissatisfactions that are too risky to express fully. So much of holding discussions with North Koreans involves coloring in the spaces they leave behind. The more you do it and the greater context you have, the more accurate you become.

This Mr. Kim had spent time abroad. He knew the world out there and fully appreciated the problems in his own country. His ambiguous sentence was his way of saying, "I want my country to be more like China."

"What do you think is more important? Theory or results?" one young lady once asked me. This was back in Pyongyang, at my favorite café, which overlooks the Taedong River. I gave some rambling academic answer, full of pretentiousness. Then she just said: "I think results are more important." I nodded, but the full impact of what she was saying didn't strike me until a couple hours later.

She was saying, "I'm not ideological. I don't care about all these political or ideological commitments. I want my country to work. I want to make money and have a good life. I want things to be better." At least that's what I interpreted it to mean.

Little quips would illustrate mild dissatisfactions and the critical think-ing that underlies them. Once, in 2016, someone in a Choson Exchange van puttering around Pyongyang pointed at a development that had been languishing for years and said, "Hey, that looks cool, it's a new shopping mall developed by the Chinese." One of the guides in the bus shot back, "We don't need new shopping malls, we need more products in our existing shopping malls."

On occasion Koreans can be explicitly negative about their country, though such moments are rare. Once I "caught" a North Korean, who was attending an international conference, reading a review of a new book about the DPRK on a hotel lobby computer.

"Oh, that's an interesting book," I said with a bit of smile, trying to signal I'd read it.

The review included discussion of the prison system and other unsavory elements of North Korea. He had a quick glance around the room. No one was in earshot. "I know so little about my own country," he told me, screw-ing up his chubby face into a frown. He took off his glasses and rubbed his forehead. "I'm sure it's all true," he sighed.

Another Korean once leaned in toward me over a hotel breakfast and said, "Look, we know our system is like capitalism now." He checked to see no other English speakers from the group were nearby. "We've got a lot of pride in some of the things we've accomplished, but we do need to learn to let go."

His comedically oversize suit—North Koreans tailor them loosely—kind of made him look like a kid who'd been dressed in hand-me-downs for a wedding, but his face was deadly serious. Letting go, for him, meant preserving some of the national story about liberation and trying to build a socialist paradise, but also recognizing that the tide of history had pulled the world in another direction. And that North Korea's refusal to participate more in that world was hurting his society.

Still, even abroad I'd not usually bring up sensitive topics directly, but I learned to ask questions that would allow the Koreans to talk about sensitive things *if they wanted to*. For example, I'd sometimes ask them, "Where in the world do you want to visit most?" I think almost all North Koreans are extremely curious about South Korea and the United States, these enemies and forbidden territories, about which they know nothing except the neg-ative coverage in official media and the often-unrealistic representations in Korean dramas or Hollywood movies.

If my conversational partner was interested in hearing from me about the United States or the other Korea, they could choose to mention those two countries. If not, we could talk about safer places, like Italy or Singapore.

One answer I heard more than once to my question was Jeju. Jeju is an island off the southern coast of the Korean Peninsula. It was a farming and fishing community, until it was transformed in the 1970s into a domestic holiday destination for South Koreans, and then in the 2000s into an international one. It is well known for its dormant volcano, Halla, and its oranges.

A North Korean could answer "Jeju," and it would be a way of indicating "South Korea" without actually saying it. We could then chat about the oranges and the restaurants and other relatively safe topics if they wanted, or they could steer the conversation to other things about South Korea if they liked.

Sometimes you could see new ideas forming among Koreans being exposed to a new country. Once in Hanoi, as we drove past shop after shop selling Ho Chi Minh paraphernalia, a middle-aged gentleman asked whose face it was. Our fixer explained that Ho Chi Minh had led an independence movement, fought the Americans, and established socialism in Vietnam. "Wow," pondered the gentleman, "He's just like our Kim Il Sung."

That may seem like a minor observation, but there must be some impact, however small, simply to know that other countries have their own versions of a Great Leader who creates and embodies all core social values. There is no cult of personality as strong as North Korea's, but others do exist, making the Kims seem less unique. (Incidentally, when visiting Washington D.C., I encourage readers to go to the Capitol Building to view *The Apotheosis of Washington*, a fresco depicting Great General George Washington ascending to heaven and becoming a god.)

Still, no other personality cult has demanded all citizens wear badges on their chest to display loyalty. It is the ultimate involuntary shibboleth, a sign that you are—or are not—part of the DPRK family.

Some North Koreans abroad don't seem to mind this, but others seem very self-conscious that it makes them stand out. More than once I've heard South Koreans whispering about the North Koreans in the immigration queue, bus, or food court. If it weren't for the badge, they wouldn't have known.

Sometimes a North Korean abroad will take off the badge as soon as they can change clothes, free to blend in at a bar or in the hotel lobby. Other times they wait to take a cue from the delegation head. If he—and it's always a he—takes it off, it is okay for the rest of the group. If not, if he is more conservative, they stay on. Regardless, for formal meetings or events they'll keep the badges on.

In general, South Koreans react one of two ways when they see North Koreans abroad. Sometimes they just ignore them, in a sort of fearful way. Once on a Singapore Air flight from Beijing to Singapore, one of our female participants was sat next to South Koreans. Her DPRK passport was out and their Korean-language Lonely Planet guide to Singapore was, too. I saw them both take note of and then studiously ignore each other for six hours.

The other way South Koreans sometimes react is to be oblivious to the awkwardness: they will sometimes just chat a North Korean's ear off. "Where are you from? What do you do? Have you been to Marina Bay Sands? Soju is expensive here, right?" etc. etc., while ignoring that the North Korean is trying their best to extricate themselves from the conversation, tension for them building with each innocuous question. Talking to South Koreans can mean trouble for a North Korean. At the very least, explaining themselves to their colleagues. At worst, having to write a formal report.

Meeting Americans abroad could be sensitive, also. If we had an American lecturer, sometimes we wouldn't introduce where they were from and just assume the Koreans didn't want to know. Sometimes, one of the Koreans would ask, however, and again, a little white lie would pop out of my mouth: "Canada, I think?"

As with other things we'd conceal from the Koreans, I'd feel bad, but justify it by saying it was better for them if they didn't know. And better for us. Still, a lie is a lie.

One instance where I was tempted to lie, but didn't, was when we took the group for afternoon tea and drinks at the house of a wealthy sponsor of Choson Exchange. This house belonged to a family that had had businesses for generations in Singapore. Have you seen *Crazy Rich Asians*? If yes: first, I'm sorry you wasted your money. Second, it was like that. If you haven't seen it, imagine a house so big that it has a glass elevator and a living room with a full fountain in it.

As we sat in this modern-day palace, one of the North Koreans leaned in toward me and whispered: "Are most houses in America like this?"

I desperately wanted to say yes, but instead I laughed and said no, this would be considered a special house anywhere in the world, but especially here where property is so expensive. We sipped our Coca-Cola in awe of the place.

Coke was always a popular choice amongst the North Koreans abroad. It's hard to find in the DPRK, and if you do it is imported from China and expensive. As of 2019, there are only two countries in the world where Coca-Cola is not produced: Cuba and North Korea.

North Koreans also love dairy. One of the women we took abroad smashed almost a pint of ice cream per day. Quality fresh milk and dairy products are extremely rare treats in the DPRK, even in Pyongyang. In 2014, on a flight to Vietnam, a genial bespectacled North Korean chap and a Vietnam

Airlines flight attendant conspired to fumble a glass of milk over my laptop, destroying the keyboard.

They were, of course, also keen on eating quality meat: as much of it as they could manage.

This once went bad when I was staying with a group of twelve North Koreans in a house that doubled as a lecture venue for a three-month mini-MBA. (I know, this sounds like a premise for a bad sitcom.) The Koreans would often cook lunch and dinner, with the men surprisingly being adept in the kitchen. Once, however, they grabbed from the fridge and stir-fried my Tofurky (registered trademark) roast that I'd hand-carried from the United States. My wife was flying down to meet me and we were going to spend that quintessentially American holiday (sorry, Canadians) with some friends in Singapore.

I couldn't believe they'd eaten it. *Hand-carried vegetarian meat-substitute for my wife.*

"Did you not realize? It was shaped in a block!"

"We thought it was processed meat! We're sorry."

"Didn't it taste different?!"

"We fried it in a spicy sauce!"

"Arggh!"

"Why are you so upset? We're sorry. We can buy you a new one."

I didn't want to tell them I'd just come from the United States, nor that it was for an American feast. I just said you couldn't find it in Singapore, and it was a gift. I couldn't believe it. Will historians remember this as the US-DPRK Tofurky incident? Is it up there with the 1968 capture of the USS *Pueblo* in terms of North Korea's victories over the United States? Clearly no on both counts, but it did strike me as somehow symbolic: The North Koreans had ruined Thanksgiving, but only because I wasn't communicating well enough with them.

Another time, in between lectures, I was reading the news and saw that the US ambassador to South Korea had been attacked with a knife, leaving a potentially life-threatening gash down his face. Mr. Jang, the true believer, passed by my table.

"Wow, did you see this news?" I asked, showing him the dramatic pictures of Ambassador Lippert's face ripped open.

"See?" he responded, "This is because they are conducting these war games that get the Korean people so upset."

I shook my head and felt a weight of disappointment press down on me. What a shitty, indoctrinated thing to have said. North Korea has consistently railed against joint military exercises between the United States and South

Korea, calling them "preparation for an invasion." Mr. Jang didn't see a dignified man who'd suffered a horrific attack. He saw an imperialist, who'd provoked the attack by representing his country.

I moved away from him; I couldn't bear it. I sat down next to the chap in the oversized suit, who looked at it and said without prompt: "I saw that, it's so terrible." He "tsked" in disgust.

And now I found my eyes welled up a little. I was so grateful to him just for being a decent person who saw right and wrong before he saw ideological enemies or allies. I'm still grateful.

It was always fun to show North Koreans new things or watch them discover things we took for granted.

This could be something small, like showing one young lady, Ms. Ha, how to put on a seatbelt in an airplane, or seeing her ask if the lady already sat next to her had misplaced her (airline) blanket on her seat. "No, no, that one's yours," the seatmate answered. Ms. Ha didn't know airlines gave out blankets.

It could be the mundane.

"What do you want to check out?" we asked Mr. Kim, perhaps the kindest man ever.

"An ATM!" he beamed. "I've only read about them and seen them in films."

But it was often more profound: I got to see many of them discover and come to grips with the internet, to start to understand the profundity of this technology that was absent from their country.

"I need to research the economy of Egypt," an older lady who'd been to China a couple of times told me.

"Okay," I said, and showed her the basics of a browser and a search engine. She typed in "economy of Egypt" into the search box. Obviously, ten million results came back.

"What do I do with all this?" she asked, drowning in data before she'd even clicked on anything.

She may have been hoping to build some sort of business with Egyptians on the back of Kim Jong Il's personal relationship with Naguib Sawaris, the CEO of Orascom. Orascom is an Egyptian conglomerate that in 2008 won the right to build North Korea's 3G network. It was also the DPRK's biggest failure, from an international business perspective. In around 2013 or 2014 we started to hear rumors that the North Koreans were preventing Orascom from repatriating their profits.

The rumor was that Orascom were being told they had to take in hard currency payments for phone and data services and convert it to won at the fictional exchange rate: about 100 won to $1. So they'd accept a ten dollar bill and give 1,000 won in phone credits to a customer, say. But then they were told they could exchange this won they held back to send abroad only at the unofficial, market exchange rate, which is around 8,000 won to $1. This would have meant Orascom was getting pennies on the dollar. My suspicion is that the profits had been held in a bank that was either mismanaged or had been told by the authorities to invest in something unproductive.

This was a really badly missed opportunity for North Korea. Orascom was the first major investment by a renowned, global corporation. Most companies doing business in the country are two-bit, small-time operations. Past deals with large Western firms had mostly gone badly. Perhaps most famously, Pyongyang bought a fleet of Swedish Volvos in the 1970s, but never paid for them. The French loans that financed the iconic Yanggakdo Hotel also went unpaid. With Orascom, Pyongyang had the chance to show the whole world that it was open for business in a new way. It failed.

Regardless, I told the lady she needed more specific search terms or to trust that in general, the top three or four results were most likely to include the information she wanted. I gave her a couple more pointers and then left her to it, struck that the vastness of the internet and its profound penetration into all aspects of our lives cannot really be described. Choson Exchange workshop leaders have explained internet-based strategies for business while in-country, but you have to see it to understand it.

In my early years of traveling to North Korea, you'd hear people say things like, "We have our domestic internet and you have your international internet," equating their small intranet with the World Wide Web, an obviously spurious comparison to an outsider like me. More recently, however, as more and more people have been abroad and used the internet and perhaps shared what that was like with friends and family back in Pyongyang, that sort of statement has disappeared. More North Koreans than ever have a vague sense that they are missing out on something huge.

That missing out includes opportunities to research and make money. The walled society will always place limits on what talented people can achieve. North Korean propaganda proclaims the country will "break through the cutting edge" and has a catchy song with that title. It just can't happen so long as people are cut off from the information flows they need to participate in.

Even the technologies the state lauds are not really cutting edge; they are from the 1970s. These include missiles and nuclear bombs as well as CNC, computer-aided machine tooling that is needed for precision in weapons making, among other things. This is not to besmirch the state's achievements: only nine countries before North Korea were able to put a satellite in orbit on top of their own indigenously developed rocket, for example. But there is a reason that North Koreans are not innovating in global markets. They are just too cut off.

They may be able to leapfrog some of the traditional stages of development, taking advantage of a well-educated workforce. But there is still a long way to go. The stage of taking on simple outsourced manufacturing, which some other Asian economies have already passed through, probably still awaits the country. Shoes, clothes, metal badges, that sort of thing.

Notes

1 Percival Lowell, *Choson, the Land of the Morning Calm: A Sketch of Korea* (Boston: Ticknor & Co., 1886), 109.

2 Lowell, *Land of the Morning Calm.*

3 Liu Ming, "Changes and Continuities in Pyongyang's China Policy," in *North Korea in Transition: Politics, Economy, and Society,* eds. Kyung-Ae Park and Scott Snyder (New York: Rowman & Littlefield, 2013), 213.

4 Bernd Schaefer, "Communist Vanguard Contest in East Asia during the 1960s and 1970s in Dynamics of the Cold War," in *Asia: Ideology, Identity, and Culture,* eds. Tuong Vu and Wasana Wongsurawat (New York: Macmillan, 2009), 117.

5 Andray Abrahamian, "Singapore as Aspiration," *North Korean Review* 14, no. 2 (2018): 87.

6 Housing and Development Board, "Public Housing—A Singapore Icon," http://www.hdb.gov.sg/cs/infoweb/about-us/our-role/public-housing--a-singapore-icon.

7 Signe Cecilie Jochumsen and Søren Smidt-Jensen, "Singapore's Successful Long-Term Public Housing Strategies," Our Future Cities, July 12, 2012, http://ourfuturecities.co/2012/07/singapores-successful-long-term-public-housing-strategies.

8 Peter Wallace Preston, *Singapore in the Global System: Relationship, Structure and Change* (Routledge: New York, 2007), 190.

14

Where Do We Go Now?

After one Choson Exchange workshop in North Korea, I came out with that usual mix of exhaustion and exhilaration. The exhaustion comes from working hard, but also from being in the middle of the control, stress, and privation that is North Korean life. The exhilaration comes in part from being back online, plugging back into social media and emails, checking news and gossip. It's like digital crack.

I sat in Beijing's Saturday morning traffic, made it home, hugged my wife, showered, and took a nap. In the evening, we went to our favorite Yunnan restaurant and then strolled down a street near the old drum and bell towers. As we approached one corner, we heard the lilting sounds of reggae rhythms being strummed out on a guitar. We poked our head into the bar from which it wafted, took a seat, and grabbed a drink. It was all Chinese kids, some with dreadlocks, jamming or nodding along to a reggae beat. On one wall were the colors of Jamaica: red, yellow, and green. Somehow, these Chinese kids were into reggae. "How did this happen?" I wondered. Was it at a US college? Was it backpacking in Southeast Asia, where reggae bars are ubiquitous? Was it from watching music videos online? I didn't know, but I did suddenly know that this was what I wanted to see in North Korea.

This. This is what I want for the North Koreans I know. Of course, I want North Koreans to have food security; for there to be an end to malnutrition and stunting; for there to be twenty-four-hour electricity; for there to be no fear of labor camps or re-education. But what I would love most of all is to walk down the streets of Pyongyang and find a reggae bar. Or an eighties bar. Or a jazz bar.

I want to see North Koreans nerd out on advanced NBA metrics; on airline liveries; Terry Pratchett's Discworld novels; on *whatever.* To be disaffected teenagers whose family and neighbors don't understand why they love cyber-punk or the J. R. R. Tolkien canon so much, but who can find a community online that sustains and enriches them.

I don't want to suggest that personal interests don't exist in the country. I've met amateur poets. I've met someone obsessed with Roman mythology. But the range of potential choices in life is narrow. I want to see them widened.

Will such a DPRK ever come to be? I don't know.

When you visit North Korea, the state wants to convey three things, in order of importance: control and stability; contentment and legitimacy; and the beauty and truth of Juche. They know that a few Westerners will buy into Juche and love it. If so, great. They won't convince many, but a few are inclined to be Kimilsung-Kimjongilists. They know that most people will not be in favor of how they've built their society—that's fine too, but at least some number will at least leave saying, "Well, it's not for us, but maybe it works for them."

They want most people to fly out of Sunan Airport thinking that even if people are unhappy, even if the system is abhorrent, that the state is in control and that the country is in no danger of collapse. And I do think the system is essentially stable. In that sense, maybe they got me. Maybe I fell for it. Or maybe it really is locked down: a combination of rigidity and flexibility that has allowed for state survival beyond expectation. The country has adapted to new economic realities while doubling down on a political system that has been mostly abandoned in the rest of the world.

What can we do when facing a state like this?

Fundamentally, there are two camps when it comes to dealing with North Korea. There are "engagers" and "hardliners." Engagers basically hope that by working with the regime and the people living in it, they can induce or support positive changes in North Korea. Some possibly think they can undermine the state. Hardliners hope that through pressuring the country, they can induce change by getting Pyongyang to crack, to capitulate.

I use the word "hope" deliberately. Both approaches have had limited success and accuse the other side of undermining their approach.

Hardliners complain that, by sending aid in the 1990s and creating the Agreed Framework in 1994, the international community propped up an odious regime that was on the edge. Letting it collapse, even with all the human suffering that would entail, would have been better than what we have now: a stabilized, nuclear state. For hardliners, North Korea is essentially an unchanging and unchangeable place at its core. Working with such a regime will only ensconce its position, if not improve it. The tight sanctions imposed on North Korea for its nuclear program are thus necessary and must continue until the regime's will is broken and it submits.

Engagers generally think by increasing interactions with the DPRK, by building connections, we can find more positive outcomes. That the more North Korean people we expose to the outside world, the more they will be advocates for better policy, greater justice, and a better quality of life in their society. Engagers bemoan US broken promises or contradictions (of which there have been several) as reinforcing the suspicious, hostile attitude that North Koreans have toward the outside world: the attitude used to justify isolation.

If you've read this book, you see that I'm an engager. This is for a few reasons, but first and foremost it's because I don't think pressure will get us to where we'd like. The country is *uniquely built to be closed*. Sanctioning and isolating it ad infinitum will, in my estimation, not cause it to collapse. This is in part because of how much control the state has over its citizens. But it's also because of how much China wants it to survive. It is very much in China's interest *not* to see the DPRK collapse. Beijing is not keen on North Korea's nuclear program, but they're less keen on a unified Korea allied with the United States on their doorstep. North Korea is an important buffer.

Moreover, the Chinese government has more information on North Korea than any other country, by some margin. Not only do they have a massive embassy and a consulate in Chongjin (the Russians are the only other country to have one there), but they can also draw information from a joint management committee in Rason, some sort of consultancy group in Sinuiju, a large business community, and the *hwagyo*—Chinese permanent residents in North Korea, a legacy of the early independence era. They will be able to sniff out a crisis and react while everyone else is twiddling their thumbs. Let's not fool ourselves into thinking pressure will cause a North Korean collapse.

Sanctions may not cause collapse—but they could incentivize Pyongyang to negotiate some of its nuclear program away. It is clear after the US-DPRK summit in February 2019 that Kim Jong Un wants to find an end to his country's economic isolation and is willing to make concessions. We'd almost certainly have to compromise on something, though: the United States currently insists on a complete denuclearization that will be difficult for Pyongyang to accept. The US side also wants to define the end-state before beginning a process of mutual concessions.

But what if Pyongyang doesn't budge and offers only a freeze and some sort of limited rollback on the nuclear program? This would surely be a win, right? It would increase security and stability in the region and beyond, a good outcome for the sanctions policy that has been called "maximum pressure" since Donald Trump took office. It would feel like failure for the

United States, however: "they developed nuclear weapons, didn't give them up, and earned a normal relationship with the outside world." Hawks argue, therefore, that we should hold back sanctions relief until nearly all of the nuclear program has been handed over.

I'm not 100 percent anti-sanctions, but this hawkish approach is not realistic. And we have to be clear-eyed regarding the limitations of sanctions. Sanctions seeking military impairment or "other major policy changes" are effective 31 percent and 30 percent of the time, respectively, according to one major study. The latter number drops precipitously when the target is an autocracy, to 9 percent.[1] North Korea's nuclear and missile programs are central to the state's conception of itself. They are the ultimate deterrent for a country that basically believes the United States and the rest of the world is out to get them. They included the phrase "nuclear-possessing" into the North Korean constitution in 2012. DPRK citizens may or may not care about the nukes, but it doesn't matter. North Korea does not have civil society platforms for citizens to express frustration against policies that brought on sanctions, as in Iran, nor an internal champion for them, as in Myanmar.

Just like in those other countries, though, sanctions pain is not evenly spread around. Compared to ordinary people, how much economic pain do the decision-makers feel? Very little. Privation gets socialized downward. The least powerful in society end up suffering the most.

So, if sanctions don't get us to a compromise and we continue to heap pressure on the country, ordinary people will just suffer greater adversity and hardship, beyond what their own country already heaps upon them. A wealthy few will coalesce around powerful state organizations. Opportunities for individuals to earn money and join the small middle class will diminish. The poorest people will have less food and fewer nutrients. People will die because they can't afford medicines. They will suffer and cope in silence, unable to affect the decisions that harm their lives.

How many North Koreans could we end up killing through trying to pressure their government? Would we accept ten thousand? A hundred thousand? What if we did it even knowing that we'd be unlikely to cause the government to collapse or get it to change course? Would that be moral?

Hawkishness, if looking to force a compromise, is defensible. But if it is in pursuit of total capitulation or collapse, it will fail. And the consequences of that failure are the increased immiseration and suffering of ordinary North Koreans.

The downside for doves and engagers is that cooperation may entrench the regime and legitimize it, if it were able to generate economic growth within its closed model. However, the regime already has some degree of legitimacy. A recent survey of new defectors by Seoul National University suggests that public support for the third generation of leadership under Kim Jong Un may be fairly solid. Among the respondents, 33% believed that over 70% of North Koreans support the leadership, 47.4% thought it was between 30% and 69%, while only 19.6% said support was below 30% of the population.[2] If the DPRK cannot deliver economic growth, which has thus far been a positive part of Kim Jong Un's brand, it will lean back on "defending the Korean people from hostile imperialisms," i.e., on militarism.

So if the regime is unlikely to collapse and still enjoys considerable legitimacy, what is the point of engaging the country? The hope on that side is that through increasing connections with the people and leaders of North Korea, we can encourage the state to become a better version of itself. There's no need to be all Pollyanna about this. A gradual transition would still almost certainly be an autocratic, Kim-family-led state. North Korea will retain some of its nuclear capability, though some kind of arms-control regime might be possible. (As is, there is nothing of the sort, of course.)

Hardliners will say "North Korea can never change." They may be right, though autocracies are more adaptable and flexible than we often think. Regardless, we have never committed to trying to create a scenario in which we really put that proposition to the test.

We've seen other examples of single-party states in the region becoming reformist and seeking increased integration with the outside world: China, Vietnam, and Laos. They all found the rhetorical and ideological wiggle room to make dramatic changes to how they organize their economies and societies. Importantly, none faced existential security threats when their openings happened: Vietnam, and its neighbor Laos, had fought off the Americans (and French, and Japanese, and French again, then finally the Chinese); China had developed nuclear weapons in the 1960s, then emerged from internal turmoil later that decade and into the 1970s. More recently, Myanmar also relaxed military control once the security threat of large insurgencies had been tamped down.

These are all dictatorships, to be sure, but we have to say that their citizens are better off due to their countries' rapprochement with the West generally and the United States specifically.[3] There would be many factors in a potential North Korean opening—notably politics and attitudes in South Korea—but the biggest is the lack of rapprochement, victory, or defeat in its conflict with the United States.

We don't know how North Korea would develop if the United States signed a peace treaty.[4] We do know that the threat of the United States rationalizes almost everything that the citizens of North Korea endure.

"Why do I need a travel permit to go to the neighboring province?"

"Because if we didn't have this system the Americans would infiltrate our country and destroy us."

"Why can't I have internet access?"

"Because if we were online the Americans would get in our systems and destroy us."

"Why isn't there enough to eat?"

"The Americans have us under an embargo."

How would the DPRK's leaders organize the country without the justification of the American threat? I don't know. But more importantly, they don't know either: they've never had to do it before.

I would like to see the United States take a gamble on this. After all, most of the South Korean public wants US troops to remain on Korean soil, even if a peace treaty is signed. If the gamble—if a process of peacemaking—fails, deterrence will still work.

What if it doesn't fail, though? How would North Korea look? My guess is that more personal freedoms would emerge, along with further reforms to the economy. Food security and health would improve. I'm sure plenty of surveillance (more with Chinese technology, probably) would remain; plenty of injustice and corruption would remain, though in both cases probably less than exists today.

Ultimately, peace is difficult. There is another divided nation we can look to: Ireland. If one looks at the example of Northern Ireland in the 1980s, cynics on all sides would have said of their enemies: they want our destruction; we can't ever trust them; negotiations will never work. And they failed. And failed. And failed again. Until they worked. Until men responsible for horrendous crimes and violence sat down, made compromises, and ultimately sold those compromises to skeptical constituents in their communities and polities. To end war, some uncomfortable facts had to be confronted. Others had to be ignored. Ultimately, something similar needs to happen on the Korean Peninsula and will require the right mix of people and conditions in both Koreas and the United States.

Maybe then I'll be allowed to call up one of my friends when I visit Pyongyang. Perhaps I can pop by his house and meet his kids. Then maybe we can find that new reggae bar and have a beer after he's put them to bed. Sure, it's in the slightly out-of-the-way-but-up-and-coming Pyongchon District, but we can easily pop over on the refurbished subway—or hell, I'll splurge on a ride-share. The band will be full of energy and he'll snap a picture on his phone and share it right away with his friend in China.

Then the next morning I'll jump on the train down to Seoul. I'll briefly put my phone down as I go through customs and immigration but pick it right up again after my passport is stamped. He and I will still be texting about how great that band was.

And I don't even like reggae.

Notes

1 Gary Clyde Hufbauer, Jeffrey J. Schott, Kimberly Ann Elliott, and Barbara Oegg, *Economic Sanctions Reconsidered* (Washington, DC: Peterson Institute for International Economics, 2007), 155–66.

2 Jeyup S. Kwaak, "North Korean Escapees Say They Perceive Solid Support for Dictator," *Wall Street Journal,* August 26, 2015, http://www.wsj.com/articles/north-korean-escapees-report-solid-support-for-dictator-kim-1440568866.

3 Looking back to the 1970s, we'd still want to take the "reform and opening" version of China, even though it now presents huge challenges to US interests and values.

4 Something, by the way, that would not likely require withdrawing US troops from South Korea. See Son Daekwon, "Evolution of North Korea's Peace Treaty Proposals and Sino-DPRK Relations Behind the Scenes," *Korea Observer* 50, no. 4 (Winter 2019): 505–33.

15

It All Falls Apart

I was stood on a mobile BBC set on the roof of a Hanoi café overlooking a lake when everything started falling apart. My phone began blowing up: Kim Jong Un and Donald Trump have left the summit venue. Wait, no they haven't. Lunch is canceled. Wait, they are leaving. There will be no agreement. Kim Jong Un stormed out. Wait, no, it was Trump. Trump's press conference is two o'clock, not four o'clock now. No, he's going straight to Air Force One and leaving.

I was shell-shocked. As the BBC's dedicated analyst, I'd spent two days outlining what the two sides wanted and what they would need to take home for the Hanoi Summit to be a success. The BBC had brought me on because I'd been working on North Korea for nearly fifteen years. That and I evince some effervescent quality that all the television greats like Oprah or John Oliver have. I'd been working on North Korea for nearly fifteen years. And I'd just flown a long way only to have my predictions be proven so brutally incorrect. On live TV, no less.

Leading up to the event there had been a summer-camp vibe to the city of Hanoi, with celebratory concerts, art, and T-shirts all over town. Triptychs of American and North Korean flags bracketing the Vietnamese one fluttered everywhere. In the days prior, pundits, journalists, and diplomats, many of whom were my friends, arrived in the city and got together to catch up and speculate on what might happen. The June 2018 Singapore Summit had been for show, but the consensus was that here real concessions would be made.

It didn't happen. Minutes after the two sides walked away from the negotiation table, Trump's motorcade zoomed through the crowds lining the street below the BBC set. But the mood was no longer jubilant. Then, bizarrely, a storm cloud descended over the nearby lake, whipping up the wind, but then moving on without dumping rain on us. If I were superstitious, I'd have said it was an omen. But it was just weather. (Right?)

The climate inside the room where Kim and Trump met had certainly darkened, and fast. They'd hardly been at the table for any time at all when, instead of trying to negotiate a limited deal to kick off a relationship-building process, early rumors made it seem as if the US side had escalated its demands to the level of a grand bargain, one that would be hard for the North Koreans to accept at this early stage in negotiations. On the other side, the North Koreans were asking for a significant amount of sanctions relief and other steps in exchange for a limited part of their nuclear program. Talks collapsed.

I wondered on air if this was going to be a missed opportunity that would last a generation. Were we in for twenty more years of acrimony, tensions, and a fundamentally closed North Korea? With the specter of nuclear war raised in 2017 followed by a warming of relations in 2018, 2019 seemed like a chance for the United States to remake its relationship with that difficult country. This new relationship would require accepting — at least for a while — that North Korea is a nuclear state, but doing so would be an attempt to create space to draw the country into the family of nations and change its strategic outlook. Instead, we achieved nothing.

North Korea is a tightly wound society, but as I'd seen from several years of spending time in the country, it is full of creative, earnest, and pragmatic people. They had been enjoying an improved situation: from about 2012 to 2016 rules governing businesses improved and while sanctions created problems, they were not yet crushing. The improved economic freedoms were good for Kim Jong Un's domestic brand. With the collapse of this summit, the prospect for sanctions relief looked poor and I worried that the willingness to experiment with economic reform would evaporate. A conservatism, already growing as the conflict with the international community escalated in 2016–2017, would entrench itself.

I also worried that the robust nature of North Korea's closed-circuit social system meant it probably could—and would—continue to survive under sanctions and pressure for decades to come. It had already survived longer than expected, beyond the collapse of communism in the rest of the world and through a devastating famine in the mid-1990s. By the time of the Hanoi Summit, the Democratic People's Republic of Korea—the DPRK—had somehow existed longer than the USSR.

Across from the roof where the BBC's cameras and lighting were set up was a place called the Seoul Restaurant. It appeared in every shot. Four years earlier I'd brought a group of North Koreans there for dinner. We'd come to learn about how the private sector and government cooperate in order to develop cities and tourism destinations. If one of them had told me, "Hey, five years from now you'll be on a roof across the street talking to millions of people about President Donald Trump and Kim Jong Un meeting," I'd have said, "Put that *soju* down and go to bed. We have a long day planned for tomorrow."

Yet here we were, with the leaders holding unprecedented talks but then abruptly parting ways. Along with the core issue of denuclearization, the two sides were supposed to agree on a number of non-nuclear issues, including perhaps an initiative to support women in North Korea. I had been setting up a nonprofit to feed into that. Instead, nothing.

I was in something of a fugue state, which sometimes happens when I talk on TV or in public. In the moment, I feel coherent and articulate, but a minute after the interview I can't really remember what I just said. The presenter, Lucy Hockings, asked me to explain the situation. I don't recall what I said. I'm sure I conveyed some shock.

This was bad. This was really bad.

That evening, a number of the aforementioned journalists, pundits, and diplomats gathered at a local bar to dissect the day. The journalists were buzzing: it was a great news day. Exciting stuff. The North Korea nerds were more dismayed. What was next, those of us hoping for a deal wondered?

Then, several drinks in, everyone's phones blew up again. The North Korean foreign minister was holding a midnight press conference. We paid up as quickly as possible and ran over to the hotel. It was, of course, far too late to get in, so we mingled pointlessly in the rain with all the other journalists who were in the same predicament. Some interviewed each other, even more pointlessly.

This was the diplomatic gamble by the United States and North Korea that I'd been hoping for. Both leaders seemed keen to make a deal that they would then have to sell to skeptical stakeholders back home. But they didn't even reach that hurdle. Why did it fail so early? More information emerged in the days and weeks afterwards. Mistakes were made on both sides. Usually, the details of an agreement to be made at an important summit like this are settled upon before the event itself. But on the North Korean side, the working-level negotiators in the run-up to the main event refused to discuss the details of denuclearization, saying only the supreme leader could do that. Kim seemed to want to leave the most crucial part of an agreement to the last minute. President Trump decided to risk going ahead with the meeting, hoping that on the day they could find common ground.

Kim Jong Un must also have thought on the day he could get what he wanted from Trump. When the gap in expectations emerged, it seemed as if the North Korean side didn't have a plan B. This was an error and Kim did not appear to have the flexibility under pressure that he needed. Perhaps the same could be said of Trump. Regardless, the US side decided after a few hours to walk away. This too was a mistake. Why not say, "Hey, take tonight to discuss some details with your team and we'll meet for breakfast and see if we can get any closer"?

In the longer run, the American side may have underestimated how hard it would be for Kim Jong Un to return back to Pyongyang empty-handed. For Trump's unorthodox presidency, coming home to criticism over this summit was a minor affair. But for Kim, returning to Pyongyang empty-handed was a major issue. Even in North Korea, the leader has "audience costs," the penalties leaders incur in the eyes of key stakeholders when they make mistakes. Kim had to go back to Pyongyang to deal with hardliners who could credibly argue that he had been engaging in high-level diplomacy for over a year now and had received no sanctions relief; that he'd risked too much by trusting the Americans, who clearly wanted North Korea to be vulnerable by giving everything up too early.

"They want us on our knees," a North Korean lamented to me a few months after the summit. He'd really wanted a deal, too. In the year following Hanoi, North Korea tightened up: external policies became more hard line; there were various crackdowns on information and market activity; ideological study sessions became tenser as people tested each other's loyalty. When there is instability at the top, elites push those stresses down through the system. "There are no real friends anymore," as another North Korean put it some months later.

Back in Hanoi, damp and cold from the rain, I traipsed back to my hotel room and fell into bed. I'd hoped that this day would be the first step toward more economic opportunities for my friends in North Korea; that they'd begin to be better connected to the outside world and live without their country's antagonistic relationship with the United States defining their lives. That today would begin building doorways into the most walled society on earth and help my friends in South Korea become more secure.

Instead, nothing.

POSTSCRIPT

The Moon or Some Other Planet

> They have the Oriental vices of suspicion, cunning, and untruthfulness, and trust between man and man is unknown. Women are secluded, and occupy a very inferior position.
>
> Isabella Bird Bishop[1]
>
> ...I have known of more than one man considered to be, or posing as, a judge of peoples and nations, who, after a prolonged stay in Japan and China, visiting their courts, factories, schools, etc., etc., to study the people, and after giving but the few hours while the vessel stayed in Korean ports in which to judge of the Koreans, has not hesitated to make lengthy and apparently learned discourses on the three nations, to the disparagement, naturally under the circumstances, of the Korean.
>
> Horace Grant Underwood[2]

Pardon this belated apology. But with this book, I'm entering a tradition. I've become an Orientalist: a Westerner who takes it upon himself the task—nay, the virtuous *burden*—of explaining Korea to a Western audience. The travelogue/memoir of a faraway land is a genre fraught with peril. It is extremely hard to represent another culture fairly, without exoticizing the subject. Western scholarship and writing have long fed into power structures that favor some groups over others, justifying some practices over others.[3] And describing Korea has always been problematic, as writers grappled with a closed and often xenophobic society, not to mention their own biases and intellectual constraints.

I have my own, of course, and if you've read the preceding text, some of these might be clear to you. (I care more about coffee than I should, for example.) I would like to spend a few pages drawing your attention to how some of the early ideas about Korea were made and conveyed. This may seem like a diversion—you came to read about today's North Korea, after all—but it is important because these early ideas *still in*form the way most of us think about the Northern part of the peninsula. Looking back at writings from over a hundred years ago, I see things I've tried to avoid, but also things I have not been able to escape as I've visited and thought about today's North Korea.

From the beginning, Westerners confronted Korea as a mysterious, alien place. A problem or puzzle to be solved. A place to project ideas onto, regardless of whether they were wanted or not. And yet, we have to try to understand other societies, right?

There is always difficulty when extremely different cultures encounter one another. From what god's-eye view are we supposed to judge a foreign culture? How can we say whether an alphabetic or logographic writing system is better? Or if communalism is superior to individualism? Or if a single-party political system is better than a multiparty system? There is simply no objective position from which to describe our social world, and every pronouncement about right or wrong implies or creates winners and losers.

On the other hand, if we fully accede to a postmodern worldview, we literally cannot pass judgments about anything. We become mired in a way of thinking in which one cannot critically describe or judge any society at all. In the end we have to find commonality where we can and to make judgments where we must without condescension and with humility. This is not easy and never has been with Korea.

Western ideas about Korea began, in a way, with China and Marco Polo's dubious account of a great land bursting with riches. His story was suspect in the sense that he failed to describe tea, chopsticks, or foot binding, among other quintessentially Chinese traditions.[4] Still, he described a vast Sinitic empire, civilized, but alien.

Subsequent descriptions led European thinkers in the eighteenth century to conclude that Confucian society was largely based on "lofty reason and good conduct."[5] Yet gradually there emerged an image of a China as a sick society ready—perhaps calling—for exploitation. The people were submissive; their leaders corrupt and their technology backwards: they were ready to be controlled by the West.

There was only one major pre-nineteenth-century publication on Korea: Hendrick Hamel's journal. Hamel was a Dutch East India Company employee who, along with thirty-five others, was stranded on Jeju Island after being shipwrecked in 1653. For violating Korea's territory, he was essentially a prisoner for thirteen years, and the second part of his journals paints an unflattering picture of Koreans:

> With regard to the moral standards, it has to be said that the Koreans are not very strict when it comes to mine and thine, they lie and cheat and that's why they can't be trusted. They are proud if they have cheated somebody and they don't think that's a disgrace.... On the other hand the Koreans are very gullible. We could fool them with anything.[6]

They are by this account so degenerate they not only cheat, *they don't even realize it's wrong.* Oh, and they are simpletons.

A gap of well over a century passed until the next major account of travels in Korea was written, after Basil Hall and Herbert John Clifford explored East Asia in 1816, including an unauthorized visit to Korea. Hall likened the country to "the moon, or to some other planet, where nothing existed in common with our previous knowledge."[7] The natives they encountered "received us with looks of distrust and alarm, were evidently uneasy at our landing, for they were crowded timorously together like so many sheep."[8] This theriomorphization of the islanders divorces their behavior from that of the human world and places it alongside livestock.

These adventurous Europeans decided "without waiting for an invitation, to take a look at the village."[9] No matter that there was no request for a visit, nor that the interlopers had not brought gifts or some form of communiqué. "This measure elicited something like emotion in the sulky natives, several of whom stepped forward, and placing themselves between us and the houses, made very unequivocal signs for us to return to our boats forthwith."[10] How rude of them. And how silly of them not to welcome superior European people and norms with open arms. Also note the phrase "something like emotion." At this point, we can't be sure the natives have feelings, like we do.

Korea remained insignificant for several more decades insofar as the Western powers were concerned: even the disappearance of the USS *General Sherman* in 1866 and the fact-finding/punitive mission Washington dispatched five years later barely created a ripple in the US media. After the United States–Korea Treaty of 1882, however, Protestant missionaries began to work on the peninsula. Accompanying them was an explosion of interest in the formerly closed country.

It was that year that perhaps the most enduring moniker was born: *Corea, the Hermit Nation.* This was the title of a very influential book by William Elliot Griffis, a minister and professor who spent much time in Japan. Guess what? He never set foot in Korea. Still, he knew that Korea was "Japan's Ireland," an inferior nation.[11] The inferiority, he concludes, is not the fault of ordinary Koreans, however.

"The ill fame of the native character for inhospitality and hatred of foreigners belongs not to the people, nor is truly characteristic of them." It is "the government which curses country and people, and in the ruling classes who, like those in Old Japan, do not wish the peasantry to see the inferiority of those who govern them."[12] It was in this rendering embarrassing to Korea's elites that the Westerner was superior in literally every possible way, from science to arts to religion. Japan, where he had direct experience, had earned his favor by consciously opening to Western, specifically American, norms.

Not all writers on Korea condescended in the same way or to the same extent. One towering figure in the missionary/author scene was Horace Allen. He arrived in Korea as a missionary in 1884, became an informal diplomat for several years, and then became minister and consul general from 1897 to 1905. Upon his recall, he wrote *Things Korean,* published in 1908. In contrast to Griffis, Allen was very sympathetic to Korea. He suggested more subtly that Korea was in need of some kind of stewardship and that the United States, by allowing Japan to turn Korea into a protectorate in 1905, had violated its treaty obligations. He wrote that "we deserted them in their time of need and ignored the solemn agreement we had entered into with them...for their abandoning the centuries-old position of exclusion and non-intercourse and emerging into the dazzling glare of treaty relations."[13]

Another Horace and titan in the missionary community was Horace Grant Underwood. He wrote approvingly of American railway development in Korea, saying "commerce and the Church go hand in hand, here as elsewhere, in forwarding His kingdom and spreading abroad the knowledge of the Prince of Peace."[14] He frequently praised Koreans as both intelligent and hardworking: it was the lack of religiously derived morals that made them deficient. His wife, Lillias Horton Underwood, no slouch, was a professional companion and published a major work on Korea in 1904, a very personal account titled *Fifteen Years among the Top-Knots, or Life in Korea.*" Koreans, she found, were "singularly winning and lovable."[15] Korea's "stupor" was not endemic, but rather the fault of a curable socioeconomic model.

She also saw how descriptions of Korea were used for political means. "The Koreans have frequently been spoken and written of as listless, dull, stupid, lazy, an inferior race: but I submit this has been said mainly by travelers who did not know them, or by those who were their enemies and had an object in making the world think them worthless."[16]

Both Horaces, sympathetic or not, were still missionaries, called on to bring the "truth" to ignorant heathens.

One missionary seemed a bit more progressive than the others: James Scarth Gale. He argued that "so much of life seems reversed or standing on its head in their universe of thought," but that Westerners must also "stand on our heads" to learn Asia's ways in a mutual effort of understanding.[17] He thought Koreans were by and large hospitable, honest, and fair.[18] He chided a colleague for breaking up a cock fight, enraging the participants, and causing a fight, calling it "a mistake," while still admiring the man's efforts.[19]

Why are these early descriptions of Korea relevant? Because they are still connected to how we think about North Korea. Recall the reportage you've recently read about the country: no doubt it was something about how degenerate the leadership is, or how dangerous their nuclear weapons or missiles are. Think about how many times you've personally read the descriptor "hermit Kingdom" or "desperate" or "dictatorship" about North Korea.

Since those early days of contact, the Far East has been cast as a latent threat to European centrality, while at the same time Confucian societies were closed and mysterious, ripe both for gaining riches and reaping souls for those that might crack them open. In a way, as far as we've come, North Korea still occupies that position. The DPRK is seen as a closed and spiritually deficient society.

As much as I look down upon and scoff at those early, essentializing, and often racist descriptions of old Korea, some aspects of them ring true to me today as I think about the DPRK. I want to avoid stereotypes, but people in North Koreans *are* nervous about talking to foreigners. Movers and shakers in the economy *do* seem to view ripping off foreigners differently to ripping off other Koreans. Elites *do* shield the people from competing worldviews, insulating themselves from judgment.

I don't wish to see proselytization take place in North Korea: they, like other cultures, are perfectly capable of finding their own set of moral and ethical standards without the importation of a Western theology. But the country would, I have to believe, be a better society if they adapted some (but not all) norms practiced in other countries, particularly around political participation and the role of markets. They would see better outcomes and greater human happiness. There are some universal, secular standards for human dignity and behavior to which we should all aspire.

In that regard, this is why it is important to liaise with North Koreans today. We should be trying to find ways to help the country's elites choose better policies and to empower them to find positive outcomes for themselves and their families. This requires a degree of sympathy and understanding, even for the fortunate in their society.

When we encounter ridiculous, cruel, or unfair practices, we have to understand that these things come from a historically contingent process. And that it will take new processes to improve them, processes in which a broader range of outsiders should be involved; currently, probably some 90 percent of North Korean interactions with the outside world are via China. This isn't good for North Korea, and it isn't good for us.

With all that said, that doesn't mean we can't laugh at the ridiculous. Indeed, if you've been to North Korea, you know you have to. Otherwise you can be driven mad.

Notes

1 Isabella Bird Bishop, *Korea & Her Neighbors: A Narrative of Travel, with an Account of the Recent Vicissitudes and Present Position of the Country* (London: John Murray, 1898), 4.

2 Horace Grant Underwood, *The Call of Korea* (New York: Fleming H. Revell Co., 1908), 44.

3 Indeed, all knowledge production does. Confucian scholarship certainly supported and reproduced the centrality of China in the region, as well as the primacy of the male and of the landed elite.

4 An observation made by Frances Wood in *Did Marco Polo Go to China?* (New York and Oxon: Routledge, 2018), and noted in Mike Edwards, "Wonders and Whoppers," *Smithsonian* 39, no. 4 (2008): 82–88.

5 Zhang Longxi, "The Myth of the Other: China in the Eyes of the West," *Critical Inquiry* 15, no. 1 (Autumn 1988): 117.

6 Hendrick Hamel, *The Journal of Hendrick Hamel*, website of Henny Savenije, chapter 12, http://www.hendrick-hamel.henny-savenije.pe.kr/holland12.htm.

7 Basil Hall, *Voyage to Loo-Choo, and Other Places in the Eastern Seas, in the Year 1816. Including an Account of Captain Maxwell's Attack on the Batteries at Canton; and Notes of an Interview with Buonaparte at St. Helena, in August 1817* (Edinburgh: Printed for A. Constable & Co., 1826), 59.

8 Hall, *Voyage to Loo-Choo*, 57.

9 Hall, *Voyage to Loo-Choo*, 57.

10 Hall, *Voyage to Loo-Choo*, 57.

11 W. E. Griffis, *Corea: The Hermit Nation* (New York: Charles Scribner's Sons, 1882), 9.

12 Griffis, *Corea*, 10.

13 Horace Allen, *Things Korean* (New York: Fleming H. Revell Co., 1908), 8.

14 Underwood, *Call of Korea*, 24.

15 Lillias Horton Underwood, *Fifteen Years among the Top-Knots or Life in Korea*, second edition, revised and enlarged (New York: American Tract Society, 1904), xi.

16 Underwood, *Fifteen Years among the Top-Knots*, 273.

17 James S. Gale, *Korean Sketches* (New York: Fleming H. Revell Co., 1898), 174.

18 Gale, *Korean Sketches*, 239, 241.

19 Gale, *Korean Sketches*, 255.